AQA English Language and Literature A

A2

Exclusively endorsed by AQA

Andy Archibald
David Emery

Series editor
Chris Purple

 Nelson Thornes

Published in 2009 by:
Nelson Thornes Ltd
Delta Place
27 Bath Road
CHELTENHAM
GL53 7TH
United Kingdom

09 10 11 12 13 / 10 9 8 7 6 5 4 3 2 1

A catalogue record for this book is available from the British Library

ISBN 978 1 4085 1385 9

Cover photograph: Photolibrary/Photoalto
Page make-up by Pantek Arts Ltd, Maidstone
Printed and bound in Spain by GraphyCems

Contents

AQA introduction

Nelson Thornes has worked in partnership with AQA to ensure this book and the accompanying online resources offer you the best support for your A2 course.

All resources have been approved by senior AQA examiners so you can feel assured that they closely match the specification for this subject and provide you with everything you need to prepare successfully for your exams.

These print and online resources together **unlock blended learning**; this means that the links between the activities in the book and the activities online blend together to maximise your understanding of a topic and help you achieve your potential.

These online resources are available on **kerboodle!** which can be accessed via the internet at **http://www.kerboodle.com/live**, anytime, anywhere. If your school or college subscribes to this service you will be provided with your own personal login details. Once logged in, access your course and locate the required activity.

For more information and help visit **http://www.kerboodle.com**

Icons in this book indicate where there is material online related to that topic. The following icons are used:

💡 Learning activity

These resources include a variety of interactive and non-interactive activities to support your learning.

✔ Progress tracking

These resources include a variety of tests that you can use to check your knowledge on particular topics (Test yourself) and a range of resources that enable you to analyse and understand examination questions (On your marks …).

🔍 Research support

These resources include WebQuests, in which you are assigned a task and provided with a range of web links to use as source material for research.

◤ Study skills

These resources support you in developing a skill that is key for your course, for example planning essays.

🔍 Analysis tool

These resources help you to analyse key texts and images by providing questions and prompts to focus your response.

When you see an icon, go to Nelson Thornes learning space at **www.nelsonthornes.com/aqagce**, enter your access details and select your course. The materials are arranged in the same order as the topics in the book, so you can easily find the resources you need.

How to use this book

This book covers the specification for your course and is arranged in a sequence approved by AQA. The introduction to the book explains what will be required of you as an English Language and Literature student. The book is divided into two units. Unit 3 is on comparative analysis and text adaptation, and will prepare you for the examination paper. Section A will prepare you for the question in Section A of the examination by guiding you through analysing and comparing different types of texts. Section B is designed to help you with the question in Section B of the exam, in which you will adapt a text for a given audience. Unit 4 will help you with the coursework part of the course.

Definitions of any words that appear in bold can be found in the glossary at the back of this book.

The features in this book include:

Learning objectives

At the beginning of each section you will find a list of learning objectives that contain targets linked to the requirements of the specification.

Key terms

Terms that you will need to be able to define and understand. These terms are coloured blue in the text book and their definition will also appear in the glossary at the back of this book.

Modern language

Words or phrases that are not in common use today but that you will need to know in order to understand a particular extract. These terms are coloured blue in the extract and their definition appears in the margin.

Link

Links to other areas in the text book, or in your experience from GCSE, which are relevant to what you are reading.

Practical activity

Activities to develop skills, knowledge and understanding that will prepare you for assessment in English Language and Literature A.

Critical response activity

Activities that focus on a specific extract to develop skills relevant to your assessment in the examination.

AQA Examiner's tip

Hints from AQA examiners to help you with your study and to prepare you for your exam.

Commentary

Examples of answers you might give to the activities. These are designed to help you to understand what type of response the examiner is looking for, not to tell you the answer. There are many equally valid responses, so you will find this book most helpful if you try the activity yourself first, then look at the commentary to read another opinion. Not all activities have a commentary.

AQA examination questions are reproduced by permission of the Assessment and Qualifications Alliance.

Introduction to this book

Integrated study of language and literature

The books in this series are designed to support you in your AS and A2 *English Language and Literature* studies. What is special about this subject is that it brings together aspects of two other kinds of A level English course – the separate *English Literature* and *English Language* specifications, and there are some real advantages in continuing your studies of English language and literature in an integrated course of this sort.

English at every level up to GCSE requires both language and literature to be studied as essential parts of the course. How can you study literature properly without being keenly interested in the medium of that literature – the ways in which words and sentences and paragraphs and chapters interrelate to create texts of various kinds? These texts may be novels, short stories, plays, documentary scripts, poems, and non-fiction texts of a whole range of types and forms.

Being inquisitive about language in all of its forms and habitats is probably the most important quality that you can bring to your studies. We are immersed in language – it's our medium of communication with other people, it's the medium of entertainment (radio, television, comedy clubs, etc.) and a medium of instruction and information (how to … books, labels on medicines). More than that, my language and your language form essential parts of our identities, our individual personalities.

If you go on to study English at university you will also encounter a subject which has largely abandoned sharp distinctions between 'literature' and 'language' study as unhelpful oversimplifications. You will inevitably be looking at how writers use language when you study a work of literature, and your knowledge about language and how it is used can help you to appreciate and understand how writers and speakers, readers and listeners can be creative and responsive in their experiences of language.

It's important not to think of A Level English Language and Literature as a mix-and-match course in which you 'do language' in one section of a unit and 'do literature' in another section. The point is that language study and literature study are *integrated* and you need to think about how your interest in language can extend and enhance your appreciation of literary texts, and equally you need to think about literary texts as examples of language being used in ways that repay close scrutiny, analysis and reflection. There are four main skills that you need to develop during the AS and A2 course:

- You need to show that you are capable of reading texts closely and thoughtfully and writing about those texts in ways that show intelligent engagement and control.
- You need to show that you understand the characteristics of various kinds of spoken language, ranging from spontaneous exchanges between friends or strangers to carefully prepared speeches that are designed to persuade large numbers of people in live events, or via television and radio.

Think about it

Have you used the AQA , Nelson Thornes and other websites to find out more about particular aspects of the course?

The AQA site (www.aqa.org.uk) includes:

- the full subject specification
- specimen question papers
- subject reports based on candidates' performance in both the January and June examinations each year.

The Nelson Thornes (www.nelson thornes.com) site includes:

- interactive resources for each unit so that you can practise the skills you need to develop.

Other sources include:

- Wikipedia (www.wikipedia.org)
- the BBC website (www.bbc. co.uk), especially for Radio 4, which has some excellent programmes about books and reading
- bookshops – become a bookshop browser, and/or use the Amazon site (www.amazon.com) to find out about particular books.

▦ You need to show that you are capable of producing writing that is appropriate to the purpose and audience specified in the task, showing conscious control of your choices of vocabulary, grammar and structure.

▦ You need to show that you are capable of writing in a focused and analytical way about your own writing – the processes you apply, the choices you make, and the evaluation of whether the text works as well as you intended.

All of these activities build directly on the skills you have developed during your GCSE course, and in your earlier secondary years, as well as in your primary school and during the pre-school years when you learnt language skills by imitating adults and children with whom you grew up. And they are skills that many of us continue to develop as the range of our experiences as readers, writers, speakers and listeners expands.

▦ The units

This course focuses on a number of literary and non-literary texts and on particular language topics. During the first year (AS) of the English Language and Literature (Specification A) course, students will have developed their understanding of a range of terms and concepts that enable them to approach texts with confidence. They should be able to apply their knowledge and analytical skills to ask the right questions and to arrive at sound judgements about how any written or spoken text communicates with readers or listeners. They should also have a working understanding of the concepts of genre, audience and purpose, and experience of having written texts for a range of purposes. The two AS units provide the context for students to develop these competences.

▦ Unit 1 (ELLA1): Integrated analysis and text production
(Examination: one hour and 30 minutes)

Two texts are studied from a list of 10 prose and drama texts and candidates answer one question on each text. One question requires an analytical response about aspects of language and style and the second question is a production task based on a thorough knowledge of the text.

▦ Unit 2 (ELLA2): Analysing speech and its representation
(Examination: one hour and 30 minutes)

The first question of the examination focuses on the analytical comparison of **two** unseen spoken texts. The second question in this unit is based on the study of one text selected from a list of eight prose and drama texts. The focus for this question is the representation of speech and other stylistic features, with an extract from the text provided as a focus for the response.

The two A2 units, which are the subject of this book, build on the knowledge, understanding and skills developed during the AS phase of the course:

▦ Unit 3 (ELLA3): Comparative analysis and text adaptation
(Examination: two hours and 30 minutes)

The first task in this unit is a comparative analysis of three linked unseen texts: a transcript of spontaneous speech, a literary text and a non-literary text. The second task is based on the study of selected sections of collections of non-fiction writing and consists of a textual recasting accompanied by a brief commentary.

Unit 4 (ELLA 4): Comparative analysis through independent study (Coursework)

This coursework unit is a based on the close analytical comparison of a particular theme or aspect of *either* one poetry text and one prose or drama text, *or* two poetry texts, selected from AQA's lists of prescribed texts for this unit.

Preparation

The English Language and Literature course is designed to develop students' increasing autonomy as effective readers and writers and to extend their range and competence as writers. As in the AS phase, the A2 units are based on the following aims:

Students should:

- approach their reading and writing in an *integrated* way building on both *linguistic* and *literary understanding* and methods
- develop their *creativity* and *independence* as they encounter both spoken and written language
- think about *texts and the relationships between texts*, which also requires that they think about the *social, cultural and historical contexts* of these texts
- develop *independent* ways of working so that their individual *skills as producers of spoken and written language* are extended, and they also become increasingly thoughtful and responsive in their *judgements and evaluations of the language encountered* as readers and as listeners.

Assessment Objectives

During the AS phase, you should have become familiar with the Assessment Objectives (AOs) that underpin all of your studies within this subject. The AOs are set by the Qualifications and Curriculum Authority (QCA), the agency responsible for overseeing the examination system, and they apply to all specifications in this subject.

Table 1

Assessment objectives	Questions to ask yourself
AO1 Select and apply relevant concepts and approaches from integrated linguistic and literary study, using appropriate terminology and accurate, coherent written expression	Can I write accurately and coherently about a range of texts of various sorts, using specialist linguistic and literary terms and concepts that will help me to be clear and precise?
AO2 Demonstrate detailed critical understanding in analysing the ways in which structure, form and language shape meanings in a range of spoken and written texts	Can I discuss and write about structure, form and language of spoken and written texts in ways that reveal my critical and analytical understanding?
AO3 Use integrated approaches to explore relationships between texts, analysing the significance of contextual factors in their production and reception	Can I use my linguistic and literary understanding to interpret and evaluate texts and to compare different texts and their social, cultural and historical contexts?
AO4 Demonstrate expertise and creativity in using language appropriately for a variety of purposes and audiences, drawing on insights from literary and linguistic studies	Can I use my linguistic and literary understanding to produce written and spoken language appropriately to communicate effectively with a range of audiences and for a range of purposes?

You will have noticed that running through the questions in Table 1 is an insistence on the need to apply your knowledge and understanding of both language and literature, and this is the key to success on this course of study.

In the introduction to the AS book, we discussed the question of what it means to become an independent reader and identified a number of strands. During the A2 phase of a course in English Language and Literature, students need to extend their knowledge and skills and apply them within the new contexts of Units 3 and 4. The relevant knowledge and skills include:

- becoming increasingly knowledgeable about language and acquiring the analytical frameworks necessary for discussing in detail how writers construct and communicate meaning
- becoming competent in making evaluative judgements and supporting them with textual evidence
- understanding (as readers and as writers) the importance of the key concepts of genre, audience and purpose, and being able to create written texts that reflect secure judgements about these concepts
- understanding the techniques necessary in both examination and coursework contexts to apply their skills, knowledge and understanding as effectively as possible.

How to read

The introduction to the AS book referred to three different kinds of reading:

- *Reading the lines*: reading for surface meanings.
- *Reading between the lines*: reading closely so that you are alert to what a text hints at or implies, as well as what is stated explicitly.
- *Reading beyond the lines*: reading creatively so that you relate books to your own experience and beliefs, challenging and extending your own thinking.

At A2 Level, you need to concentrate on developing your analytical skills so that you are able to *read between the lines* in sophisticated ways and *read beyond the lines* so that you can answer questions like:

- What do I think and feel about this text, and has it affected me and my beliefs and values?
- What do I think about this text in terms of the writer's techniques: how has he or she won me over as an enthusiastic admirer of the text, or failed to do so?
- Which other books or real experiences does this text remind me of, and does it make me re-evaluate them and my own responses to them?

At this halfway stage of the four-unit course, it is worth reconsidering the quotations which were presented in the introduction to the AS book. Ask yourself whether you respond to them differently now, compared with when you first thought about them. If you feel that the implications of each question are a little richer than they seemed when you first read them, you are almost certainly working along the right lines as you follow this course!

Think about it

Think about the different types of reading in relation to the following quotations about how we read and what the effects of reading can be:

'Some books are to be tasted, others to be swallowed, and some few are to be chewed and digested.'
  Francis Bacon (1561–1626)

'A conventional good read is usually a bad read, a relaxing bath in what we know already. A true good read is surely an act of innovative creation in which we, the readers, become conspirators.'
  Malcolm Bradbury (1932–)

'Reading a book is like re-writing it for yourself ... You bring to a novel, anything you read, all your experience of the world. You bring your history and you read it in your own terms.'
  Angela Carter (1940–92)

'There is creative reading as well as creative writing.'
  Ralph Waldo Emerson (1803–82)

'Books give not wisdom where none was before. But where some is, there reading makes it more.'
  John Harington (1561–1612)

'What is reading, but silent conversation?'
  Walter Savage Landor (1775–1864)

Comparative analysis and text adaptation

Introduction to Unit 3

This unit covers:

■ **AO1** Select and apply relevant concepts and approaches from integrated linguistic study using appropriate terminology and accurate coherent written expression.

■ **AO2** Demonstrate detailed critical understanding in analysing the ways in which structure, form and language shape meaning in a range of written contexts.

■ **AO3** Use integrated approaches to explore relationships between texts, analysing and evaluating the significance of contextual factors in their production and reception.

■ **AO4** Demonstrate expertise and creativity in using language appropriately for a variety of purposes and audiences, drawing on insights from linguistic and literary studies.

■ The written examination unit

This unit contains the only written examination you will be taking in your second year, and it extends the knowledge and skills which the AS level programme introduced and developed. It contains *two* sections:

■ Section A, which contains three unseen passages for comparison (worth 60 per cent).

■ Section B, in which you are asked to recast an extract from a set text for a different audience and purpose (worth 40 per cent). You will also be asked to write a short commentary which explains the language choices you made in your recasting, and their intended effects on your readers.

It is well worthwhile keeping in your mind the four Assessment Objectives for the whole examination, because they will be tested in this synoptic unit. Although all elements are important, if you look carefully at each of them, there are certain key words or phrases that stand out and examiners focus on.

■ AO1 focuses on your accurate use of appropriate critical terminology.

■ AO2 focuses on how well you can demonstrate the connections between the language used and the meaning conveyed.

■ AO3 considers your skill in comparing texts from different contexts.

■ AO4 tests your own ability to use language appropriately and creatively.

Additionally you will have to demonstrate all the skills you have developed over the duration of the course, which can be described as examination technique, such as timing, and relevance.

Therefore we can sum up the main requirements of the unit in the following three questions:

What do I have to know?

- appropriate framework terminology
- the content and aims of at least one set text.

What do I have to do?

- answer two questions in 2½ hours
- read and analyse literary and non-literary texts
- read and analyse a transcription of a piece of spontaneous speech
- compare texts by showing how language is used to convey ideas and attitudes
- recast one (or possibly two) short extracts from a set text to make it (or them) suitable for a new audience and purpose
- explore and explain your own language choices
- write fluently and accurately.

What are the keys for success?

- reading the unseen texts both quickly and accurately
- focusing on the relevant information
- maintaining a relevant focus on the question
- showing how meaning is conveyed in the texts
- producing a fully developed answer in the time available
- ensuring that you do not run out of time.

1 Exploring texts

This chapter covers:

- how to tackle the analytical comparison task in Section A

- examples of the types of extracts you will encounter

- strategies for exploring and analysing texts.

When you are faced with three unseen texts which you have to compare, you need to be methodical and thorough in your approach. You have 1½ hours for this task, and it is essential you do not go over the time allocated and steal precious minutes from your recasting task. You need to maximise your chances of scoring as many marks as possible, and you cannot do this if you do not allow yourself sufficient time for the recasting and commentary in Section B.

What sort of unseen texts can you expect?

- There will always be a transcription of a piece of spontaneous speech.

- There will always be a literary text. This is likely to be a piece of narrative prose (an extract from a novel) or a poem. It could be an extract from a play.

- The third text will be non-literary, and this is where there can be the widest range of possibilities. The non-literary text could be biography/autobiography, travel writing, informative writing, advertising, journalism, **rhetoric**, etc. Note that prepared speech or rhetoric forms part of the non-literary section, so it could be possible to be given two spoken extracts (one spontaneous and one prepared) and one literary piece.

The task is always going to be similar in approach with only minor differences to accommodate the specific texts. Although it is always challenging to be faced with unseen texts, a methodical approach will help you to navigate your way successfully through them.

Link

Examples of the type of extracts you could be given in the examination can be found on pp6–28 and 31–8.

What is the best way to approach the task?

Before you begin to write your response in your answer book you need to spend time working on the texts themselves. Bearing in mind the information you have been given, skim read the texts to gain an overview of each and the relationship between them. Then, using the techniques you have developed throughout the course, re-read them more intensively, annotating them to identify their key features and any significant points of comparison you find. You should spend up to half an hour reading them through and annotating closely to ensure you have a good grip on them. The work you do in this first half hour is critical. It prepares the way for a well-focused and thorough exploration of the three texts. In the remaining hour for Section A you need to convey a clear and precise comparative reading of the texts, and inadequate or rushed preparation is bound to undermine the effectiveness of your answer.

As you read the texts you need to identify and consider the *language features* and *how the text is constructed*. Think about:

- structure and organisation
- vocabulary (that is, use of nouns, verbs, adjectives, adverbs, lexical frequency, etc.)
- imagery (that is, use of **simile** and **metaphor**, etc.)
- grammar (that is, sentence types, length, structure, etc.).

AQA Examiner's tip

Make sure that you spend enough time reading and re-reading the texts in Section A. This forms the foundation of your response. You should spend about twenty minutes to half an hour reading, annotating and making notes before you start to write your response.

A close consideration of these features should lead you to be able to identify the:

▦ mode

▦ domain

▦ genre

▦ degree of formality

▦ historical or social context.

These, in turn, should enable you to answer the following questions:

▦ What is the **aim** or **purpose**? What seems to you to be the intention of the writer or speaker? What is being communicated? Is it, for example, to inform, persuade, interact, express feelings or convey an idea? Is there an identifiable primary and secondary purpose? (For example, an advertisement will aim to persuade or influence, but it also may need to inform.)

▦ Who is the text aimed at? Is it a broad **audience** as in the case of a novel, which is often the reading public in general, or a much narrower audience, such as children or mothers? Is it a speech aimed at the nation or a conversation between friends?

▦ Is it in the written **mode**, the spoken mode or does it have elements of both (i.e. is it mixed mode)?

▦ Is it an identifiable type of writing or speech that belongs to a particular **domain** or field, such as the law, journalism, advertising, etc.? The language used will vary according to the function it is fulfilling in a particular context.

▦ Is it prose, poetry or drama? Can you narrow it down further and identify a sub-**genre**; for example, is it a specific type of fiction (such as a thriller, romance or historical novel) or a particular type of journalism (such as a magazine article or a leader in a popular newspaper)?

▦ Is it very **formal** (as in an academic textbook or lecture), very informal (as in a personal letter or a conversation with a friend) or are there elements of both formality and informality (as you might find in a newspaper advertisement or a discussion on the television)?

▦ Does it belong to a clearly identifiable social or historical **context**? (For example, is it a job interview or a conversation in a pub, does it relate to a specific historical event such as a wartime speech or is it a marriage proposal found in a Jane Austen novel?)

The key is to ask yourself *questions*. It does not matter if you have no answers straightaway. Train yourself to ask, for example:

▦ why did the speaker or writer use that particular word or phrase?

▦ why was that expression used?

▦ what is the effect?

Remember that a novel or poem is a consciously crafted work and the writer has taken great care with the choice of language. Think why the writer chose to use these words or metaphors. This is also true for the non-literary extract, although less so for spontaneous speech. Of course, conscious crafting can occur in spoken language, and clearly is to be found in examples of rhetoric, but it is probably less likely in unprepared speech. The various features we identify are generally not *consciously* planned.

💡 Key terms

Aim or purpose: the reason why the text has been written. The writer could, for example, be trying to argue a case or persuade the audience to have a certain point of view.

Audience: the readers the writer had in mind when writing the text.

Mode: the medium of communication used, usually speech or writing.

Domain: the type of writing to which a text belongs, for example, journalism, literature, advertising, law, conversation.

Genre: a class or category of text, with its particular conventions of language, form and structure, for example, short story, science fiction novel, Shakespearean comedy.

Formal: a formal text is one that rigidly follows certain rules or traditions of form. An informal text is usually more relaxed.

Context: the social situation, including audience and purpose, in which language is used; the social situation is an important influence on the language choices made by speakers and writers.

AQA Examiner's tip

Ask yourself questions like these during the first half hour of the examination, after your initial read-through of the text. Mark the text and make notes.

Link

The extracts that you should use for this question are Texts 1 to 8, which can be found throughout pp6–28.

■ **Practical activity**

Below you will find some short examples of written and spoken texts. They are not linked as in the examination but they are typical of the sort of extracts you might find on your examination paper.

Try to identify and explore as many language features as possible that may help you to write about the texts. Remember to think about the following:

- Structure: How is each text structured? If you can identify sections what is communicated in each? What is the text about?

- Language: How does the writer or speaker use language to convey meaning to the audience? What is the writer's or speaker's aim? Think especially about:

  a vocabulary

  b imagery

  c grammar.

- Speech: As one of the extracts on the examination paper will be a piece of spontaneous speech, it is worth thinking about any features of speech or representations of speech that may be in any of the extracts. For example, is it a transcription or is the writer trying to convey the spoken word within the written mode? If the latter, how is this done and what is communicated to us as readers? Answers to these questions will provide useful material for you to use in your comparative response.

🔍 Prose

An extract from a novel can be difficult to contextualise, even with the help provided on the examination paper. However, in addition to thinking about the bullet points above, there are a few standard questions to ask yourself:

- Is it a first person or third person narrative? What effects are achieved? Is there a discernible **narrative voice** and, if so, how does it affect the reader's response?

- Is there a sub-genre that can be identified (for example thriller, crime, science fiction)? If so, this ought to give you a clue as to the audience or aim.

- Does the writer use representations of speech? If so, you can comment on how the writer does this and compare it with the transcription.

Text 1: from *For Whom the Bell Tolls* by Ernest Hemingway

The following text is taken from Ernest Hemingway's novel *For Whom the Bell Tolls*. It is set during the Spanish Civil War of the late 1930s, which was between the communist Republican forces and the fascist troops under General Franco. This extract describes an attack on a small group of communist guerrillas by fascist aircraft. Passionaria was the name given to Dolores Ibarurri, a passionate advocate of the communist cause. Her famous saying was, 'Better to die on thy feet than live on thy knees'.

Lying flat on his belly and watching the planes come, Ignacio gathered the legs of the tripod into his two hands and steadied the gun.

"Keep thy head down," he said to Joaquin. "Keep thy head forward."

"Passionaria says 'Better to die on thy –'" Joaquin was saying to himself as the drone came nearer them. Then he shifted suddenly into "Hail Mary, full of grace, the Lord is with thee; blessed art thou among women and blessed is the fruit of thy womb, Jesus. Holy Mary, Mother of God, pray for us sinners now and at the hour of our death. Amen. Holy Mary, Mother of God," he started, then he remembered quickly as the roar came now unbearably, and started an act of contrition racing into it, "Oh, my God, I am heartily sorry for having offended thee who art worthy of all my love– "

Then there were the hammering explosions past his ears and the gun barrel hot against his shoulder. It was hammering now again and his ears were deafened by the muzzle blast. Ignacio was pulling down hard on the tripod and the barrel was burning his back. It was hammering now in the roar and he could not remember the act of contrition.

All he could remember was at the hour of our death. Amen. At the hour of our death. Amen. At the hour. At the hour. Amen. The others all were firing. Now and at the hour of our death. Amen.

Then through the hammering of the gun, there was the whistle of the air splitting apart, and then in the red-black roar the earth rolled under his knees and then waved up to hit him in the face and then dirt and bits of rock were falling all over and Ignacio was lying on him and the gun was lying on him. But he was not dead because the whistle came again and the earth rolled under him with a roar. Then it came again and the earth lurched under his belly and one side of the hilltop rose into the air and then fell slowly over them where they lay.

Critical response activity

Did you ask yourself any of the following key questions?

1 How is the extract structured?

2 What does Hemingway convey to us in each of the sections?

3 How does Hemingway use language to convey these feelings and sensations?

4 How does the narrative voice affect the reader's response?

5 How does the writer employ speech in the extract?

6 Is there an identifiable sub-genre, and does this help us to form an idea about audience or possible purpose?

Commentary

1 How is the extract structured?

Although an extract is part of a larger whole, and therefore not something that can be seen as entire in itself, there are arguably three sections we can identify here:

- the anticipation of the attack
- the attack itself showing the resistance put up by the guerrillas
- the final section which closes the battle and in which the fascist planes drop their bombs on them.

2 What does Hemingway convey to us in each of the sections?

The first section focuses on the feelings of Joaquin, his political convictions, his fear and his belief in God.

The second section focuses on the physical experience of the conflict, the chaos and Joaquin's fear of death.

The final section conveys the physical sensations experienced by Joaquin and the others as bombs were dropped on them, leading to their deaths.

3 How does Hemingway use language to convey these feelings and sensations?

Joaquin's fear: We notice the way his thoughts move quickly from a political slogan to the Hail Mary and an act of contrition. He feels he is about to die and wishes to make his peace with God. However, it is the way his prayers are said that reveals his fear. What do the adverb 'suddenly' and the verb 'shifted' convey? Speed of movement? The awareness that political slogans are hollow at the moment of death? His deep belief in God? The 'roar' of the aircraft which came 'unbearably' suggests he is overwhelmed by the noise of the aircraft. At first the aircraft were just a 'drone', a metaphor which suggests what? Does it remind us of a distant hum of insects? But the insects change to lions and the noise is so loud that he is unable to cope. The verb 'races' and the adverb 'quickly' are two more indicators of panic as the act of contrition changes into the Hail Mary. There is no time to separate the two and he is overwhelmed by a sense of personal chaos.

In the second section he becomes fixated by the thought of his imminent death. How is this shown? Hemingway uses repetition and **minor sentences** (groups of words that begin with a capital letter and end with a full stop but do not contain a verb) to show his mind revolving around the likelihood of death. Each repeated minor sentence ('At the hour of our death. Amen. At the hour. At the hour. Amen.') highlights the same thought, from which he cannot escape and which even dominate the battle.

The physical experience of the battle: What do we notice about the nouns, adjectives and verbs in the second section ('hammering explosions'; 'gun barrel hot'; 'it was hammering' (twice); 'deafened', 'muzzle blast', 'burning', 'roar')? They are all very physical and stimulate the reader's senses of hearing and touch. 'Hammering' is repeated three times (once as an adjective and twice as a verb) to convey the loud and repetitive sound of the machine gun. What is the effect of nouns such as 'explosions', 'blast' and 'roar', and verbs such as 'deafened'? Do they help convey the chaotic noise of the battle? Images of heat are also present. The gun barrel was 'hot' against his shoulder and the barrel was 'burning' his back. Why?

The final section describes the bomb hitting the hillside and the explosion which follows. Look carefully at the sentence structure here. What do you notice? The first sentence uses the coordinating conjunction 'and' four times. Why? Does each coordinating clause describe one event (for example, the bomb dropping, the explosion, the ground blowing up) to reveal the speed of the events, one happening after the other, and the chaos and destruction caused? Explore the language in each of the clauses. What is the effect of 'splitting apart' to describe air? Why does he describe a sound ('roar') in terms of colour ('red-black')? Why does he start the next sentence with another coordinating conjunction ('But')? What does 'But' mean? Does its separation from the previous sentence help emphasise his astonishment that he has not been killed yet? How many words in the final section are to do with sound and movement, and what are their effects?

> **AQA** Examiner's tip
>
> Think about your reasons for picking out and naming features such as types of sentences and repetition. These features are useful only when you can use them to support a point you are making about the text. Simply finding and naming them will not further your analysis.

4 *How does the narrative voice affect the reader's response?*

This is clearly a third person account, although a good deal of it is presented through the experiences of Joaquin so it combines the insight we get from the first person account with the reliability of the third person account. Can you identify elements of the text where we get this combination of objectivity and subjectivity?

5 *How does the writer employ speech in the extract?*

How far could you describe the exchanges between Ignacio and Joaquin as conversation? How would you describe them? Can you think of any reason why Hemingway used the archaic determiner 'thy' instead of the more usual 'your'? Could it be connected to the fact that he wants to convey the comradeship that is linked with the older singular form of the second person (still found in the Spanish *tu* but lost in English)? Most of the 'speech' is an internalised monologue. How does Hemingway use adverbs like 'suddenly', and verbs like 'racing', to help convey the way in which Joaquin's words and thoughts were expressed? What does this convey to the reader?

6 *Is there an identifiable sub-genre, and does this help us to form an idea about audience or possible purpose?*

As the text is focused on a battle, it may suggest that the sub-genre is adventure or warfare, but it is clearly impossible to generalise from such a small extract. Here the aim seems to be to convey the reality and the horror of conflict from the point of view of the participants, and, if we know something about the background of the Spanish Civil War, to involve us in the politics of the time. His emphasis on the genuine fear his protagonist feels, and his descriptions of the horror and chaos of the battle, suggest he may wish to show his readers something of the reality of war, to engage them with the humanity of those involved and to observe the way in which people can feel that religious truths are more powerful than politics. However, it would be unwise to go further, and rash to predict that it could be a novel that would appeal more to men than women. Assertions such as this are very dangerous, and usually inaccurate.

Text 2: from *Sons and Lovers* by D. H. Lawrence

Critical response activity

Now try this extract from *Sons and Lovers* by D. H. Lawrence, applying the skills you have already practised above. Remember to ask yourself the key questions.

Lawrence wrote *Sons and Lovers* in 1913, and it is set in the coal-mining district of Nottinghamshire, where he himself grew up. In the following extract Walter Morel, a coal miner, is returning to his wife and family, having been out spending his wages on drink. Mrs Morel has just had their first baby.

On the Friday, he was not home by eleven o'clock. The baby was unwell, and was restless, crying if he were put down. Mrs Morel, tired to death, and still weak, was scarcely under control.

"I wish the nuisance would come," she said wearily to herself.

The child at last sank down to sleep in her arms. She was too tired to carry him to the cradle.

"But I'll say nothing, whatever time he comes," she said. "It only works me up; I won't say anything. But I know if he does anything it'll make my blood boil," she added to herself.

Link

See Unit 1 of *AQA English Language and Literature A AS* for more about the benefits and limitations of first and third person accounts.

Link

To remind yourself of the key questions, look back to the practical activity box on p6.

She sighed, hearing him coming, as if it were something she could not bear. He, taking his revenge, was nearly drunk. She kept her head bent over the child as he entered, not wishing to see him. But it went through her like a flash of hot fire when, in passing, he lurched against the dresser, setting the tins rattling, and clutched at the white pot knobs for support. He hung up his hat and coat, then returned, stood glowering from a distance at her, as she sat bowed over the child.

"Is there nothing to eat in the house?" he asked insolently, as if to a servant. In certain stages of his intoxication he affected the clipped, mincing speech of the towns. Mrs Morel hated him most in this condition.

"You know what there is in the house," she said so coldly, it sounded impersonal.

He stood and glared at her without moving a muscle.

"I asked a civil question, and I expect a civil answer," he said affectedly.

"And you got it," she said, still ignoring him.

He glowered again. Then he came unsteadily forward. He leaned on the table with one hand, and with the other jerked at the table drawer to get a knife to cut bread. The drawer stuck because he pulled it sideways. In a temper he dragged it, so that it flew out bodily, and spoons, forks, knives, a hundred metallic things, splashed with a clatter and clang upon the brick floor. The baby gave a convulsed start.

"What are you doing, clumsy drunken fool?" the mother cried.

"Then tha' should get the flamin' things thysen. Tha should get up, like other women have to, an' wait on a man."

"Wait on you – wait on you?" she cried. "Yes, I see myself."

"Yes, an I'll learn thee tha's got to. Wait on me, yes, tha sh'lt wait on me –"

"Never, milord. I'll wait on a dog at the door first."

"What – what?"

He was trying to fit in the drawer. At her last speech he turned round. His face was crimson, his eyes bloodshot. He stared at her one silent second in threat.

"P-h!" she went quickly in contempt.

He jerked at the drawer in his excitement. It fell, cut sharply on his shin, and on the reflex he flung it at her.

One of the corners caught her brow as the shallow drawer crashed into the fireplace. She swayed, almost fell stunned from her chair. To her very soul she was sick; she clasped the child tightly to her bosom. A few moments elapsed; then, with an effort, she brought herself to. The baby was crying plaintively. Her left brow was bleeding rather profusely. As she glanced down at the child, her brain reeling, some drops of blood soaked into its white shawl; but the baby was at least not hurt. She balanced her head to keep equilibrium, so that the blood ran into her eye.

Walter Morel remained as he had stood, leaning on the table with one hand, looking blank. When he was sufficiently sure of his balance, he went across to her, swayed, caught hold of the back of the rocking-chair, almost tipping her out; then, leaning forward over her, and swaying as he spoke, he said, in a tone of wondering concern:

"Did it catch thee?"

Commentary

1 How is the text structured?

How many sections are there, and what do the different sections deal with? Note especially the way in which Lawrence intersperses authorial comment and description with spoken language. Think about the effect of this structure.

2 What does Lawrence convey in the sections or in the passage as a whole?

Trust your own response to the passage. Do you find it moving? Did you find it engaging? What feelings are generated?

3 Identify some specific features of language which Lawrence uses to do this.

Find and comment on his use of verbs and adverbs, nouns and adjectives. Identify and comment on Lawrence's use of simile and metaphor. (Note: although there are examples of **alliteration** in this passage, there are other features that are more worthwhile mentioning. In this case, the alliteration simply emphasises a meaning already communicated by the language.)

4 How does the narrative voice affect the reader's response?

For this you need to look closely at the paragraphs in which Lawrence's authorial comment and descriptions influence our responses.

5 How does the writer employ speech in the extract?

There are some interesting comments to make on how Lawrence represents **dialect**, and contrasts to be made between the different forms of speech used. How does Lawrence use adverbs and adverbial phrases to communicate the way the words are spoken? How do these affect our responses? What different effects are created by the spoken exchanges where there are no explanatory details, merely the words themselves?

6 Can we form some idea about the aim of the text, and the audience?

Bearing in mind the dangers of drawing broad conclusions from a small extract, do we nevertheless feel that Lawrence is using the experiences of his two characters to involve us in the emotions of a working-class married couple at the beginning of the 20th century? Does he have more sympathy for the wife or the husband, or neither?

Poetry

Of course, the literary extract could be a poem. However, if you do not feel confident tackling poetry, remember that there is no need to panic. Just remember that the method is essentially the same as for prose, although there are a few specialist terms you need to be aware of. Here are a few pointers that you may find helpful:

Link

To refresh your understanding of the use of dialogue in novels, look back to Chapter 16 of *AQA English Language and Literature A AS*.

Link

For more information on the representation of accent and dialect, see pp98–100 of *AQA English Language and Literature A AS*. Although this deals with use of dialect in spoken language, the effects are similar in literary texts.

Link

See the Useful Framework Terms for specific help in identifying these features. These can be found on pp152–9.

11

1 When you have read through the poem carefully a couple of times, you will begin to get some inkling of the audience and purpose. In many cases, the poet will be writing both personally and for a wider readership. There is likely to be an important idea, emotion or message that the poet wants to communicate to the wider world. Ask yourself what this might be.

2 The mode will be written, the domain literature and the genre poetry, but we cannot necessarily assume that the **tenor** will be formal. The language will be shaped by the poet to fulfil a specific purpose and may vary from the formal to the informal.

3 Is it in the first person? Is there a 'voice' you can identify? Do identifiable feelings or emotions come across?

4 Because poetry is a highly condensed form of language, poets use words in a variety of ways to convey meaning. Keep a look out for:
- simile and metaphor
- **ambiguity**
- **paradox**.

These are techniques poets often use to convey a range of ideas in a compact form.

5 When you are exploring the language, take special note of the **connotations** of verbs, nouns and adjectives.

6 Also look at the form. Poems are likely to be either in free verse, where there is often no clearly discernible regular **rhythm** or rhyme scheme, or in a very precise and identifiable metrical form. Ask yourself why the poet has chosen a particular form and what the effects are. Ask yourself if the rhythm gives emphasis to any particular words, phrases or ideas.

7 Look for any sound patterns, especially rhyme (if any), repetition, alliteration, **assonance** and **onomatopoeia**. Ask yourself what effects they achieve.

8 Finally, when comparing the poem to other texts, draw attention to any specific poetic features you have noticed that help convey the poet's meaning, and make comparisons or contrasts with the ways in which language is used in the non-literary extract or in speech. There are likely to be many contrasts, but there may be similarities, too. For example, do the rhythms resemble normal speech or are they very different, and why?

Let us have a look at a poem and apply some of these principles.

Text 3: *Naming of Parts* by Henry Reed, from a series of poems called *Lessons of the War*

The following poem was written by Henry Reed in 1942 during the Second World War, and describes a situation in which new recruits are being given some basic training on the use of their rifles. It belonged to a series of poems by Reed called *Lessons of the War*.

Naming of Parts

To-day we have naming of parts. Yesterday,
We had daily cleaning. And to-morrow morning,
We shall have what to do after firing. But to-day,
To-day we have naming of parts. Japonica
Glistens like coral in all of the neighbouring gardens,
    And to-day we have naming of parts.

This is the lower sling swivel. And this
Is the upper sling swivel, whose use you will see,
When you are given your slings. And this is the piling swivel,
Which in your case you have not got. The branches
Hold in the gardens their silent, eloquent gestures,
    Which in our case we have not got.

This is the safety catch, which is always released
With an easy flick of the thumb. And please do not let me
See anyone using his finger. You can do it quite easy
If you have any strength in your thumb. The blossoms
Are fragile and motionless, never letting anyone see
    Any of them using their finger.

And this you can see is the bolt. The purpose of this
Is to open the breech, as you can see. We can slide it
Rapidly backwards and forwards: we call this
Easing the spring. And rapidly backwards and forwards
The early bees are assaulting and fumbling the flowers:
    They call it easing the Spring.

They call it easing the Spring; it is perfectly easy
If you have any strength in your thumb: like the bolt
And the breech, and the cocking-piece and the point of balance,
Which in our case we have not got; and the almond-blossom
Silent in all of the gardens and the bees going backwards and forwards,
    For to-day we have naming of parts.

Commentary

Once we have read the poem two or three times we can ask ourselves some of the key questions.

1 How is the text structured?

The most obvious thing to note is that the poem has five stanzas. Some of the stanzas (1 and 5) appear just to express the thoughts of the soldier-narrator who may be talking to us, the readers, while others (2, 3 and 4) also contain the words of the instructor. Why could Reed be doing this? How does this give overall cohesion to the poem? Could it be to create a contrast? Clearly, some of the stanzas are reflective in **tone** while others are largely giving information. Why would Reed want to make such a contrast? The answer to this question will guide us towards identifying the **theme** of the poem.

2 What does Reed convey to us in each of the sections and in the poem as a whole?

Stanza 1: This stanza seems to find the narrator talking to us, telling us precisely (three times) that he and his fellow recruits are about to be shown how to identify the various parts of a rifle, but he also pauses to tell us that the japonica is flowering in beautiful colour nearby. Why? Do we get a sense of boredom or irritation on the part of the poet? If so, how? Do we get the feeling that he would rather be doing something else, and that he finds this a waste of time?

Stanza 2: This stanza introduces us to the voice of the instructor, and the language describing the rifle. This is followed by the voice of the narrator describing the garden. What contrast does this make? What does 'eloquent' mean? What is an 'eloquent gesture'? What are the soldiers missing, according to the narrator? What does the narrator seem to feel about this? Is he sad, angry, or what? What tells you this?

Stanza 3: Does this stanza follow the pattern of the previous one? Why? What idea does it seem to reinforce? What is the difference between the soldiers and the natural world? Beauty? Growth? New life? Is there a contrast with the sterility of the soldiers' actions?

Stanza 4: Does this stanza follow the pattern of the previous two? Which word is used twice but with different meanings? What is the difference between 'the spring' and 'the Spring'? Is one associated with the rifle as it is being prepared to fire, while the other is used to convey new life at the start of a new year? What is Reed saying about humanity and war, and nature and the natural world. What is he saying about the relationship between them?

Stanza 5: Like the opening stanza, the closing stanza focuses on the thoughts of the narrator. Is he using his final stanza to underline his point? Is he maintaining the contrast between the sterile world of the soldiers and the fertile world of nature? If so, how? What does he identify as missing in the world of the soldiers? What meanings can you give to the phrase 'the point of balance'?

3 How does Reed use language?

It is important to remember that it is the writer's use of language which conveys ideas and attitudes, and it is our identification and exploration of the way the writer uses language that scores marks in examinations. For our purposes, 'use of language' is a blanket term that covers imagery, syntax and word classes, as well as other ways in which meaning is conveyed, such as ambiguity and paradox. In any discussion of language and meaning, these various elements interact. Language is all of a piece, and when, for example, we are discussing how the use of a particular word class helps convey meaning, we may find it naturally links to a comment on imagery or on syntax.

The language selections which follow below are pointers you may like to consider.

Stanza 1

- ■ Imagery: 'glistens like coral'. Reed uses a simile linking the japonica to coral. What are the points of comparison? Colour? Richness? Rarity? How does the verb 'glistens' add to the beauty of the flowers? What are its connotations? It is a sensuous verb. Which senses does it engage? How does this simile introduce the key idea of the poem in stanza 1?

- ■ Word classes: Adverbs: 'To-day' (repeated four times) and 'Yesterday to-morrow'. How does Reed use these adverbs to convey a sense of the soldier-narrator feeling trapped in time, and being made to undergo some sort of ordeal he cannot escape? Does its everyday reality contrast with the world of nature he can see, but is separated from?

- ■ Conjunctions: The coordinating conjunctions 'and' and 'but' are used to add meaning to the poem. Beginning a sentence with 'And' (line 2) is unusual. What difference in emphasis does the full stop make? Would the meaning have been exactly the same if a comma had been used? Do we get an increased sense of the narrator's frustration? Although the second 'And' (line 6) does not begin a new sentence, it begins a new line and helps to create a sense of the writer's growing feelings of irritation. Reading between the lines we may detect the

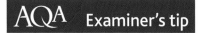

AQA Examiner's tip

Remember that at this level examiners do not have a check-list against which you will be assessed. An examiner has an open mind and is going to respond to what you say. Different candidates can focus on different features and draw different conclusions but still all get top marks if the discussion is handled well.

narrator's unspoken feelings as the words in italics – 'And to-day [*of all days, when the Japonica is glistening in the garden*] we [*are compelled to*] have naming of parts.' The use of 'But' (line 3) when combined with the repetition of 'to-day' seems to convey a similar effect. There is an almost weary acceptance of the inevitable waste of three days on aspects of the rifle.

- Syntax: The verse consists of five short declarative sentences, two of which are constructed to begin with conjunctions as we have already seen. The effect of these has been considered in the section on conjunctions above. However, Reed uses the compound sentence in lines 4–6 for a special effect. How is the compound structure which balances separate ideas round a coordinating conjunction ('and') used? Does it convey the contrast between the beauty of nature, which the narrator is cut off from, and the mundane reality of the instructor's lesson?

Critical response activity

Using these suggestions for stanza 1 as a guide, have a look at the other stanzas and see what you can find to discuss on Reed's use of language.

Commentary

You may have focused on the following:

Stanza 2

- Word classes: What is the effect of the repeated use of adjective-noun combinations which form part of the **semantic field** of rifles? How do these contrast with the adjective-noun combinations in the second part of the verse? How can the branches be both 'silent' and 'eloquent'? What are the branches 'saying'? What point is Reed making?

- Syntax: Note the use of basic explanatory declaratives. What is the effect of the full stops and the use the conjunction 'And' to begin a new utterance and sentence? Does this help Reed to convey the speaking voice of the instructor as he pauses between each piece of information? How do the subordinate clauses in sentences 2 and 3 of stanza 2 relate to the practicality or usefulness of the information given by the instructor? How does the repetition of the subordinate clause in lines 4 and 7 of stanza 2 ('Which in your case'/'Which in our case' 'you have not got'/'we have not got') with its minor variations help Reed to convey his meaning? What difference in meaning can you see?

Stanza 3

- Word classes: What is the effect of using the adjective 'easy' as an adverb instead of the more grammatically acceptable 'easily'? Does it give a sense of the instructor's voice? Of colloquial English? What is the effect of the adjectives 'fragile' and 'motionless' to describe the branches?

- Syntax: How is the syntax used to help convey the 'voice' of the instructor? You might like to consider the combination of declaratives and an imperative. What does Reed gain by continuing to contrast the language of narrator and the instructor? What is the difference in tone?

Stanza 4

- Word classes: How does Reed continue to use nouns from the semantic field of rifles and nature? How does he use the ambiguity found in the common and proper nouns 'spring' and 'Spring'? What are the connotation of the verbs 'assaulting' and 'fumbling'? What are these used to convey?

Stanza 5

■ Word classes: How does Reed use ambiguities ('Spring', 'bolt', 'breech', 'cocking piece', 'point of balance') to convey his feelings? What does he seem to feel? Anger? Frustration? Or what? Do they help to convey the conflict between fertility and sterility? What are the meanings of 'the point-of-balance'?

4 Is there an identifiable narrative voice?

There appear to be two voices in the poem: the voice of the narrator and the voice of the instructor. How does the poet differentiate between the two? Why has the poet chosen to contrast the two voices? Is one reflective and does it address the reader, and share thoughts with the reader? Is the other is more practical and more colloquial, giving instructions to the recruits? Is there a difference between the attitudes of each? Is the instructor solely focused on the gun and its various parts? Is the narrator aware of the wider implications of war and its effects on people? In the poem we can argue that Reed is creating representations of speech. How do they differ from spontaneous speech? In what ways are Reed's speech representations shaped and structured to help him convey his thoughts and feelings in the poem?

5 How has Reed used sound and form patterns?

You do not have to have a detailed knowledge of verse forms and the technical vocabulary of poetry to be able to respond to this question. Poems are carefully structured works, even if they give the impression of being unstructured!

■ Patterning: Clearly, this poem has a regular pattern within each of the verses. Reed has used it to make contrasts between the soldiers and the world of nature, through careful use of echo and repetition. How does Reed use repetition to link the soldiers and the instructor, and to contrast them with the natural world (for example, 'Which in your case you have not got' in stanza 2 and 'Which in our case we have not got' in stanza 5, as well as most of stanza 5)? Where else do you see this?

■ Rhyme: Reed has not chosen to use rhyme. The stanzas are unrhymed. What reasons can you suggest for this? Could it be to present a more natural speaking voice? Are there any other reasons?

■ Rhythm: All language has rhythm. A poet will often use a regular number of stressed words or syllables in a line to help emphasise key ideas. It is a link between sound and meaning. Just look at a few lines and see if you can spot Reed putting **stress** on specific words to underline his meaning (for example stanza 5, 'They call it easing the Spring; it is perfectly easy'). The rhythm underlines the point he is making, while the use of the pause and the half line further emphasises the idea that it is perfectly easy to be part of the natural world if we are able to reject war. Reed makes sure the lines are not end-stopped but that the natural speaking voice is conveyed through the use of **enjambement**. However, a poet will often put words or phrases at the beginning or the end of a line to make them stand out. Where has Reed done this? Look, for example, at stanza 2 lines 3 and 4, and the final line in each stanza.

■ Link

For more on representations of speech, see Unit 2 of *AQA English Language and Literature A AS*, beginning on page 84.

▦ Sound: Reed does use alliteration and assonance, but in a subtle way, to help him underline his meaning. Can you see a contrast in stanza 2 between the rather harsh-sounding repetition of the 's' sound to describe the 'sling-swivels' on the rifles with the flowing vowel sounds of 'silent' and 'eloquent' to describe the blossom? This contrast would help him stress the difference between the sterile weapons of war with the fertile beauty of nature.

6 Is there a theme we can identify? Is there a specific audience?

Is this an anti-war poem? Is Reed focusing on some of the ways war affects people? How does he use his narrators to do this?

Here are two more poems you could explore, using some of the techniques outlined above.

Text 4: *Inventory* by Liz Lochhead

The first poem is by the Scottish poet, Liz Lochhead. Liz Lochhead was born in Motherwell in 1947 and in this poem tells us about her feelings after a break-up in a relationship.

> You left me
>   nothing but nail
>   parings orange peel
>   empty nut shells half filled
>   ashtrays dirty
>   cups with dregs of
>   nightcaps an odd hair
>   or two of yours on my
>   comb gap toothed
>   bookshelves and a
>   you shaped
>   depression in my pillow

AQA Examiner's tip

Remember, the alliteration and assonance only add to the music of Reed's poem and support the meaning. You can use these features to support the points you make about the meaning, but it is important not to give them too much weight.

▦ Critical response activity

1 Can you see any connection between the form and structure of the poem and the title? How has she used her structure to support the meaning she wants to communicate to the reader?

2 How does the lack of punctuation in the poem enable you to read the lines in more than one way? Where do we pause when reading the lines? How many different meanings can we find?

3 This is a poem that has to be 'read' with the ears as well as the eyes. How many interpretations can you give to 'a you-shaped depression'? How many other lines could carry more than one meaning?

4 Is the poem just a clever puzzle or do you think that the way she compresses her feelings into 12 lines conveys them effectively to the reader? You need to justify your thoughts.

Text 5: *The Five Students* **by Thomas Hardy (1840–1928)**

The sparrow dips in his wheel-rut bath,
　　The sun grows passionate-eyed,
And boils the dew to smoke by the paddock-path;
　　As strenuously we stride, –
Five of us; dark He, fair He, dark She, fair She, I
　　All beating by.

The air is shaken, the high-road hot,
　　Shadowless swoons the day,
The greens are sobered and cattle at rest; but not
　　We on our urgent way, –
Four of us; fair She, dark She, Fair He, I, are there,
　　But one – elsewhere.

Autumn moulds the hard fruit mellow,
　　And forward still we press
Through moors, briar-meshed plantations, clay-pits yellow
　　As in the spring hours – yes,
Three of us; Fair He, fair She, I, as heretofore,
　　But – fallen one more.

The leaf drops; earthworms draw it in
　　At night-time noiselessly,
The fingers of birch and beech are skeleton-thin,
　　And yet on the beat are we, –
Two of us; fair She, I, but no more left to go
　　The track we know.

Icicles tag the church-aisle leads,
　　The flag-rope gibbers hoarse,
The home-bound foot-folk wrap their snow-flaked heads,
　　Yet I still stand the course, –
One of us . . . Dark and fair He, dark and fair She, gone:
　　The rest – anon.

■　Critical response activity

Consider these points whilst analysing *The Five Students* by Thomas Hardy:

■ Look at the way the poem is structured. What happens in stanzas 2–4? What happens to each of the companions?

■ Are there any other patterns you can see in the poem? How does Hardy use images of time? What is the time of day in each of the stanzas? What is the season of the year? What is he using this dual-time scheme to symbolise? How does he use the weather?

■ Why does he echo the final two lines of each stanza throughout the poem?

■ How do the language and imagery of each stanza reflect the time of day, the season of the year and the age of the companions?

■ How do the rhythms of each stanza reflect the speaking voice? How is pause used in the final stanza?

■ What is the tone and mood of the poem?

■ What is Hardy trying to communicate to his readers in the poem?

Commentary

As you read through Hardy's poem you may like to consider the following words and phrases from the poem. Think about them carefully; ask yourself what they connote in their context and how they help Hardy to convey his meaning. There may also be others not listed below that you feel are equally important.

Stanza 1
- verbs: 'grows', 'boils' ('to smoke'), 'stride', 'beating'
- adverbs: 'strenuously'
- nouns: 'sun', 'dew'
- adjectives: 'passionate-eyed'.

Stanza 2
- verbs: 'is shaken', 'are sobered', 'swoons'
- adverbs: 'elsewhere'
- nouns: 'day'
- adjectives: 'shadowless', 'urgent'.

Stanza 3
- verbs: 'press', 'fallen'
- adverbs: 'forward still'
- nouns: '(hard) fruit', 'moors', 'clay-pits'
- adjectives: 'mellow', 'briar-meshed'.

Stanza 4
- verbs: 'drops', 'draw' ('in')
- adverbs: 'noiselessly', ('And') 'yet'
- nouns: 'earthworms', 'night-time', 'fingers', 'beat'
- adjectives: 'skeleton-thin'.

Stanza 5
- verbs: 'gibbers', 'wrap', 'gone'
- adverbs: 'hoarse', 'still', 'anon'
- nouns: 'icicles', 'foot-folk', ('The') 'rest'
- adjectives: 'home-bound', 'snow-flaked'.

Critical response activity

Consider the following questions:

1. Did you notice the change in the *verbs*? They move from dynamic active verbs that are full of life and vigour, through to passive verbs, and on to verbs which connote age and death. What is the reason for this?

2. What did you notice about the *adverbs*? How do the adverbs of manner change? How does Hardy use the adverbs of time? What is significant about the fact that 'still' is used twice (once in connection with 'forward' and 'press' and once in connection with 'stand'). Does one convey a sense of desperate action and one of resigned stoicism?

3. Many of the *nouns* relate to nature and the natural world. How does Hardy use them to reflect the change in the time of day/the season of the year/life and death?

4. How does Hardy use *adjectives* to reflect the attitude of the travellers? In what ways do they also help convey the passage of time?

🔍 The non-literary extract

The non-literary extract, of course, can be taken from many different genres and domains. To prepare yourself for this you need to familiarise yourself with as wide a range of texts as possible in your everyday reading. After all, it could be a piece of journalism, travel writing, a prepared speech, advertising, biography, autobiography, an extract from an academic text book and so on. However, the methodology for tackling the non-literary extract is the same as for all the other texts.

■ Find the structure.

■ Look closely at the language.

■ Identify the purpose and audience.

■ Look for any representations of speech.

Text 6: from *Snakes and Ladders* by Gita Mehta

The following text is an extract from Gita Mehta's book *Snakes and Ladders*, a series of essays about what she sees as the paradoxes and contradictions of modern India. In this extract, she ponders the poverty and wealth found side by side.

'You must have seen the people foraging through that huge garbage dump on the outskirts of Delhi,' the Indian paper tycoon remarked.

'The beggars looking for food?' I asked. 'Of course I've seen them'. 5

But that was all I had done. Seen them, then quickly turned away, covering my nose although the car windows were up and the banks of the four-lane highway were planted with bougainvillaea bushes to hide a square mile of 10 fetid garbage with vultures circling overhead.

'They're not beggars,' the tycoon corrected me. 'They are rag-pickers – supplying raw material to us in the paper industry.'

I was shocked. 'You mean people working in 15 those subhuman conditions are on your payroll? You hire them to live like that?'

'Of course I don't bloody hire them,'he said in irritation. 'They collect rags and sell them to a contractor. If you are looking for a convenient 20 phrase you might say those people are self-employed.'

Well, talk about the unacceptable origins of capitalism.

'Actually, it's only an extension of the kind 25 of work they have always done,' the tycoon explained kindly. 'They're all untouchables by caste. Local sweepers.'

Intrigued by these self-employed people, so evidently masters of their own destiny, I got out 30 of the car and made my way towards the tiny figures in the middle of that grey landscape.

The handkerchief covering my face did little to protect me from the fetid quicksand under my feet. Why hadn't I realized this garbage dump 35 would not be solid ground? That I would be sinking into effluvia from the deaths, marriages, examination papers, hospital refuse of a giant metropolis of a million people.

Beyond the dump flowed the holy Jumna River. 40 On the far bank I could see the stone battlements of the Red Fort, where languid Moghul emperors had once enjoyed the evening breeze in their marbled wind pavilions while their subjects promenaded on the river bank below. One 45 emperor had even famously sighed, 'If there is a paradise on earth, it is this, it is this.'

Today, to the left of the battlements a power station belched grey smoke into the air, colouring the mile of garbage a uniform grey like filthy flannel. Sunk to 50 my knees in spongy refuse, not daring to look down to see what might be clinging to my legs, I ploughed my way towards a thin woman wearing a short peasant skirt and a torn jacket. She looked middle-aged but could as easily have been in her twenties. 55 In one hand she carried a long iron spoke, hooked at the bottom, which she plunged into the waste. Further on, I could see other scavengers fishing up bits of rusty iron or stained rags. Children, their heads barely clearing the surface of the garbage, 60 worked beside their parents.

The exhausted woman examined me suspiciously when I greeted her. Was I a government inspector who was going to challenge her right to be there? Or a do-gooder who would take away her children, 65 contributing their pittance to the family's survival?

Commentary

1 How is the text structured?

As you know, there is no absolutely correct answer to this question. However, could we argue that there are broadly two sections: the first her conversation between Mehta and the tycoon, and the second her exploration of the dump together with her meeting with the rag-picker?

2 What does Mehta communicate to us in each of the sections?

In her opening exchange with the tycoon she reveals something about herself. Her own ignorance? Her own complacency? Or what? What alters her attitude and inspires her to find out more about the rag-pickers? What characterises the attitude of the tycoon? What suggests he feels at the very least not responsible for the rag-pickers, and possibly even that he is doing them a favour? In the second section, does she use her own reactions to shape our feelings towards the place? Towards the pickers? What would these be? Horror? Disgust? Sympathy? What evidence can we find to support our views? Why are these two sections, which take her and us from ignorance and complacency to engagement and emotional involvement, important to Mehta? How do they help her address her audience and fulfil her aim?

3 How does she use her language to convey her thoughts and feelings?

Remember that you are looking to explain to the examiner the ways in which the writer conveys her meaning, through the words she chooses and the way she combines those words in phrases or sentences. Suggestions of the effects that Mehta achieves in some of her paragraphs are listed below. Take a close look at these and try to identify the key words, images or structures she uses. Suggestions on where to focus your attention are in brackets:

lines 1–3: the desperate plight of the rag-pickers and the complacency of the tycoon ('foraging', 'huge garbage dump' 'remarked')

lines 4–7: her own ignorance of what, in retrospect, she is ashamed ('beggars' 'But', 'all', 'quickly turned away', 'covering my nose', use of full stop)

lines 6–11: the neglect of the poor by the authorities as a reflection of her own lack of concern; her moment of insight ('four-lane highway', 'bougainvillaea bushes', 'fetid garbage', 'vultures')

lines 12–28: contrasting attitudes to the plight of the poor ('tycoon', 'beggars' v. 'rag-pickers' v. 'suppliers' v. 'self-employed', 'Actually…' 'only…' 'always', 'raw material to paper industry', 'shocked', 'subhuman conditions'; implied tone)

lines 23–24 and 29–32: moral outrage (address to reader, use of monitoring feature 'Well', 'unacceptable origins'; use of irony, 'tiny figures')

lines 25–28: condescending attitude of tycoon to Mehta ('explained kindly')

lines 33–54: attitude to working conditions ('fetid quicksand, use of question, effluvia, use of list, contrast of past and present, 'languid Moghul emperors … in marbled wind pavilions' v. 'a power station belched grey smoke into the air', 'filthy flannel' 'spongy refuse')

lines 54–61: effects on people ('looked middle-aged' 'scavengers' 'children', 'heads barely clearing the surface')

lines 62–66: complexity of problem and moral ambiguity ('exhausted', verbs 'suspiciously', use of questions, woman's point of view, 'do-gooder' 'contributing to … survival').

AQA Examiner's tip

Remember that this commentary is made up of suggestions. If you thought of other interpretations or other answers to these questions and you are able to back them up with reference to the text, your ideas are equally as valid. Trust your own interpretation.

4 Is there an identifiable voice?

This is a personal account in which the writer aims to take her readers along with her as she discovers more about the lives of the rag-pickers. Can we see a change in her tone as the account proceeds? How does she first characterise her attitude? What makes it change? What differences can we see between the way she speaks to the tycoon and the way she speaks to her readers? How does she convey her shame to her readers about the fact she had tried to avoid facing up to the issue of the rag-pickers? Can we detect a tone of **irony** in her voice as she tries to come to terms with the attitude of the tycoon?

5 In what ways are representations of speech used in the extract?

Although this is not a novel, Mehta seems to use some of the techniques of the novelist to engage us and to help her make her point. What do the verbs 'remarked', 'corrected' and 'explained' in lines 3, 12 and 27, and the adverbial phrases 'in irritation' and 'kindly' in lines 18–19 and 27, suggest about the attitude of the tycoon? Where does Mehta address the reader? How does she convey feelings through her tone?

6 Can we identify the aim/audience?

This is an extract which takes the reader along a path of discovery with the author. Although there is a sense of moral outrage at the treatment of the rag-pickers and horror at the conditions in which they work, by the end of the extract we begin to grasp the complexity of India and the difficulties that lie in making snap moral decisions. The suspicion of the woman and her antagonism to Mehta make us aware that to ban this work and 'save' the children may condemn her and her family to death. Mehta is addressing those of us who are unaware of these issues.

Prepared speech

It is possible that you may be given an extract from a piece of prepared speech to discuss. This would give you many opportunities to compare prepared and spontaneous speech.

The text below is an example of a political speech made after an event of high national significance. It is George W. Bush's address to the American people following the attack on the World Trade Center in New York on 11 September 2001.

Although given at a time of high emotional intensity, it is nevertheless a carefully crafted piece of political rhetoric. Look at it closely and try to identify those elements which make it effective in achieving its aim. As in the extracts so far considered, look at the structure and organisation, the narrative voice, the language and imagery, and the rhetorical features. Before you begin to read the text, it is reasonable to make an assessment of the aim because of your existing knowledge of the context in which it was written and delivered. However, delay your final judgement until you have completed your analysis.

Text 7: Address to America by George W. Bush, 11 September 2001

Good evening.

[1] Today our fellow citizens, our way of life, our very freedom came under attack in a series of deliberate and deadly terrorist acts. The victims were in airplanes or in their offices: secretaries, business men and women, military and federal workers, moms and dads,

■ **Link**

Before you have a look at the example below, it would be a good idea to remind yourself of the section on prepared speech in Chapter 14 of *AQA English Language and Literature A AS*.

AQA **Examiner's tip**

It is not only politicians and campaigners who prepare speeches before delivering them. To be ready to analyse prepared speech in the exam you could also look at speeches prepared for occasions such as lectures, weddings, funerals, news reports and other presentations people might make as part of their job.

friends and neighbors. Thousands of lives were suddenly ended by evil, despicable acts of terror. The pictures of airplanes flying into buildings, fires burning, huge structures collapsing have filled us with disbelief, terrible sadness and a quiet, unyielding anger. These acts of mass murder were intended to frighten our nation into chaos and retreat. But they have failed. Our country is strong.

[2] A great people has been moved to defend a great nation. Terrorist attacks can shake the foundations of the biggest buildings, but they cannot touch the foundations of America. These acts shatter steel, but they cannot dent the steel of American resolve. America was targeted for attack because we're the brightest beacon of freedom and opportunity in the world. And no one will keep that light from shining. Today, our nation saw evil – the very worst of human nature – and we responded with the best of America. With the daring of our rescue workers, with the caring for strangers and neighbours who came to give blood and help out in any way they could.

[3] Immediately following the first attack, I implemented our government's emergency response plans. Our military is powerful and it's prepared. Our emergency teams are working in New York City and Washington DC to help with local rescue efforts. Our first priority is to get help to those who have been injured and to take every precaution to protect our citizens at home and around the world from further attacks. The functions of our government continue without interruption. Federal agencies in Washington which had to be evacuated today are reopening for essential personnel tonight and will be open for business tomorrow. Our financial institutions remain strong, and the American economy will be open for business as well.

[4] The search is underway for those who were behind these evil acts. I have directed the full resources of our intelligence and law enforcement communities to find those responsible and to bring them to justice. We will make no distinction between the terrorists who committed these acts and those who harbour them.

[5] I appreciate so very much the members of Congress who have joined me in strongly condemning these attacks. And on behalf of the American people, I thank the many world leaders who have called to offer their condolences and assistance. America and our friends and allies join with all those who want peace and security in the world, and we stand together to win the war against terrorism.

[6] Tonight I ask for your prayers for all those who grieve, for the children whose worlds have been shattered, for all whose sense of safety and security has been threatened. And I pray they will be comforted by a Power greater than any of us, spoken through the ages in Psalm 23: 'Even though I walk through the valley of the shadow of death, I fear no evil for you are with me.'

[7] This is a day when Americans from every walk of life unite in our resolve for justice and peace. America has stood down enemies before and we will do so this time. None of us will ever forget this day, yet we go forward to defend freedom and all that is good and just in our world.

[8] Thank you. Good night. And God bless America.

Please note, original US spellings have been retained

Commentary

This is not a long speech. It was delivered soon after the news of the attack had spread, and people were still in a state of shock. The organisation of the speech is therefore important, as such a speech needs to speak to the nation as a whole, to offer leadership, while giving reassurance that matters are under control and something is being done. This is a speech that is designed to push all the right buttons to create that sense of togetherness needed at a time of crisis, and possibly to prepare the nation to support the military action that the administration had decided to pursue.

1 Can you identify the structure?

There are only seven sections in the speech, organised into seven paragraphs. However, as the speech is designed to be heard rather than read, each of these sections or 'paragraphs' needs to address a key issue or address a need in the audience. What is each section designed to offer? How far do you agree with the following suggestions?

1 This section promotes a sense of national unity, and connects audience to victims, harnessing an emotional response in the listeners.

2 This section provides a sense of community and unity and reasserts national pride which has been severely bruised.

3 This section provides reassurance that the situation is under control.

4 This section informs the listeners of what action has been taken to satisfy the desire for justice.

5 This section links America to the international community in a battle for peace and security.

6 This section shows an awareness of the sufferings of the bereaved and invokes the higher power of God (implicitly reinforcing the belief that God and America are on the same side).

7 This section ends on a note of optimism, re-emphasising national unity and moral values.

8 This section provides a familiar and reassuring conclusion.

2 Can you identify the voice?

In a written examination you can only be presented with the text of a speech. The **intonation** and other features of the oral delivery, which help constitute the 'voice' of the speaker, cannot be easily conveyed. However, if we pay close attention to the language and structure we will be able to 'hear' the speaker, and make some meaningful comment on the 'voice'. In many ways such a task is the opposite of that in AS Unit 1, where, in the B options of each question on a set text, you have to convey the voice of a character. In ELLA3 it is an analytical task, and in this specific case, we know that the speech is given by the President of the United States at a moment of national crisis. It is fair to ask yourself what such a speech would have to do. Does the speech convey that sense of gravitas and leadership that is required in these circumstances, and if so how? Does it attempt to rally the people? Does the President attempt to orchestrate the national response to the event? To try to answer some of these questions we might notice the effects achieved by the use of the inclusive determiner 'our' three times in the opening line and twice more before the end of the first section, along with the personal pronoun 'us'. Where do we find the continued use of the first person pronoun (both singular and plural) and determiner elsewhere in the text? Where in the opening section does the President try to articulate the response of people to the events they have witnessed on television? When we identify a presidential voice speaking with and for the people ('disbelief, terrible sadness and a quiet unyielding anger') and giving shape to the emotions that people have felt, how far does this help ensure support for any political or even military action which may follow? If we look at key words and phrases in the sections which follow, such as:

- 'defend a great nation' (paragraph 2)
- 'military powerful and prepared' (paragraph 3)
- 'no distinction between those who committed acts and those who harbour them' (paragraph 4)
- 'war against terrorism' (paragraph 5)
- 'go forward to defend freedom' (paragraph 7),

how far do these convey the powerful voice of conventional leadership?

3 How does the speaker use language?

If we look carefully through the speech we notice a heavy use of **emotive language**, including abstract value-laden *nouns*, for example: 'evil', 'freedom', 'justice', 'peace', 'security', 'opportunity', 'business', along with similar emotive and value-laden *adjectives*, such as 'evil', 'despicable', ' quiet', 'unyielding', 'good', just, etc. Why have these been used and how do they work in context? How far do they depend on the speaker's tapping into an automatic reaction of approval or disapproval in his listeners? Are there any other nouns used in a similar way in this speech? What, for example, is a terrorist? Someone once said that one person's terrorist is another person's freedom fighter. How is this word used by the President in this speech and for what ends?

Comment on the use of **collocations** in the opening paragraph to identify the range of victims: (business men and women, military and federal workers, moms and dads, friends and neighbours). Can you see a careful structuring of the pairs? How is the President giving a familiar, domestic perspective to a national event that many Americans had difficulty in comprehending? Why is it important to do this?

Verbs used in a text are always worth examining. Find dynamic verbs which are used to present vividly the horror of the events, verbs used to convey the strength and resolve of the nation, and verbs which are used to hint of action to come. Why is 'defend' used in paragraph 7 ('we go forward to defend freedom')? In what light does it present American future actions? Why is that verb used rather than one such as 'attack' (for example 'We shall use all our resources to attack our enemies')? Where does it place the burden of responsibility for future events?

4 How are the sentences structured to enable them to be uttered effectively in this particular context?

If we examine the sentences in the opening section we notice that they are almost all **simple** or **compound** and their structures are balanced to enable the speaking voice to emphasise key ideas. They are not too long as the various ideas need to be weighed by the listener and their importance absorbed. Sentence 1, for example, addresses the audience directly and inclusively, identifies the subject with two parallel phrases ('our way of life', 'our very freedom'), uses a simple but powerful dynamic verb ('came [under attack]'), and concludes with an adverbial phrase containing two emotive adjectives ('deliberate', 'deadly') linked and given added weight by the alliteration that enables them to be emphasised. At times in the speech a sentence is split by a full stop, instead of a

AQA **Examiner's tip**

Remember that features such as intonation, pauses, gestures, facial expressions, etc., are not shown in the text of a speech. Like a drama text, a prepared speech gains its impact from both text and performance. Whilst an understanding of this fact is essential to your success in analysing prepared speech, your analysis should focus on the text that you are provided with in the exam.

Key terms

Emotive language: language which is specifically chosen to appeal to the reader's or listener's feelings or emotions.

comma or a semi-colon, and the conjunction 'but' is used to begin a new sentence instead of linking the clauses ('But they have failed'). This use of the short simple sentence allows the speaker to pause and emphasise the contradictory point that the conjunction 'but' is making, that the aim of the attack, which was to frighten the nation into 'chaos and retreat', has *totally* and *completely* failed. It is interesting to note that the nouns 'chaos' and 'retreat' are linked here. The semantic field connected with 'retreat' is battle and warfare, and the opposite of a retreat is an advance. If the attack has failed it surely implies that not only will the nation not disintegrate into disorganisation but it will itself move forward and attack. The simple sentence that ends the section 'Our country is strong.' now seems to imply that this strength will be used and some military action will follow before long.

How many other simple and compound sentences are there in the speech, and how are they used to support the meaning delivered by the spoken voice? How are the conjunctions 'and' and 'but' (especially in section 2) used to support the meaning?

5 How is imagery used to support the meaning?

Section 2 seems to contain the bulk of the metaphors. What aspects of the meaning of 'foundations' is transferred from buildings to America in the second sentence of section 2? Similarly, how is the literal meaning of 'steel' used to enhance its metaphorical use in connection with American resolve? Can you also comment on the use of 'but' in this sentence to balance the two clauses by acting as a pivot? How does it support the meaning? Why does the speaker change the verb 'shatter' from the first clause to 'dent' in the second clause? Can you also comment on the way the imagery of light is used in this section? Is there any other imagery you can find in the speech? Could the phrase 'war against terrorism' be regarded as a metaphor?

6 What use is made of specific rhetorical devices?

As this is a political speech addressing the nation, the use of rhetoric is inevitable. We have touched already on some of these features in the sections on language, syntax and imagery above. However, they can also be looked at separately. Do remember that it is not an exercise in feature spotting. Speakers use rhetorical devices because they achieve a specific effect, and it is the effect that is important, not the device.

Where is **alliteration** used to underline the speaker's meaning or to allow him to give extra emphasis to words?

Antithesis: Where do we find ideas contrasted in parallel constructions (usually, but not always, balanced around the conjunction 'but')? What do such **antithetical** structures enable the speaker to emphasise?

Hyperbole: Can you find any examples of exaggeration used to enhance the meaning?

Triplets are just one example of **listing** and their use in political speeches was explored at length in Max Atkinson's book *Our Masters' Voices* (Routledge 1984). How is a list used for effect in section 1 and triplets used in sections 1 and 6?

There are many **repetitions** and **patterns** used throughout the speech. The speech opens with an anaphoric triplet, one that repeats 'our' at the beginning of each of three successive phrases. Why is this a particularly effective opening? You could comment on the use of 'our', the movement from the concrete ('citizens') to the abstract ('freedom') or the euphony of the structure.

■ Key terms

Alliteration: the repetition of an initial consonant sound.

Antithesis: the juxtaposition of contrasting words or phrases to create a sense of balance or opposition between conflicting ideas.

Antithetical: opposite and contrasting.

Hyperbole: deliberate exaggeration.

Triplet: a pattern of three repeated words or phrases.

Listing: deliberately placing a number of items next to each other to ensure they are memorable for either listeners or readers.

Repetition: repeating words or phrases for emphasis or to create a rhetorical effect.

Patterns/patterning: a regular order or arrangement of elements in the text to try to ensure they are memorable for either listeners or readers.

A common pattern that we have already touched on is the use of parallel clauses largely in compound units. Can you find examples of the use of parallel clauses in section 2? How do they enhance the meaning and help the speaker to emphasise specific ideas?

References: Although not strictly speaking a rhetorical device, how does the use of the biblical quotation in section 6 help consolidate the speaker's view that America is now engaged in a war with evil forces?

Do we wish to revise our original thoughts about the aim of the speech? Having looked closely at some aspects of the speech, what can we say is its main or primary purpose? Are there any secondary aims?

Critical response activity

Using some of the above ideas and others of your own, explore Text 7 on pp22–3 further and illustrate how it fulfils its aims and achieves its effects.

Spontaneous speech

There will always be a piece of spontaneous speech in the examination. In ELLA3 you could find a conversation between a number of participants or a single speaker. One of the problems you face when trying to explore the language of spontaneous speech in an examination is that you are not given a recording of the words to listen to. You have to work out as much as you can about the way in which the words are spoken from the language on the page and from the transcription conventions used, which at best can only be approximations. It is rather like discussing a piece of music without a recording, and only being given the sheet with the notes on to work from. You have to bring the music to life inside your head. In the same way, you need to reproduce in your head the 'music' of the conversation with all stress and intonation patterns. It is useful to count out the pauses in seconds, too, to give you a sense of the length of the silences.

Look at the following transcription of a conversation between two men about a driving incident. You will need to read it more than once. Try reading it silently under your breath and give the pauses due time so that you begin to pick up a sense of spoken voice.

When you feel you have a clear grasp of the extract, ask yourself how the speakers communicate their impressions of the incident.

Text 8: A driving incident

Key:
(.)	micropause
(1.0)	pause in seconds
underlining	emphasis on a particular word

A. yes I remember there was a terrible story (1.0) <u>horrifying</u>
story that was told by a colleague of mine when I used
to teach years ago (1.0) who erm (.) this chap lived in erm
(1.0) in a semi deta (.) detached house and next door (1.0) there was
(.) a man who'd just bought a new car (1.0) and he was   5
telling me that one morning he was looking through the
window (1.0) and this (.) man allowed his wife to drive the
car very unwisely and she was having a first go in it
(1.0) (B: mm) (.) and (1.0) he backed it out of the garage (1.0) so that
it was standing on the driveway (.) and he'd closed the   10

Link

Since there will always be a piece of spontaneous speech in the examination it is sensible to revise what you learned about speech in *AQA English Language and Literature A AS*. The section on spontaneous speech is Chapter 13, but the other sections on speech in Unit 2 will also be useful.

 Examiner's tip

Reading through the text in your mind in real-time can be difficult when you feel under pressure in the exam room! But the time you spend doing it will help you to understand the text and pick out key features of speech. Remember to make notes as soon as you have finished so that you have a record of the features you noticed.

garage doors (1.0) (B: yeah) (.) and (1.0) she came out of the
house (1.0) to (.) take this car out and go shopping for the
first time (1.0) so she came out very gingerly (1.0) and
opened the door (.) and sat in the car (1.0) and (1.0) er (.) began
to back (.) very very (1.0) gently taking (.) <u>great</u> care you   15
see that she didn't do anything to this (.) to this new
car (1.0) and (1.5) as she backed (1.0) there was an unpleasant
(.) <u>crunching</u> sound (B: <u>laughs</u>) and she <u>slapped</u> on the brakes
and looked around frantically (1.0) and realised that she
hadn't opened the (.) gates (.) that (.) let on to the main   20
road you see (B: oh) (.) and she'd just backed into these
<u>very</u> gently and sort of touched the bumper and
bent the gates slightly (B: mm) (1.0) and this put her into a bit
of a flap (.) (B: mm) so (1.0) before she could do anything about
this she had to pull forward (B: mm) (.) in order to er to   25
open the gates (1.0) so she (1.0) took the car out of reverse
(.) put it into (.) first gear and pulled forward
very gently (B: yeah) (1.0) but (1.0) unfortunately (.) she (.)
misjudged the distance to the garage doors (.) so that as
she pulled forward (.) she ran into the garage doors (.)   30
<u>thump</u> (B: <u>laughs</u>) and smashed in the front bumper of the
car (.) and (B: oh) bent the garage doors (B: yeah) (1.0) so she
<u>stopped</u> in time (.) you see (1.0) and by this stage she was
getting into a bit of a flutter (.) (B: <u>laughs</u>) so (.) she got
out of the car (B: <u>laughs</u>) <u>shaking</u> like a leaf (1.0) went (.)   35
behind the car and opened the gates (.) that let on to the
main road (B: yeah) and then she was (.) determined not to
be defeated by this state of affairs which was pretty
terrifying got into the car (1.0) and (1.5) started the engine (.)
looked through the back window very very carefully (.)   40
and (.) backed out with the <u>utmost</u> deliberation (.) into the
main road (.) and managed it absolutely <u>perfectly</u> (1.0) but
the only trouble was (.) that (.) she'd left the driving side
door open (.) and had forgotten to close it (.) so that as
she backed out through the gates into the main road she   45
tore off the door (B: <u>laughs</u>) (1.5) apparently at which stage
she just <u>collapsed</u> and went into a state of hysteria

B. (<u>laughs</u>) oh God (.) I thought you were going to say she was
going to hit the milkman or something

A. no no   50

B. hm (1.0) t oh blimey

Critical response activity

1 What sort of things do you need to look for in this extract? Remember to
work from your reading of the extract. Avoid simply spotting features.

2 It appears to be a story about a very unfortunate incident which caused a
woman a good deal of distress. However, does the speaker (A) encourage
a sympathetic response in the listener (B)? What role does the listener
play in the extract? Is he merely a sounding board or does he play an
important, if minor, active part in the dynamic?

Commentary

1 What can we deduce about the context?

It appears to be part of a friendly conversation which centres upon one main speaker telling a story. How can we tell the participants are friends?

2 Who is the audience and what do we learn about the audience?

A is telling the story and B is the audience. What sort of **feedback** does he give? Does he encourage the speaker and show approval of the story or does he show disapproval? How do you know? Do you think most women would have responded in a similar way? If not, why not? What does this suggest about the importance of the audience? Would the narrator have told the story in the same way if his audience had been a woman? Is there a shared attitude between speaker and listener?

3 What appears to be the aim of the narrative?

The stated aim is to tell 'a terrible story (1.0) horrifying story'. However, does the evidence of the extract suggest that this is the whole truth? How far is it meant to elicit sympathy for the woman driver and how far is the aim to tell an amusing story at the expense of 'women' drivers in general? Is the story horrifying or funny? How do you know? How important is our awareness of the context and the audience?

4 Is there an identifiable structure?

The spontaneous speech extract in ELLA3 could be a conversation between two or more people, or could be, as in this case, a narrative in which a single speaker takes the dominating role. If the latter is the case, then it is worth asking yourself if Labov's narrative model can be applied to the text.

William Labov, professor of linguistics at the University of Pennsylvania, has written extensively on the ways in which oral narratives are constructed. He found from his research that oral narratives of personal experience are not random and lacking in organisation, but have a structure that is clear and well defined. He identifies six key stages in his narrative model which are:

- the abstract (which signals that the story is about to begin)
- the orientation (which provides a focus by dealing with the who, what, when and where of the story)
- the complication (which is the basic narrative that develops the story)
- the resolution (which draws events to a conclusion and tells the listener what finally happened)
- the evaluation (which makes the point of the story clear and draws a conclusion)
- the coda (which signals to the listener that the story has ended).

Of course not all narratives will contain all of the above, but most narratives will contain most of the stages, and identifying them helps you to comment on the structure and organisation of the piece. How many of these sections can you find in the above narrative?

5 Is there a clear narrative voice?

Because spoken language has many linguistic and **paralinguistic** opportunities to convey meaning to listeners, we need to think how the speaker communicates the story to the listener and what *features of speech* help him do this. Some will be deliberate, such as the use of

In this example, we have been told within the background information (on p27) that both speakers are men. In the examination, if information is not given on the sex of the speakers it is important not to assume that speakers are either male or female. You may make a suggestion as to whether you think the speaker is male or female if it furthers your argument and you are able to support your suggestion from the text.

emphasis and **pause** for effect, but some will be simply the result of the nature of spoken language, such as **false starts** and **repairs**, **hesitations** or **fillers**. Where does the speaker use stress and pause to help him tell his story more effectively, for example to help him build to a climax which will shock or amuse his listener? Think about some of the following: 'crunching' (line 18) 'thump' (line 31) 'utmost deliberation' (line 41) 'perfectly' (is there added irony here?) (line 42) 'tore off the door' (line 46).

Looking through the extract there do not appear to be very many hesitations, false starts, fillers or repairs. Why do you think this is? Is it anything to do with the fact that this is a rehearsed narrative? Why do such false starts and repairs as there are occur in the first few lines? There are two examples of the **monitoring** feature 'you see' (lines 21 and 33). What function do these perform in helping to connect speaker and listener in a lengthy narrative? In lines 43–44 the speaker repeats the same piece of information in slightly different words: 'she'd left the driving side door open (.) and had forgotten to close it'. Why does this occur? Is it an unintended repetition or is it a deliberate emphasis of a point prior to the climax of the story?

If we also look at the **syntax** we can comment on how that enables a speaker to engage and maintain the interest of the listener. As you know it is important to speak about **utterance** units and not sentences in your analysis of speech, and these utterance units are very often linked by coordinating conjunctions forming a compound structure. This drives the narrative forward. Look at the number of units that are linked by 'and' here. The subordinating conjunction that is most used in the text is 'so'. Why do you think this finds its way so frequently into a narrative such as this, which explores a sequence of events?

Link

Remember that the definitions of words that appear in bold are in the glossary at the back of this book (pp160–3). Check terms that you do not remember as a quick revision exercise.

6 *How does the language used by the speakers reveal their attitudes to the events?*

Don't forget that the question asks us to comment on how the speakers communicate their impressions of the incident. In other words, do their thoughts and feelings come across and what features of language reveal these to us? If we look carefully through the text we will identify various words and phrases that reveal a lot about how the speaker and the listener view the events. What do the following appear to indicate about the speaker's attitudes towards the woman and the incident?

- 'allowed' (verb) line 7
- 'unwisely' (adverb) line 8
- 'gingerly' (adverb) line 13
- 'very very gently' (adverb phrase) line 15
- 'frantically' (adverb) line 19
- 'unfortunately' (adverb) line 28
- 'getting into a bit of a flutter' (verb phrase) line 34
- 'shaking like a leaf' (verb phrase) line 35
- 'determined not to be defeated' (verb phrase) line 37
- 'hysteria' (noun) line 47.

7 *What can we say about speaker B?*

How far does Speaker B share the attitudes and values of Speaker A? His contribution up to line 47 consists of non-linguistic noises which act as feedback ('yeah', 'mm') and laughter. Do his final two utterances (lines 48–49 and 51) add anything to your understanding?

Exploring the Section A question

Sample question

This is an example of a typical task you are likely to find in Section A. Each of the texts has been annotated with the sort of jottings you might include as ideas come into your mind as you read.

Section A – Examination style questions

Analytical comparison

1 Read the three texts printed on the following pages. The texts are all concerned with specific places.

- Text A is the opening of the novel *1984* by George Orwell.
- Text B is an extract from a non-fiction text.
- Text C is a transcript of an adult talking about a recent holiday.

Compare texts A, B and C, analysing how the writers and the speaker communicate their impressions of the places they are writing about.

Your analysis should include a consideration of the following:

- the writers' and speaker's choices of vocabulary, grammar and style
- the relationship between the texts and the significance of context on language use.

(60 marks)

Link

The texts will appear immediately after the question on your exam paper. In this book, Text A can be found on p3, Text B on p34 and Text C on p38.

Text A

George Orwell wrote this as the opening to his novel *1984*. The novel was published in 1948. Here Orwell describes his hero, Winston Smith, arriving home to his apartment.

Adjectives: setting the scene, focusing on senses, adds immediacy

3rd person narrative; Winston Smith sounds British, Smith suggests Everyman figure

Irony

Sensuous

It was a **bright cold day** in April **and** the clocks were **striking thirteen**. **Winston Smith**, his chin nuzzled into his breast in an effort to escape the **vile** wind, **slipped** quickly though the glass doors of **Victory Mansions**, though not quickly enough to prevent a swirl of **gritty dust** from entering along with him. The hallway **smelt** of **boiled cabbage and old rag mats**. At one end of it a coloured poster, too large for indoor display, had been tacked to the wall. It depicted simply an

Compound sentence structure

Odd/alien

Disconcerting, unpleasant

Furtive

Grimy, dirty

Poverty, unpleasant conditions

Annotations (left side):

- Adjective makes it overpowering
- Failure of the system
- Specific age, not old
- Precise adverbial phrases
- Sinister
- Depersonalised
- Dull, political propaganda is of no interest to Winston
- Technological progress
- Military, political
- Dingy, neglected
- Dull, drab existence
- Controlling
- Intrusive, technology
- Simile: noise, insect, disease, nuisance

Annotations (right side):

- Strength, power
- Masculine, attractive
- Alien concept
- Untreated, painful medical condition
- Powerful verb, connotes hypnotic power
- Friendly/frightening juxtaposition. 2nd person, surveillance, capitals for emphasis
- Intrusive
- Vulnerability
- Shortage of basic necessities
- Unwelcoming, pathetic fallacy
- All-knowing, hypnotic
- Alien word
- Repetition, key word
- Alien term in simple sentence, capitalisation for significance, situation of adverb for emphasis

Extract text:

enormous face, more than a metre wide: the face of a man about forty-five, with a heavy black moustache and ruggedly handsome features. Winston made for the stairs. It was no use trying the lift. Even at the best of times it was seldom working, and at present the electric current was cut off during daylight hours. It was part of the economy drive in preparation for Hate Week. The flat was seven flights up, and Winston, who was thirty-nine and had a varicose ulcer above his right ankle, went slowly, resting several times on the way. On each landing, opposite the liftshaft, the poster with the enormous face gazed from the wall. It was one of those pictures which are so contrived that the eyes follow you about when you move. BIG BROTHER IS WATCHING YOU, the caption beneath it ran.

Inside the flat a fruity voice was reading out a list of figures, which had something to do with the production of pig iron. The voice came from an oblong metal plaque like a dulled mirror which formed part of the surface of the right-hand wall. Winston turned a switch and the voice sank somewhat, though the words were still distinguishable. The instrument (the telescreen it was called) could be dimmed, but there was no way of shutting it off completely. He moved over to the window, a smallish, frail figure, the meagerness of his body merely emphasized by the blue overalls which were the uniform of the Party. His hair was very fair, his face naturally sanguine, his skin roughened by coarse soap and blunt razor blades and the cold of the winter that had just ended.

Outside, even through the shut window-pane, the world looked cold. Down in the street little eddies of wind were whirling dust and torn paper into spirals, and though the sun was shining and the sky a harsh blue, there seemed to be no colour in anything, except the posters that were plastered everywhere. The black-moustachio'd face gazed down from every commanding corner. There was one on the house-front immediately opposite. BIG BROTHER IS WATCHING YOU, the caption said, while the dark eyes looked deep into Winston's own. Down at street level another poster, torn at one corner, flapped fitfully in the wind, alternately covering and uncovering the single word INGSOC. In the far distance a helicopter skimmed down between the roofs, hovering for an instance like a blue-bottle, and darted away again with a curving flight. It was the police patrol, snooping into people's windows. The patrols did not matter, however. Only the Thought Police mattered.

Summary of annotations

What have we been told about the extract?

- It is the opening of a novel.
- It is set in the future.
- It appears to have a political focus.

What have we noticed?

■ The opening sentence creates an unexpected and unusual context.

■ The location is unpleasant and the machinery inefficient.

■ There are details which create an alien/sinister/frightening world.

■ The central figure is frail/unwell/suffering from an ulcer/not old.

■ The place is dominated by a sinister image of a man.

■ It is a third person narrative.

How is the extract structured?

■ It establishes setting, atmosphere and the central character.

■ It introduces a world which is both familiar and alien.

■ It establishes a culture of spying and surveillance.

What language features have we identified?

■ Use of nouns and adjectives to create unpleasant or sinister context: 'vile wind', 'boiled cabbage and old rag mats', 'varicose ulcer', 'enormous face', 'a fruity voice', 'telescreen', 'smallish, frail figure', 'coarse soap', 'blunt razor blades', 'cold', 'harsh blue', 'every commanding corner'.

■ Use of proper nouns and names to provide ironic comments: 'Winston Smith', 'Victory Mansions', 'Big Brother'; or a sinister atmosphere: 'the Thought Police'.

■ Use of verbs which create a sensuous response in the reader: 'smelt'; or a sinister atmosphere: 'watching', 'gazed', 'contrived', 'snooping',

■ Use of similes to convey attitudes: 'a helicopter skimmed down between the roofs, hovering for an instance like a blue-bottle.'

■ Use of **juxtaposition** (friend/threat) to create a sinister atmosphere: 'BIG BROTHER IS WATCHING YOU'; 'a heavy black moustache and ruggedly handsome features'.

■ Use of contrasting sentences for emphasis: 'The patrols did not matter, however. Only the Thought Police mattered.'

■ Use of sentence structure for specific effects: compound sentence to open the novel connecting two ideas by 'and' – one familiar, one unfamiliar.

■ Frequent use of simple sentences to focus on specific details, for example smell ('The hallway smelt of boiled cabbage and old rag mats.'), visual details ('On each landing, opposite the liftshaft, the poster with the enormous face gazed from the wall.'), plus use of two adverb phrases in initial position to add precision.

Initial responses

These observations ought to enable us to make a start on answering some of the key questions we identified earlier: 'What is the aim or purpose of the writer?' 'What is the domain and genre of the text?' 'What sort of audience does it seem to be aimed at?' At this stage we can only begin to give some tentative answers since, as we focus more closely on the language, our understanding ought to deepen. However, some ideas will be beginning to take shape in our minds. It is worth remembering that we will not be able to use everything that we have found. Our comparative essay needs to be selective and focused, and there is only about an hour in which to write it. Inevitably some things we might like to put in will have to be left out. That will not matter as long as we go into detail about what we do say.

AQA Examiner's tip

Comments on syntax take time to present properly. Sentences need to be quoted in full, not abbreviated to the beginning and end and connected by dots. An examiner does not have the time to search through the texts to find and check your reference. The discussion needs to be detailed so the examiner can check that the analysis is accurate. Avoid generalising about simple and complex sentences.

AQA Examiner's tip

You do not have to include in your answer everything you have found. Be selective and make your chosen points in as much detail as you can. The golden rule is: 'Write a lot about a little rather than a little about a lot.'

What appears to be the aim or purpose of the writer?

It is always tricky to ask yourself this question, since you can never be sure unless you can speak to the writer (and even then you can never be totally sure if you can trust the answer). So all we can do is look at the evidence before us and make a reasonable judgement. However, it seems fairly clear that here Orwell is *writing a novel for a general adult readership*, which, at its time of writing, was set in a future scenario. Its *central focus* appears to be political as it is concerned with describing a society which is intimidated by the oppressive power of the State, but which does not seem to function very efficiently or provide a pleasant environment in which to live.

It is the *opening* of a *novel*, so these features are there to establish the setting and introduce a key character. It is written in the *third person*, so the author is able to step back a little from the action and present the reader with an overview.

Once you have a few ideas down on paper, the whole task does not look quite so awesome.

■ Text B

The following extract is from *The Iron Coast* by Jane Gardam, in which she writes about the North Yorkshire coastline.

Annotation	Text	Annotation
Metaphor, positioned at the opening: shape, size, colour; slightly sinister		Ancient, subject focus of paragraph
		Verb and adverb: impressive dominant

A great black tooth, the ruined abbey of St Hilda, stands high on the cliff above Whitby, facing every wind that is flung against it. The Saxon abbey St Hilda founded, and then this towering Norman one, have stood above the Bay of the Watchtower by the side of the Roman signal station for 1,300 years. It is a place so holy that kings and queens chose to be buried there for centuries, and birds have always been said to be afraid to fly over it because Hilda's magnetism causes them to drop dead to the ground.

Twenty-five miles north of Whitby, on the Yorkshire bank of the mouth of the Tees, spreads the twentieth-century Hell's kitchen of one of the great chemical works of the world, with the nineteenth-century graveyard of the steelworks in front of it and the remains of the streets of poor industrial towns tangled in its entrails. Out of the tops of the refinery chimneys flames like lurid petals bend in the wind. The wind takes the fumes and smoke across the coastal plain, deep down into the lungs, withering up gardens and struggling attempts at trees, and across to Scandinavia which it coats with bitter, orange dust. In between is a stretch of

Annotations:
- Power of nature, sense of awe at resilience
- Focus on unique features
- Foregrounded, two adverbial phrases to fix the setting, travel writing genre
- Metaphor: flames, cooking, horror, damnation
- Metaphor: death, destruction
- Metaphor: animal, devouring
- Hell imagery
- Defiance, personification
- Adverb, endurance
- Adverb, historical perspective
- Attraction, force, supernatural power
- Verb, size/awe
- Size, economic power, irony?
- Emotive, sympathy
- Beauty/horror juxtaposition
- Destructive of natural growth
- Unpleasant taste, unnatural colour barrenness, destruction

Left margin annotations:

- Aim to introduce little known area
- Visual simile: sharp narrow
- Metaphor: insects, insignificance, numbers
- Adjective: horror conditions
- Emotive verb: bubble over
- Simple declarative, emphasis
- Adjective: connotes strength
- Anecdote to support argument, add immediacy
- Historical importance, travel genre, background, impressive

Main extract:

coast not well known, a plain so low and bare that it is invisible from the sea and a church spire rises from the water like a needle. The coast appears to begin with the long lines of the Cleveland Hills several miles inland, and the broken cone of Roseberry Topping*, like a midget volcano. Along the hills is one black dot, the memorial to Captain Cook who was born in a cottage on the marshy fields. Salts and ores have been worked between Roseberry and the sea since medieval times and probably since the Romans, but it was the discovery of massive deposits of iron in the hills during the nineteenth century that brought the poor and homeless and workless swarming here from all over England and starving Ireland. Within one generation the estuary began to seethe with people like the mud flats of Bangladesh. Middlesbrough and 'Teesside' were born.

The Iron Coast feels different from anywhere else. There is a hard, quiet unhappiness about it, and the plain and seaboard tend to be avoided rather than explored. The young do their best to get away. Even a century ago Dickens, who was usually ready for anything and a good east-coast man, was too impatient here. He got out of the train at Redcar station, walked down to the promenade with his carpet bag, looked quickly north and south, walked back to the platform and caught the next train on to Scarborough. Yet this small rag of the country has bred international heroes, saints, scientists and geniuses. It has twice raised armies that came within a thread of changing a dynasty and once ordered a clipping and reshaping of the powers of the monarchy that has survived nearly 800 years.

Roseberry Topping – The name of a distinctive hill.

Right margin annotations:

- Simile: humour, size
- Historical fact, travel genre
- Adverbial, reference to past
- Conjunction used as pivot
- Syndetic list
- Simile: cultural, historical link to developing countries
- Personification
- Adverb, argument
- Syndetic list, impressive

Summary of annotations

What have we been told about the extract?

- It is an example of travel writing.
- It deals with the North Yorkshire coast.

What have we noticed?

- The opening sentence creates a spectacular impression of the ruined abbey of St Hilda, using, among other features, metaphor ('A great black tooth'), elevated language ('facing every wind that is flung against it') and myth ('birds have always been said to be afraid to fly over it because Hilda's magnetism causes them to drop dead to the ground').
- The text covers three locations in three paragraphs.
- There are details which create a mysterious, magical impression.
- There are details which create an alien, frightening impression.
- The writer uses similes and metaphors in order to create vivid images and to evoke a mysterious mood which is both ominous and inviting.

■ The writer emphasises the history of the area and stresses its importance.

How is it structured?

■ Whitby: its location, history and folklore.

■ Middlesbrough: its location, industrial past and present.

■ The Cleveland ('Iron') coast: description, its history, impact.

What language features have we identified?

■ Use of nouns and adjectives: to give a sense of time or history: 'ruined abbey', 'Saxon abbey', 'towering Norman one'; to provide emotive response: 'bitter, orange dust', 'great chemical works', 'lurid petals', 'hard, quiet unhappiness'; to create a unique focus for the place: 'magnetism', 'graveyard'.

■ Use of proper nouns to give a sense of location: 'Whitby', 'Bay of the Watchtower', 'Middlesbrough', 'Teesside'; or history 'St. Hilda'.

■ Use of verbs to create a sense of the power of nature and the strength of the place: ('facing', 'flung'); the encroachment of industry ('spreads' 'tangled'); the destructive power of industry ('withering up', 'coats'); the swift growth and agitation ('seethe'); or living growth of place ('were born').

■ Use of adverbial phrases (appropriate for travel writing as they help fix place or time) often foregrounded for emphasis.
'Twenty-five miles north of Whitby, on the Yorkshire bank of the mouth of the Tees ...', 'for 1,300 years...', 'Out of the tops of the refinery chimneys', 'In between is a stretch of coast ...', 'since medieval times and probably since the Romans.'

■ Use of metaphors/similes (used to convey attitudes, influence feelings – a literary device):

Metaphors: 'A great black tooth' (visual, sinister, living creature, opening position for emphasis); 'Hell's kitchen' (sensuous and emotive, heat, flame, colour, damnation); 'tangled in its entrails' (sinister, living creature, devouring, consuming); 'swarming' (people as numerous, insignificant as insects); 'Iron coast' (strength, endurance, ruggedness, solidity, reliability)

Similes: 'flames like lurid petals' (combines Hell and a garden to convey beauty and horror of place); 'like a needle' (visual image, sharp, narrow, pointed); 'like a midget volcano' (visual, not threatening, humour, reduces scale); 'like the mud flats of Bangladesh' (links 19th century England to developing countries' poverty, and conveys numbers and insignificance of people as individuals).

■ Use of sentence structure: sentence structure is used to harmonise with and enhance meaning. For example, compound-complex sentence pivots on 'but' to compare medieval and 19th century history. The declarative opening places it into its historical context ('Salts and ores have been worked between Roseberry and the sea since medieval times and probably since the Romans'). The pivotal coordinating conjunction 'but' which opens the second part of the sentence signals a change to something more significant in more recent history ('it was the discovery of massive deposits of iron in the hills in the nineteenth century'). This is followed by the subordinate clause that explains the consequences ('that brought the poor and homeless and workless'). The use of the syndetic list emphasises the different types of people and their numbers and the sense that they followed one after the other. The connotations of 'swarming' and 'starving' reinforce the numbers. The compound-complex sentence provides a wealth of information and contrasts with the use of the simple sentence which emphasises the new beginning by its shortness and simplicity 'Middlesbrough and "Teesside" were born.'

Initial responses

While this is clearly in the domain of *travel writing*, we must notice that Jane Gardam is doing much more than inform her readers about the Iron Coast. She uses language carefully selected to elicit a strong response from her readers, to influence our impression of the various places along the coast, and to convey her own attitudes and feelings of awe at its age, its beauty, its destructive power, etc. Although she does give us plenty of facts, as we would expect in a piece of travel writing, she also uses the techniques of the writer of fiction to engage our attention and influence our responses. As she points out, the area of England she is talking about is not well known, and so her aim appears to be to interest her reader and possibly to encourage us to visit a place off the normal tourist itinerary. She writes in the *third person*, which gives her account a greater sense of objectivity. The audience, as with Orwell's novel, appears to be the general adult reader.

▨ Text C

One of the difficulties with 'reading' a transcription is that you have to hear it in your head. After all, you are trying to recreate spontaneous living language. It may take a couple of readings for you to get a sense of the intonation and the emphasis, but it is essential that you try to do this in order to get a clear grasp of the text. As discussed on p27, it is rather like being given a piece of sheet music and asked to hear the sounds in your head. It is sometimes useful to read it 'aloud' but very quietly, under your breath. To do this successfully you will have to put in the pauses. Count the seconds for a long pause. A speaker may be hesitating for many reasons and the context will give you some ideas. It may just reflect uncertainty, but it may be because the speaker is debating how best to express a point. Once you have 'heard' the language, this extract ought to be the easiest to deal with because you hear and interpret spoken language every day of your life and you are instinctively attuned to 'reading' the subtleties of meaning in the human voice. You just have to transfer your understanding to the example you have been given. Remember that it is important to get to grips with the meaning of the text and the connection between the language and how the meaning or the attitudes of the speakers are conveyed. It is not an exercise in feature spotting.

The following is a transcript of an adult talking about a recent holiday in the American state of Florida. To allow you to see all of the annotations this transcript has been reproduced in three sections over pages 38–40.

Hedge begins criticism hesitantly, suggests English reticence?, apparent response to a question

Lines 1 and 2 constitute the abstract in Labov's narrative theory (see p29)

Hesitation suggests pause to consider

Emphasis shows negative attitude; end-clipping, casual

Lengthy pauses to allow time to consider; begins Labov's orientation

Superficial, soulless; paired adjectives show dislike

Key

(.)	micropause
(1.0)	pause in seconds
::	elongation of sound
underlining:	emphasis on a particular word

Adjective emphasised; first line of criticism is superficiality, falseness

Fillers, hesitations and hedge suggest unwillingness at first to criticise

I suppose one o'the most (.) er:: (0.5) disappointin' places I've ever been to is (.) erm (1.0) Disneyland (.) in Florida (2.0) erm (3.0) what I didn't like about it was the (1.0) and complete artificiality about the whole thing (.) I thought it was very plastic (.) it was all veneer (.) indeed it wa it was (.) very squeaky clean (.) that sort of antiseptic (1.0) er type of (.) place (.) which (.)is obviously all erm (1.0) I suppose (2.0) erm(.) manufactured (.) very deliberately of course (.) but (.) which leaves the whole place rather characterless (.) and er (1.0) I felt that the whole sort o'deal in (.) Disney was (.) very superficial (.) and ultimately I just got (.) very tired with the sort of whoop-whoop culture that the Americans so seem to

not genuine, artificial; begins Labov's complications

Short pause plus conjunction suggests shift of emphasis to focus on criticism

Falseness emphasised

Adjective: superficial, lacking distinctive features

Slang using sound and emphasis to parody people's flashy behaviour and attitudes

Criticism builds, linked by coordinators

Summary of annotations

What have we been told about the extract?
- There is a single adult speaker.
- The speaker is presenting views about a recent visit to Florida.

What have we noticed?
- Single speaker, an account. Addressee's presence is understood.
- Extract follows Labov's narrative structure.
- Speaker criticises Disneyland.
- Criticism covers three areas: artificiality, exploitation and food.
- Speaker feels deceived by hype.
- Speaker contrasts English and American values both explicitly and implicitly through language choices.

How is it structured?

Although not strictly a story, there is a single speaker and the discussion follows the outline identified by Labov in a number of respects:
- the Abstract (lines 1–2) establishes focus of narrative ('disappointin'')
- the Orientation (lines 3–6) identifies the problem ('artificiality')

■ Link

To find out more about Labov's narrative structure, see p29.

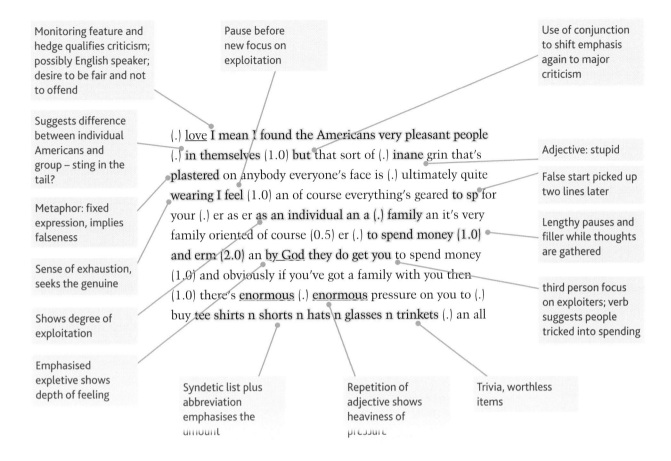

Monitoring feature and hedge qualifies criticism; possibly English speaker; desire to be fair and not to offend

Pause before new focus on exploitation

Use of conjunction to shift emphasis again to major criticism

Suggests difference between individual Americans and group – sting in the tail?

Adjective: stupid

False start picked up two lines later

Metaphor: fixed expression, implies falseness

Lengthy pauses and filler while thoughts are gathered

Sense of exhaustion, seeks the genuine

Shows degree of exploitation

third person focus on exploiters; verb suggests people tricked into spending

Emphasised expletive shows depth of feeling

Syndetic list plus abbreviation emphasises the amount

Repetition of adjective shows heaviness of pressure

Trivia, worthless items

(.) <u>love</u> I mean I found the Americans very pleasant people (.) in themselves (1.0) but that sort of (.) inane grin that's plastered on anybody everyone's face is (.) ultimately quite wearing I feel (1.0) an of course everything's geared to sp for your (.) er as er as an individual an a (.) family an it's very family oriented of course (0.5) er (.) to spend money (1.0) and erm (2.0) an by God they do get you to spend money (1.0) and obviously if you've got a family with you then (1.0) there's enormous (.) enormous pressure on you to (.) buy tee shirts n shorts n hats n glasses n trinkets (.) an all

- the Complication (lines 6–22) provides the criticisms of the place
- the Resolution/Evaluation (lines 22–24) makes the comparison with home.

The listener is introduced to the topic by the speaker so the focus is clear (the sense of let-down he felt on visiting Disneyland, Florida). His criticisms are then presented, before the speaker concludes with a comment that sums up the essence of the problem (the poor quality of the food when compared to what he was used to in England). This comparison gives a sense of completeness to the narrative.

What language features have we identified?

- Language used to criticise artificiality:
  - adjectives: 'plastic', 'antiseptic', 'manufactured', 'characterless', 'superficial', 'inane'
  - nouns: 'veneer'
  - phrases: 'squeaky clean', 'whoop-whoop culture'.
- Language used to criticise exploitation:
  - verbs: 'geared', 'get (you) to spend'
  - adjectives and nouns: 'enormous' and 'pressure'.

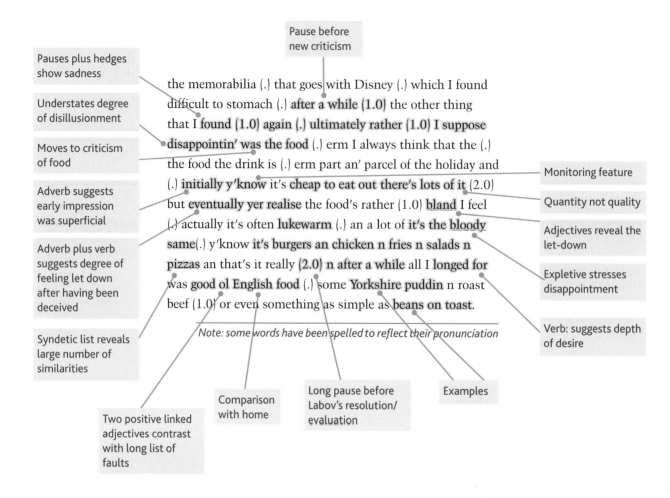

Pause before
new criticism

Pauses plus hedges
show sadness

Understates degree
of disillusionment

Moves to criticism
of food

Adverb suggests
early impression
was superficial

Adverb plus verb
suggests degree of
feeling let down
after having been
deceived

Syndetic list reveals
large number of
similarities

the memorabilia (.) that goes with Disney (.) which I found
difficult to stomach (.) after a while (1.0) the other thing
that I found (1.0) again (.) ultimately rather (1.0) I suppose
disappointin' was the food (.) erm I always think that the (.)
the food the drink is (.) erm part an' parcel of the holiday and
(.) initially y'know it's cheap to eat out there's lots of it (2.0)
but eventually yer realise the food's rather (1.0) bland I feel
(.) actually it's often lukewarm (.) an a lot of it's the bloody
same(.) y'know it's burgers an chicken n fries n salads n
pizzas an that's it really (2.0) n after a while all I longed for
was good ol English food (.) some Yorkshire puddin n roast
beef (1.0) or even something as simple as beans on toast.

Note: some words have been spelled to reflect their pronunciation

Monitoring feature

Quantity not quality

Adjectives reveal the
let-down

Expletive stresses
disappointment

Verb: suggests depth
of desire

Two positive linked
adjectives contrast
with long list of
faults

Comparison
with home

Long pause before
Labov's resolution/
evaluation

Examples

■ Language used to criticise food:
  – adjectives: 'bland', 'lukewarm'
  – adjectives in contrast: 'good, ol' English'
  – verbs: 'longed for'.

■ Demotic language: 'bloody', 'by God' – expressions of the speaker's frustration or irritation.

■ Colloquial language: 'whoop-whoop'. There is relatively little in this extract and so this example stands out as it uses onomatopoeia/sound to parody the sound made by the crowd.

■ Mode features/features of speech identified:
  – **hedges**: 'I suppose' (twice), 'erm', 'rather' (twice), 'I felt', 'I mean'. These modify the speaker's expressions of criticism and suggest he feels slightly uncomfortable about being too damning
  – monitoring features: 'I mean', y'know (see hedges above)
  – fillers: various uses such as filling thinking spaces with noise, sounds leading up to words to be emphasised, and occasionally used as hedges

- pauses: minor pauses for breath, but occasionally longer pauses while thoughts are gathered or before a word to give added emphasis
- emphasis: 'disappointin'' (twice), 'manufactured', 'whoop-whoop', 'inane', 'by God', 'enormous' (twice), 'bland', 'bloody'. Emphasis tends to be used at key points in the development of the discourse or to stress a topic the speaker feels particularly strongly about
- end-clippings: 'disappointin''
- false starts: 'to sp for your (.) er as er as an individual …' reveals the ongoing thought processes as the speaker focuses on reformulating and then communicating key ideas.
- repetitions: 'enormous (.) enormous' to intensify the pressure placed on people to buy.

- Grammatical features:
  - compound utterances and use of 'and' to link ideas together with 'but' to show contrast or change of direction
  - syndetic lists: 'tee shirts n shorts n hats n glasses n trinkets' (used to indicate the large range of worthless items visitors are pressured to buy); 'burgers an chicken n fries n salads n pizzas' (used to indicate the large number of foods which he feels are always on offer). The use of the reduced form of 'and' in the syndetic list strings out the items and helps the speaker to emphasise and the listener to grasp the sheer number of items in question.

- Gender hints: no clear indication as to gender of speaker. Use of expletives and focus on English food towards the end possibly suggests male speaker.

Link

For more about false starts, see the paragraph on 'initial responses' below.

Initial responses

An analysis or exploration of a piece of spontaneous spoken language by a single speaker requires a different approach to the analysis or exploration of written texts. The main difference is that the written texts are consciously and carefully crafted as we have already seen in the examples earlier. The final version is the product of a number of drafts. However, when we speak spontaneously the process of 'crafting' occurs as we speak. Our language and our thought processes are interconnected and reflect each other. This accounts for the false starts and hesitations in spoken language as we reshape and re-express our ideas, or pause as we think of the best ways to communicate what we want to say. In our exploration of speech therefore we need to take this into account. It is unlikely, for example, in Extract C that the speaker had planned what he was going to say in advance. It seems he was responding to a question from the addressee on the lines of 'Did your holiday in Florida come up to your expectations?' or 'What's your most disappointing holiday experience?' and the criticism begins to build as he recalls his experiences of Disneyland. That he felt let down by Disneyland comes across in the emphasis placed on *disappointin'* in the first line, and after having taken a little time to gather his thoughts (in the two- and three-second pauses) he criticises what he felt was the most significant weakness, its artificiality (hence the emphasis in line 1). This is described by the speaker in a number of different ways ('plastic', 'veneer', 'antiseptic', etc.) leading up to the summative point – that the place is manufactured (the second emphasis in the extract). Recollections of his feelings about the place at the time (his sense of being exhausted by manufactured enthusiasm) leads him to a criticism of the shallowness of the Americans in holiday mode, but, tempered by a wish not to offend or be unfair, he draws a distinction between the holiday crowds and individuals. Having come to the end of this point (after 'ultimately quite wearing') he pauses for a second before moving on to the next area for criticism, the commercialism. That this point has not been fully shaped in his mind is clear from the false starts that now occur. The thought process seems to be on these lines:

1 'an of course everything's geared to sp' (spend money)
2 'for your' [family to spend money]
3 [you] 'as an individual an a family'
4 ('an it's very family oriented of course')
5 'to spend money …'

The speaker intends to make the point that Disneyland is geared to getting people to spend money but decides to extend the general point of line 1 (above) by adding the focus of 'your family' in line 2, but before he says that he further broadens it by adding the idea of 'you as an individual and your family' (in line 3). He then includes the parenthetical idea (line 4) about the place being focused on families before eventually arriving at the main point (in line 5) about spending money. The journey he has made in his thinking is reflected in the presence of language features which are typical of speech. He now explores his second main line of criticism, the commercial exploitation of the visitors, and then pauses again before moving on to the final area for criticism, the food: '(1.0) the other thing that I found (1.0) again ultimately rather (1.0) I suppose disappointin' was the food'. The pauses and the hedges imply his reluctance about finding yet another area to criticise. Furthermore, the use of 'disappointin'' again, reflects his reticence. Disappointment is a fairly mild way to describe the let-down of the experience, and the list of examples that occurs in the text indicates that disappointment understates his true emotions.

3

Writing a comparative essay

How to present your comparison

Now that you have got plenty to say about the three texts, you need to structure your response so that you gain as much credit as possible.

The Assessment Objectives

The examiner assesses your work against Assessment Objectives (AOs) that have been laid down in the marking scheme for the examination as a whole. For this question the Assessment Objectives to be used are AO2 and AO3.

- AO2 requires us to *demonstrate detailed critical understanding in analysing the ways in which structure, form and language shape meanings in a range of spoken and written texts.* In other words, we have to show how the language is used by the writer/speaker. The organisation of the text and the mode and/or genre all influence the ways meaning is communicated to the reader/listener.

- AO3 requires us to *use integrated approaches to explore relationships between texts, analysing and evaluating the significance of contextual factors in their production and reception.* In other words, we have to compare and contrast the texts we are given to work with, identifying similarities and differences, and also we have to consider how the contexts in which they were produced and the audiences they were produced for are reflected in the language choices made by the writers/speaker.

AQA Examiner's tip

These Assessment Objectives tell you what the examiner is looking for and what they will award you marks for. Read them carefully to make sure that you are focusing on the things that will help you score highly in your examination.

Your answer

It is vital that you use a framework or scaffolding for your answer. It needs to be organised carefully to ensure you cover the AOs outlined above. There should be around five or six sections of varying length depending on how much you have to say in each. Each section may be split into more than one paragraph.

The most common approach is to make some broad comparative points about all three texts, and then to take one of the texts as your focus or anchor. This anchor is your starting point and should be explored in some detail, including specifically those aspects which can be compared or contrasted to the other texts. Then bring in Text 2 for comparison and analysis. When these two texts have been explored, bring in Text 3, explore it in some detail and link it to the other two.

Section 1 (the introduction)

What do the three texts have in common? Make a broad statement about what links the three texts and then move on to compare the *mode* and *genre*, and consider the apparent *audience* and *aim* of each extract. You need to establish the type of texts you are dealing with, whether they are *literary* or *non-literary*, and the *degree of formality* they exhibit. Bear in mind that a writer of literature is likely to try to use language to involve the feelings or emotions of the reader, while the writer of the non-literary extract may be reporting something in a more factual way, and may be writing to inform as well as to entertain. The spontaneous speaker will be

AQA Examiner's tip

One of the first things you should do when you open your exam paper is assess what types of texts you have been given. This will help you when you come to consider the purpose of each text and how these purposes are similar or different.

using language in a much more immediate way with probably little time for reflection or careful selection. Nevertheless, these generalisations do not apply to all texts, and it is essential to analyse the textual evidence rather than impose preconceptions about what you might regard as typical features of particular kinds of text.

If the non-literary text is an extract from a speech, then there will be evidence of rhetorical devices.

Section 2

It is often sensible to approach the analysis of the texts in the order that they appear on the examination paper. However, this is not a fixed rule. You can approach the texts in the way that suits you best. Whichever text you choose to begin with, you need to explore how the writer or speaker uses language to communicate meaning to the reader or listener. Comment on:

- vocabulary (remember word classes and look for significant use of nouns/verbs/adjectives/adverbs. What connotations do the words carry?)
- use of imagery (quote and comment on the effects of similes and metaphors. Show in detail how they work)
- grammar and syntax (for example, adverbial phrases and their position in the structure of sentences, types of sentence, spoken English features, etc.)
- phonological features (for example, alliteration, assonance, onomatopoeia, **prosodic features**).

If you do begin with the literary text, note whether it is poetry or prose. Remember that the language of poetry is normally more metaphorically dense and the structure tighter than in prose. On the other hand, if you begin with the spontaneous speech, explore all of the above, but remember the differences between speech and writing. The various features of speech, the hesitations, the false starts, the hedges, the emphases, etc., all reflect the speaker's attempt to communicate meaning, thoughts and feelings. Explore them in detail.

Section 3

Begin your discussion of Text 2. Comment on what appears to be the aim and how the language is used to fulfil that aim and communicate meaning. Comment also on the nature of the audience and how this may affect language choice, but in the process make comparisons or contrasts with Text 1. State in what ways the context, aim and audience differ from Text 1 and how these differences affect language use. For example, Text 2 may be more factually informative or amusing than Text 1 and will have a different focus of interest. Identify this different focus. Be as specific as you can be. Compare examples of language use from Text 1 and Text 2. Try to explore as many of the following as you can:

- words and their meanings and connotations
- the different ways the same word classes function in the two texts
- imagery (for example, use of simile and metaphor)
- whether one uses more colloquial or informal language (for example, slang, dialect, jargon) than the other and why
- whether one uses more formal or standard language than the other and why

AQA Examiner's tip

Your answer will be more impressive if your essay can compare texts at the same time as exploring them. Rather than talking about each text in turn and then talking about the links, try to make comparisons throughout your essay. A strong understanding of the purpose of each text will help you do this.

- whether one uses spoken features and why (for example, representations of non-linguistic noises such as 'mmm', incomplete sentences, direct address, etc.) and how it contrasts with the more formal language of the other text
- whether one uses more imagery than the other and why
- whether the language is very context-dependent (that is, our ability to grasp the meaning depends on our understanding of the context).

Section 4

Now begin your discussion of Text 3 and link and compare all three texts. What is the aim and audience? Look closely at the language, grammar, etc. How does the language or form:

- convey the meaning
- fulfil the aim
- address the audience
- differ from the other two extracts.

Also, ask how far does its aim and audience appear to be similar or different?

Section 5

Sum up your observations in a conclusion that brings together all three texts.

Now let us look at an answer produced by a student to the above task.

4

Examples of answers for Section A

- exploring two examples of student responses

- looking at examiner comments and mark schemes.

AQA Examiner's tip

Don't worry if you do not have time to cover all of the points you noted in your plan. The examiner understands that you have a limited amount of time and wants to see what you consider most important. Make sure that you use your most convincing points first, then move on to the less important points if you have time.

Link

Features of speech

Student A has made a note here to consider Labov's narrative model in the answer. To remind yourself about Labov's research, look back to p29.

☑ Examples of students' answers

Any answer to the question produced within the time limits of the examination is unlikely to include all the points and ideas that we can find when we are annotating the texts. Often, under the stress of the examination, we may need to omit some interesting points identified in our initial exploration. That does not matter. This is an examination exercise attempted under strictly controlled conditions, and not a piece of coursework for which we have (almost) unlimited time to draft and redraft our ideas. What the examiner is marking is what can reasonably be produced by a student working under examination pressure. Consequently the following example does not include all the ideas identified in the planning stage, and, if the student had had longer to produce the response, more points would have been covered.

■ Student A

Student A's plan

Approaches

- Attitudes to places.
- Mode differences.

Introduction – overview

Links/audience/aim/mode/tenor

Text A aim: political criticism, genre sci-fi novel/fiction

- Language establishes setting and mood/creates cohesion.
- Imagery is minimal. Strong narrative focus.
- Syntax – use of simple sentence.

Text B aim: create vivid impression of place, genre travel writing, non-fiction

- Language – emotive/persuasive/shows liking for places.
- Imagery – extensive use of metaphor and simile: literary.
- Syntax – complex.

Text C aim: express criticism of Disneyland (link to Text A)/spontaneous/one speaker/structured (Labov)

- Language – critical: expresses attitude.
- Fos – reveals spontaneous nature.

Student A's answer

A unifying link between the three texts is the way in which places are presented. However, this topic is dealt with from a different angle in each. Text A is an extract from a novel, and is in the written mode, permanent and fictional. It is context independent and message oriented. Text B is an extract from a piece of travel writing and is also in the written mode, permanent but non-fictional. Text C, however, is a transcript of the spoken mode which was not originally intended to be permanent. It contains hesitations and contractions together with some mild taboo language and is largely context dependent. However, it does have some aspects of formality in that there is one speaker who is giving his feelings about Disneyland, giving it a low interaction. It is reasonable to assume that the audiences for Texts A and B are literate, educated general readers, while the audience in Text C is far more limited, being the person or persons sharing in the conversation.

The aims and attitudes of the speaker and writers to the shared topic vary considerably, too. Orwell presents a political vision of a future world which is both familiar and unfamiliar. It is a world of shortages and shabbiness with a pervasive culture of surveillance. Jane Gardam, however, brings to life the history and culture of part of the North Yorkshire coast to readers who are unfamiliar with it. Although the domain is non-fictional travel writing, she uses many of the techniques of the writer of fiction, such as emotive language and imagery, to convey her admiration, and possibly encourage her readers to pay a visit to North Yorkshire. However, the speaker in Text C criticises Florida as an example of the superficiality and commercialism of modern American culture.

Orwell begins his political criticism by creating an atmosphere of grimy seediness. He does this through the use of sensuous language and adjective-noun combinations. The adjective 'gritty' combined with the noun 'dust' creates a collocation that produces both a physical sensation in the reader and an awareness of the unkempt condition of the streets through which Winston had to walk. The adjective 'vile', in 'vile wind', further develops the sense of discomfort. At the beginning of paragraph 2 Orwell introduces the sense of smell in addition to the sense of feeling in the extremely unpleasant 'The hallway smelt of boiled cabbage and old rag mats'. The connotations of poverty and food rationing created by the reference to boiled cabbage reinforce the impression that the people living in 1984 exist on only the basics, and this impression is further strengthened when we are told of the lift that was not working as the current had been cut off as part of an 'economy drive'. This collocation connotes economic shortages. The hardness of the life for the citizens of 1984 is emphasised by the quality of basic necessities such as soap and razor blades, which are described as 'coarse' and 'blunt', these adjectives suggesting the most basic material and their inadequate supply. Overall the physical atmosphere seems dominated by the weather which is twice described as cold and colourless ('there seemed no colour in anything') despite a harsh blue sky – a use of the pathetic fallacy by Orwell where he uses the weather to suggest the depressed mood of his character, Winston Smith.

In paragraph 1, Student A approaches the task through mode comparison linked to audience. This is a useful way to get into the task, and is an approach that can be used for many of the texts that are set in Section A.

It is always difficult for us to be sure precisely of writers' or speakers' aims, although we can make a reasonable assumption from our exploration of the language. Nevertheless, we need to avoid being too dogmatic. In paragraph 2 Student A now goes on to compare in general terms what each of the writers and speaker seems to be aiming to achieve. This concludes Section 1.

In paragraph 3 Student A begins the analysis with Text A and focuses on exploring Orwell's language, using framework terminology to show how meaning is conveyed, and how Orwell's attitudes and feelings emerge. This concludes Section 2.

In paragraph 4 the exploration now moves to Text B and focuses on how Jane Gardam uses her language to express her meaning and her attitudes. There is some comparison with Text A, although the main focus is on B. The student continues to use appropriate framework terminology and introduces a discussion of imagery.

In Text B, Jane Gardam also makes use of emotive language, but instead of directing it towards the end of political criticism, she uses it to awaken in her reader a sense of awe at the magnificence of the 'Iron Coast'. The use of 'iron' as an adjective carries with it from the beginning connotations of strength and solidity, and it is the strength and power of the landscape and the enduring nature of the places that she writes about. Her description of Whitby abbey seems to personify endurance. Where Orwell combined nouns and adjectives, Gardam combines verbs and adverbs. The verb/adverb combination 'stands high' in the opening sentence connotes pride and defiance as does the use of the verbs 'facing' and 'flung' in 'facing every wind that is flung against it'. Gardam creates a picture of a ruined building defying the elements, and uses a striking metaphor to describe the abbey: 'A great black tooth'. This not only creates an impressively huge silhouette to stimulate the visual imagination of the reader, but also is placed at the beginning of the sentence to give it greater prominence. Whereas Orwell's opening paragraph was focused on the unpleasant weather in order to support his criticism, Gardam's opening paragraph uses the weather to focus on the strength and endurance of the abbey, which dominates Whitby. She also uses the adjective 'towering' to describe its impressive size.

In paragraph 5 Student A continues to explore the effects of the language and imagery and compares Gardam's emotive use of simile and metaphor with Orwell's very limited use.

However, it is in paragraph two that Gardam makes best use of emotive language and imagery to convey the power and the frightening magnificence of the Middlesbrough chemical industry. She opens her topic sentence with two adverbial phrases to place the chemical industry precisely in the geography of the Iron Coast and to hold back the imagery for greater impact. She uses a complex series of metaphors to communicate its size and impressiveness. While acknowledging its greatness on an international level ('one of the great chemical works of the world') she compares it to 'Hell's kitchen' which connotes both horror, fire and damnation, implying that it is a terrifying place that, while bringing some prosperity to the region, has done so at the cost of its soul. She tells us it is responsible for the death of the nineteenth century steelworks through the use of the image of the graveyard ('the nineteenth-century graveyard of the steelworks in front of it'), and she gives it the persona of a wild and dangerous predator that has overcome but not totally absorbed its victims through the use of the metaphor of entrails which suggests the ways it has spread ('the remains of the streets of poor industrial towns tangled in its entrails'). The combination of beauty and horror is further developed by the simile 'like lurid petals' which describes the flames from the refinery chimneys by combining the image of the delicate flower with the adjective 'lurid' which suggests its unnaturalness. The extended use of simile and metaphor can be contrasted with Orwell's more limited use of imagery. There are only two similes in Text A, one where he conveys the irritation Winston Smith feels by comparing the snooping helicopter to a noisy troublesome insect and the other which compares the telescreen to a 'dulled mirror'. The latter is used simply to enable the reader to visualise more precisely what the telescreen looked like.

The sentence structure also helps Gardam focus on the meaning. In the final sentence of paragraph two the destructive nature of the chemical works is emphasised by the 'fumes and smoke' which 'wither up' the gardens and the trees, and 'coat' Scandinavia with 'bitter, orange dust'. The connotations here of unnaturalness create an ambiguity in her use of the adjective 'great' to describe the works. It is great in size, power and economic impact, but certainly not ecologically, and this ambiguity conveys ambivalence in Gardam's attitude. This compound-complex sentence with its linked adverbial phrases helps Gardam convey the pervasiveness of the pollution. The fumes and smoke go far ('across the coastal plain … across to Scandinavia') but also deep inside people ('deep down into the lungs').

A similar sort of ambivalence is found in the final paragraph of Text B. It is a place of 'hard, quiet unhappiness'. The adjectives 'hard, quiet' here suggest a tough stoicism born out of suffering among the people. She uses the metaphor 'this small rag of the country' to further suggest its apparent worthlessness. However, the adverb 'yet' which begins the final sentence with its list of achievers and achievements leaves us with a positive view and an awareness of Gardam's admiration.

Orwell, in contrast, does not show any ambivalence in his distaste for the world of 1984. Where Gardam used the size of the historical monuments and the chemical works to convey the impressiveness of the Iron Coast, Orwell uses the size of the poster of Big Brother to show how it is used to intimidate the people. The adjective 'enormous' combined with the post qualifying phrase 'more than a metre wide' convey its physical dominance. The caption over the bed 'watching' to convey to the readers that all their movements are seen, and the use of the second person personal pronoun in the direct object 'you' makes it more personal and threatening. The use of the phrase 'Big Brother' creates a sinister effect, as it undermines the associations of care and protection that normally come with the adjective/noun combination and replace them with a sense of threat. This is no brother and he is big both in a physically threatening and an emotionally dominant way. This threatening surveillance is emphasised by the simile of the helicopter hovering 'like a bluebottle' and 'snooping' into people's windows. This image and verb suggests, however, something irritating and persistent rather than truly terrifying, and contrast with the more frightening image of 'Hell's kitchen' used by Gardam to describe the chemical works. Orwell makes use of syntax to suggest the true terror of that society – the Thought Police – by placing this in a simple sentence which begins with the emphatic adverb 'only'.

Text C is the most different, partly because of the mode, which is spontaneous and spoken, and therefore ephemeral. It has some similarities to the other two texts in its aim, which is to convey the speaker's feelings about a place, in this case Disneyland, and he uses language to express his dislike, but additionally there are a number of prosodic features which writers cannot use. As there is a single speaker, Labov's narrative structure can be applied to the extract. The abstract establishes the topicality and the first pause of a second suggests the speaker is pausing to think. However, the hedges ('I suppose'/'erm') and pauses (there is in total a 5 second pause – a 3 plus a 2 linked by a filler) show the spontaneity of the language and may suggest the speaker's hesitation before launching into the criticisms, which follow on fairly rapidly in the orientation. The initial hedges of the speaker may be compared to the ambivalence we saw in Gardam.

In paragraph 6 a brief discussion of syntax is included to support the reading conveyed by the language and imagery.

Before Student A returns to Text A by way of comparison, paragraph 7 is used to comment briefly on the language of the final paragraph of Text B.

In paragraph 8 the comparison becomes more integrated. Student A compares how Gardam's feelings were revealed through her use of language with the way we begin to understand Orwell's attitudes through his use of language and syntax. This concludes Section 3.

The discussion now moves in paragraph 9 to Text C, and makes links with the other texts in terms of mode and aim. It then goes on to consider the structure.

The spoken voice, unlike the written text, allows the use of stress to give emphasis to key ideas, and here the speaker wishes to stress two ideas about the place – it was 'disappointin'' and its 'artificiality'.

In paragraph 10 Student A considers the language and syntax of Text C in some detail.

Structurally the complication criticises various aspects of American life such as its superficiality (the adjective 'characterless' suggests its emptiness of any solid value), its commercialism ('an by God they do get you to spend money' where he uses an emphatic oath to ram home the point) and its inadequate food ('bland'/'lukewarm') before using the resolution to compare it with the solid and reliable values of home ('good ol' English food'). In the complication we see the tendency of the speaker to use the coordinating conjunctions 'and' and 'but' to link together criticisms in a list-like, compound structure. This builds the criticisms up in a simple way. For example, 'an of course everything's geared to sp for your (.) er as er as an individual an a (.) family an it's very family oriented of course (0.5) er (.) to spend money and erm (2.0) an by God they do get you to spend money and obviously ...' This utterance clearly contrasts with the carefully structured language of Texts A and B. It reveals how through a series of false starts the speaker develops and builds his criticism. The use of syndetic lists a little further on creates an impression of the large number of items the visitor is pressured to buy: 'tee shirts n shorts n hats n glasses n trinkets an all the memorabilia that goes with Disney ...' The reduced spoken form 'n' further helps emphasise the range of goods through the speed with which the utterance is delivered. This prosodic feature is not something the writers of Texts A and B are able to use.

In paragraph 11 Student A looks closely at the use of adjectives in Text C and makes a broad comparison with the use of adjectives in Texts A and B. This concludes Section 4.

However, in a similar way to which the writers use adjectives to express their criticisms of their subjects the speaker employs adjectives throughout to show his dislike of Disneyland and the cumulative effect of these is emphatic. He moves from 'disappointin'' through 'plastic', 'squeaky clean', 'antiseptic', 'manufactured', 'characterless' to 'superficial'. These adjectives convey his feeling that Disneyland lacked genuineness. It was artificially produced for consumption by the public. 'Antiseptic' is especially damning as it connotes sterility, a lack of any form of real life. 'Manufactured' is given extra emphasis by the use of stress within the utterance and by the fact that there is a two-second pause before it is used. This pause suggests that the speaker has spent time considering his choice of word in order to make it as accurate a summary of his feelings as possible. These adjectives are further supported by nouns such as 'veneer' connoting a surface appearance and 'artificiality' (the latter intensified by the modifiers 'absolute and complete') to also indicate the total lack of genuineness in the place. He sums up his dislike of the superficiality of American culture by coining a new adjective which uses sound and emphasis. He describes it as 'whoop-whoop' which very informally and colloquially creates a child's cry of excitement in order to suggest its immaturity. The speaker also combines emphasis with mild taboo language to similarly emphasise his points ('a lot of it's the bloody same').

The final paragraph concludes with some general comparisons between the three texts summing up some of the points that have been discussed in the answer. The approach that has been largely taken is the anchor text approach, where one text is discussed in detail first of all, and then a second text is added and compared. Finally the third text is added, explored in detail and linked with the other two texts.

In Text C the spontaneity and informality of the text contrasts the spoken mode with Texts A and B, the two examples of the written mode. The attitudes found in all three texts vary in line with the different aims. Text A's political criticism of a society found expression through the description of the place; Text B's admiration for the Iron Coast found expression through the description of its history and culture; and Text C's dislike of aspects of American culture found its expression through an account of a visit to Florida.

Examiner's comments

This is a good answer, because it is not only comprehensive in its coverage of the texts, but shows a detailed exploration of the way the writers' and speaker's language choices express various shades of meaning. It attempts to deal with language, imagery and syntax, and links the texts with a discussion of mode, aim and audience. It avoids the trap of feature spotting.

If we measure it against the mark scheme for this question, we see that it fulfils many of the criteria identified in the top band.

The two assessment objectives for this Unit are AO2 and AO3. AO2 is marked out of 45 and AO3 is marked out of 15, making a total of 60 marks for this section. This clearly places AO2 as the more important Assessment Objective, and we can see how it places at the very centre of the Objective the requirement to relate structure, form and language to meaning. AO3 focuses largely on rewarding the comparisons between the texts.

	Marks out of 45	Demonstrate detailed critical understanding in analysing the ways in which structure, form and language shape meanings in a range of spoken and written contexts. AO2	Marks out of 15	Use integrated approaches to explore relationships between texts, analysing and evaluating the significance of contextual factors in their production and reception. AO3
Band 4	39–45	Profound analysis of literary or linguistic texts; sense of overview; illuminating reading of text. Possibly conceptualised or individualistic in approach. Conceptual comment on cohesion and textual structure. Cogent comments on features of speech and how speech works.	13–15	Assimilates and contextualises references with originality. Total overview that may offer observations on wider contexts. Exploratory. Significant similarities and differences are analysed in an original/personal, possibly conceptual manner. All texts effortlessly integrated.
	34–38	Secure and coherent reading and analysis underpinned by good textual evidence; textual grasp very evident. Close focus on details with a range of examples discussed. Coherent comment on form and structure; thoughtful points made on speech and how it works.	11–12	Skilful and secure comparison; clear sense of context/variation/contextual influences underpins reading. Close focus on texts. Coherently compares and contrasts writer's choice of form, structure, mode, language. Confidently compares modes.

Student B

There are a number of pitfalls some students fall into when they respond to this question. Student B has made a number of common errors which you need to avoid.

Student B's plan

None

(You really do need a plan to keep you on track and to ensure you cover the key points.)

Extract from Student B's answer

There is no detailed comment on the way language works. The quotations do not seem to be clearly linked to the argument, but appear to be randomly chosen. The limited discussion is generalised and obvious. There is narrative account rather than analysis.

Text A is aimed at a very broad audience: 'Winston Smith … slipped quickly through the doors of Victory Mansions …' The text contains a lot of ideas that many people would be able to understand, the use of description and adjectives suggest that anyone can read the text. The description is very detailed: 'The hallway smelt of boiled cabbage and old rag mats.' The imagery describes the appearance of the place and allows the reader to visualise a picture of what the author is trying to describe. The writer takes us with Winston Smith as he enters Victory Mansions and has to walk up the stairs because the lift is not working, and describes to us his flat with the telescreen, and the picture of Big Brother that can be seen on the corner of the house opposite.

Although the writer implies that a comparison of texts is going to follow, no detailed comparison is made. Technical terms are used without examples, the convention of using the writer's surname is ignored and there is no linguistic examination of the quotation.

If we compare Text A to Text B, the use of field specific lexis is combined with some description and is aimed at people interested in the Iron Coast. Jane aims her text mainly at tourists interested in history: 'A great black tooth, the ruined abbey of St Hilda, stands high on the cliff above Whitby.'

The analysis of the quotations is vague, and tells the examiner nothing about how language works. Sentences like 'it makes the reader want to read on' are meaningless and should be avoided. The attempt to use framework terminology ('strong nouns') is vague and inaccurate, and there is no clear indication of the writer's attitudes. In the final attempt at analysis the examiner does not know whether the student understands the link between the imagery of 'Hell's kitchen' and the writer's attitude.

The descriptions in this text are different to that of text A: 'Out of the tops of the refinery chimneys flames like lurid petals bend in the wind'. It is very detailed and tells us what the place is like and is very informative which is what tourists want, thus making the text aimed at a specific audience, and when comparing the imagery to Text A it is quite vivid and entertaining: 'Roseberry Topping like a midget volcano'. This sort of imagery makes the reader want to read on. The use of strong nouns clearly expresses the author's attitudes towards the iron coast: 'The Iron Coast feels different from anywhere else. There is a hard, quiet unhappiness about it.' and she seems to feel quite involved in it through the use of descriptions 'like Hell's kitchen'. The word 'kitchen' is very specific when writing about the place because it shows exactly what it was like.

The final paragraph just spots features within the text without linking them to aim or audience, makes inaccurate comments ('no grammar') and makes vague and generalised comments.

Comparing these texts to Text C this is aimed at a more informal audience. The speaker uses fillers and non-standard English to help him continue his speech. 'that sort of antiseptic (1.0.) er type of (.) place (.) which (.) is obviously all erm (1.0) I suppose (2.0) erm (.) manufactured'. The use of the pauses and hesitations shows it has no grammar and the use of hesitations and repetitions could represent thinking time for the speaker. He also uses taboo language: 'a lot of it's the bloody same (.) y'know' Here he uses swearing and the emphasis on bloody suggests that he wants his audience to pay attention to what he is talking about. The speaker has strong views against Disneyland.

Examiner's comments

Although this is an extract from a longer answer it clearly shows a number of the problems students need to avoid at all costs. It is full of generalisation and half-understood ideas. Quotations are not explored in detail, and there is no discussion of how language conveys meaning. Attitudes are mentioned only in the broadest terms and there are a number of inaccurate comments that reveal a limited grasp of framework terminology. If we measure this against the mark scheme, we see that it fulfils many of the criteria for the lower bands (lower band 1 is generally reserved for answers that are very weak indeed or very short):

	Marks out of 45	AO2	Marks out of 15	AO3
Lower Band 2	16–19	Basic and generalised analysis; responds to surface features in a broad fashion. May take a narrative approach with occasional simplistic comments. Lacks details or engagement and very few speech features, not related to the context at all.	4	May see how context influences language use; general awareness of writer's techniques and impact on meaning. Responds to obvious or broad links or comparisons. Sometimes comments on less important links. May lack details and evidence.
Upper Band 1	11–15	A little understanding; very limited analysis; sometimes responds to surface features/odd textual references but main focus is on textual narrative or general points. Speech points are totally general.	3	Superficial idea of context. Occasional insight but not sustained; one area of study noted, others are ignored. Lacks details and probably little evidence used.

How can I improve my performance on Section A?

The best way to improve your performance on Section A of this paper is to practise as much as you can. Look at the annotations for the three texts again, and write your own response under examination conditions. It will be different from Student A's answer but could be just as good. Try to make sure it fits the Band 4 criteria in the mark scheme on p51.

5 Exploring the Section B question

AQA Examiner's tip

ELLA3 is a *closed book* examination, which means that you are not allowed to take your texts with you into the examination. This means that the only text you will have in the examination will be that chosen by the examiner and printed on the paper.

The danger with Section B of ELLA3 is that you may be tempted to relax a little after having worked very hard for 1½ hours on the unseen comparative analysis. If you do, you may find that you do not give this section the attention you should. Do not forget that it is worth 40 per cent of the total marks for the paper! However, Section B is to some extent less demanding than Section A in that it is based on two set texts, *at least one* of which you will have studied during the second year of your course. But remember that it is a *closed book* examination.

The tasks

There are two tasks on *each* set text. Once you have found the part of the question paper that relates to the set text you have studied, you will see an extract (or possibly two shorter extracts) from your chosen set text.

Task one

The first task (worth 25 marks, which is 25 per cent of the Unit 3 examination paper) is a recasting task and will vary from year to year. You will be asked to select appropriate material from that extract and adapt it for a different specified purpose, context and audience. You may be asked to produce a fictional piece (such as a diary entry) or a non-fiction piece (such as a speech). However, it is essential that the final product *uses your own words* as far as possible and is based on the extracts you have been given. You will be judged on how well your piece fulfils the criteria of purpose, context, audience, and also on the accuracy and appropriateness of the language used.

Possible tasks in written mode:

- entry for an encyclopaedia (for adults or children)
- editorial or article for tabloid or broadsheet newspaper
- leaflet
- report
- advertisement
- review
- letter
- magazine article
- newspaper article.

Because this paper is synoptic it is intended to test the skills that have been covered in the other three units (that is, your AS units and Unit 4). This means that as well as being asked to produce a written text, such as a letter or article, you could be asked to write the script for a speech or a talk.

Possible tasks for scripting a text for spoken delivery:

- broadcast (for radio or television)
- speech
- talk.

Link

To revise features of some of these forms, look back to Chapter 9 of *AQA English Language and Literature A AS*.

If you are asked to write the text for a speech or talk, your spelling and punctuation will be taken into account just as it is in a text which is intended to be read.

Task two

The second task (worth 15 marks, which is 15 per cent of the Unit 3 paper) is a commentary in which you are asked to comment on the language choices you made in your recasting, and this will remain the same every year. You will be asked to write a short but detailed commentary in which you discuss some of the language choices you made when writing your piece. The aim of this exercise is to enable you to show that you understand how language conveys meaning, and that you are sensitive to how and why we use language in different contexts and for different audiences and purposes.

The Assessment Objectives

The AOs for this section are AO1 and AO4.

The *recasting* (task one) focuses on AO4: Demonstrate expertise and creativity in using language appropriately for a variety of purposes and audiences, drawing on insights from linguistic and literary studies.

While the *commentary* (task two) focuses on AO1: Select and apply relevant concepts and approaches from integrated linguistic study, using appropriate terminology and accurate coherent written expression.

The texts

It is a requirement that both the set texts in Unit 3 are non-fiction, and each belongs to a different genre of writing. For the first years of the Specification the genres are journalism and travel writing, and the texts contain extracts by various writers. The texts are *Cupcakes and Kalashnikovs*, a collection of women's journalism edited by Eleanor Mills, and *A House Somewhere*, a collection of travel pieces edited by Don George and Anthony Sattin.

It is unlikely that you will be required to study the whole of either collection for the ELLA3 examination in any one year. It is probable that sections from each text will be set, and this will enable you not only to thoroughly absorb the pieces, but give you enough time to develop your understanding of the contexts in which they were written. A sound grasp of context as well as content will ensure that you are both familiar with any extract that may appear on the examination paper and enable you to concentrate more effectively on selecting the most appropriate material for the recasting task, which requires you to adapt it for the new purpose and audience.

Cupcakes and Kalashnikovs

Cupcakes and Kalashnikovs, as its title may suggest, contains examples of writing by women journalists, and presents a female perspective of the world, covering all aspects of society from the domestic sphere to war. The pieces date from 1888 to 2005 but the majority span the whole of the 20th century, and reflect women's views on major historical events, even during those times when it was often inconvenient for men to hear a woman's voice. The sections in the collection include 'Politics, Race and Society', 'Emancipation and Having it All', 'Crime and Punishment',

'Sex and Body Image', 'Interviews and Icons', in addition to 'War' and 'Home and Family'.

Journalism usually finds itself at the sharp edge of history, and this collection presents us with vivid and personal responses to issues and events that have shaped the world we live in today. Some of the pieces reflect the growth of the feminist movement, but most either pre-date or post-date that period. Without exception they all give an honest and often moving account of major episodes and events from the last hundred years.

A House Somewhere

A House Somewhere is also a series of personal accounts, but focuses on places rather than world-shaking events. However, it has an original slant on the travel-writing genre. Whereas most travel writing is concerned with describing the journeys of travellers to and through different places of interest, usually ending back home where the adventure started, this collection concerns the writers' thoughts and feelings about places where they moved to and settled down. It gives us an insight into foreign countries from the point of view of the people who left their homes to live there, and so we get a sense of the magic of the places that drew these people to stay.

■ Strategies

As you only have an hour to complete this task, you need to be very disciplined in how you allocate your time. 15 minutes to plan and prepare the task, 25 minutes for the actual writing of task one and 20 minutes for your commentary seems about right.

Planning and preparation (15 minutes)

This stage breaks down into four key areas:

- analysis of the task
- imaginative grasp of the context
- selection of key material
- organisation of response.

You must read the task carefully and ensure you understand *what* you are being asked to do and *who* you are writing for. It is surprising how many students fall at this first hurdle. Then try to place yourself imaginatively in the context. In other words see it, as far as you can, as a real task, and not as an examination exercise. Think carefully about the sort of text or talk you are being asked to write. For example, if you are going to write a magazine article, make sure it is something that you feel really could appear in the pages of your chosen journal. Once you know what you are aiming to produce, you then need to select the necessary material from the source. As you read the text, it is a good idea to use a pencil to jot down in the margin, in your own words, the key ideas you could include in your answer. You could also use a highlighter to mark all the material you feel would be helpful for the task. Only select information which is apt. Finally, jot down an outline structure for what you are going to write. This ensures that your writing has some cohesion and you avoid repetition or omission of key ideas. Pay special attention to how you introduce your response. Try to give it a sense of authenticity.

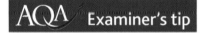

AQA Examiner's tip

You must ensure that you give yourself enough time to write a good commentary as it is worth a vital 15 per cent, and there is nowhere to steal the time from if you overrun.

Writing the task one response (25 minutes)

This stage breaks down into five key areas:

- relevance
- adaptation
- context
- register
- accuracy.

1 Relevance: If you did your job properly in the planning and preparation stage you will have identified the material *relevant* for the task. This means you can now concentrate on *how* you are going to present the material, rather than what you are going to present. Keep the task firmly in mind as you make a further selection from what you have highlighted. It is unlikely you will be able to use *all* the highlighted material, so keep to the point of the task. Place yourself imaginatively in the context as you begin to write, and try to ensure your introduction clearly shows you are addressing the task.

2 Adaptation: *Never copy out or lift parts of the original.* The text has to be *adapted* to the new audience and purpose which means you have to *use your own words*. Copying from the original is penalised because you are not adapting for your new audience and purpose. Remember, too, that the task is adaptation *not invention*. You are *not* asked to use the text as a springboard but as a source of information. This means that you must not elaborate on the source material by substantially adding to it from your own knowledge or imagination.

3 Context. Make sure that your text reflects the context specified in the task. After having placed the response in its context, keep to the source material.

4 Register: Think about your audience as well as your task. Make sure you are writing in an appropriate *register*.

5 Accuracy: As you write, avoid making errors in spelling and punctuation or in English expression. This is the only question in ELLA3 in which your spelling, punctuation and expression will be evaluated, and candidates who make basic technical errors or cannot use English accurately will lose marks.

There is a suggested word limit for the exercise of between 300 and 400 words. This is a guide, not an absolute requirement, so you could write fewer than 300 or more than 400 words. However, if you do not write enough you are not likely to cover all the necessary ideas, and to write many more is to risk losing control and running short of time on the commentary. In both cases, producing a response outside the recommended limits is likely to be self-penalising.

The commentary (20 minutes)

To write a successful commentary you need a structured approach (a **framework**). You should need to ask and answer the following questions:

Who?

- Who are you writing for? (or who is being addressed in a spoken presentation?)
- What is the context? The answer to this question will help you identify the choices when you ask 'what?' and 'how?'.

What?

- What am I aiming to do?

AQA Examiner's tip

Before the exam, investigate how many lines of your own handwriting make up 300–400 words. You can use this as a guide to pace yourself when writing your commentary, to make sure you write the right amount of words in the examination.

Key terms

Framework: a structured approach.

■ What is the aim or purpose? The answers to these questions will help you explore the choices when you ask 'how?'.

How?

■ How has the text been presented? What choices of language, style and form have been made to meet the requirements decided when you asked 'who?' and 'what?'. Think about:

■ emotive language:
  – What are the connotations of the words that have been used?
  – Do the words appeal specifically to the senses? If so, which words and how?
  – Which nouns, verbs, adjectives and adverbs have been used and what effects do they create?
  – Have I used imagery, such as similes, metaphors and personification effectively? What effects are created?

■ factual language:
  – Is the writing informative, objective and unemotive?
  – What nouns, verbs, adjectives and adverbs have been used and what effects do they create?

■ informal language:
  – Have I used colloquial language, slang or other words that create an informal tenor?

■ formal language:
  – Have I used objective, unemotive language and has it created a formal tenor?

■ syntax:
  – What types of sentences have been used and what effects have they created?

■ sounds:
  – Have any phonological devices such as alliteration, assonance or onomatopoeia been used, and if so why?
  – What effects have they created?

■ layout or design:
  – Has the text been set out in a way designed to appeal to the eye?
  – If so, why? What effects are created?

The commentary requires a succinct but detailed discussion of the language choices you made and the form you used in order to complete the task and address the audience. To enable you to explore in detail the effects of the language chosen, you need to explain who you were writing for and in what context. The areas you could consider might include some of the following:

■ vocabulary
■ imagery
■ sentence structure
■ degree of formality
■ phonology
■ literary devices
■ layout and design
■ but *not* content.

6 | Examples of answers for Section B
A House Somewhere

Let us now apply these principles to a typical task similar to ones you are likely to find in Section B on one of the set texts, starting with task one.

 ## Task one: the recasting

Examination-style questions

Dinner of Herbs – Carla Grissman

Read the source material which follows and answer both parts of the question:

Text A is from Carla Grissman's book *Dinner of Herbs*, published in 2001, in which she describes some time she spent living in a village in Turkish Anatolia in the 1960s.

BBC television is planning to broadcast a documentary programme examining Kemal Atatürk's influence on the development of modern Turkey.

Using Grissman's material as your source, write the script for a short introductory section to the programme in which the presenter will give some background information on Atatürk's attempts to modernise the traditional life and culture of Turkey.

You should select and adapt relevant information from the source material using your own words as far as possible. Your introduction should be approximately 300–400 words in length.

In your adaptation you should:

- use language appropriately to address purpose and audience
- write accurately and coherently applying relevant ideas.

(25 marks)

Link

The extract that accompanies this question can be seen on pp60–2.

Stage 1: Planning and preparation

1 Thinking about the task

What is the task?

An introduction to a television documentary programme. Audience: general adult viewer.

2 Imaginative grasp of the context

What characterises this type of introduction?

Possibly a presenter speaking to the camera at the beginning of the programme.

What must the presenter communicate?

Background information on Turkey at the time of Atatürk, the problems and an outline of his modernisation programme.

How must the presenter do this?

The presenter must be aware that the audience may possess some knowledge about Turkey from holiday visits but probably knows little about its history or about Atatürk himself. The presenter therefore must be careful neither to patronise the audience on the one hand nor to assume too much knowledge on the other. In order to engage the viewers the presenter should take them from the known to the unknown and address them in a friendly but knowledgeable way.

3 Selection of key material

Reading the text is an active process, the aim of which is to identify key information for the task and determine an approach. Pencil notes down the side of the extract are useful in summarising important ideas in your own words, and a highlighter is effective in selecting key areas. The following text has been annotated and highlighted showing some of the points that *could* be made.

Text B: *Dinner of Herbs* by Carla Grissman

Carla Grissman describes the evening meal during the holy month of Ramadan when the men of the village congregated together in one of their houses to break the fast at sunset. Kamüran is a village religious leader who is helping to look after Grissman.

> **Islamic culture: men and women eat separately**

Everyone ate quickly and the dishes were taken away while still half full, to be given to the women in the next room. There was hardly any conversation. Before the end of the meal, the Imam abruptly began a prayer and the men dropped their bread and raised both hands in front of them, palms upward, and murmured the words with him. His prayer was in Arabic, learned by rote a long time ago, the words now unintelligible and their meaning lost, but no-one would think to wonder what it meant. When the meal was finished, the trays were lifted away and the men got to their feet and queued up to wash at a tin basin in the corner of the room where one of the sons held the soap and towel and poured water over their hands. The men spread out and sat in a packed line against three sides of the room. The father or his son swept the floor clean with a short straw broom and went around dropping little tin ashtrays in front of every second person. For a few seconds everyone shifted and moved to get comfortable on their haunches and soon the room began to cloud with cigarette smoke.

> **Automatic, unthinking ritual**

Then again without warning the Imam rose and went to stand at the wall facing south. The men rose and formed in lines. In one gesture, they all turned their caps around so that the visor lay in the back. The first evening I did not know what was happening and I stood up too in confusion. Hacı Ismail said, 'You stay. There in back, sit, sit.' There were three rows of eight or nine men and the room suddenly seemed very small. The Imam called out the beginning of the prayer, and instantly all the men in their dark anonymous clothing and matted wool socks full of holes were fused, their shoulders almost touching, into a single obedient body. The act of prayer is a prescribed ritual and movements never vary. A man stands erect, his hands open at either side of his face and his thumbs on the lobes

> **Attempt by villagers to get around Atatürk's edict**

> **Power of Islam, unity in prayer**

of his ears as he says the first words: 'Allah is most great'. Still standing, he continues to pray, then bows from the hips with his hands on his knees. He stands upright again, then sinks to his knees and puts his hands and his forehead to the ground. He sits up straight on his heels, then again puts his hands and his forehead to the ground. These movements are repeated several times. The prayer too does not change. It is of praise and gratitude, a simple act of worship, not a petition for favours or a personal dialogue with Allah.

> **Devotion to Islam is deep and unquestioning**

> **Atatürk wanted to make Turkey a modern secular state and neutralise the power of religious fanatics. Decided to outlaw the fez as a symbol of Islamic power**

All the things I had been reading began to take on meaning. In 1923 one of the dramatic reforms in Kemal Atatürk's secularization of Turkey was the demand that Western hats be worn instead of the fez, which to him was the symbol of Muslim fanaticism. This caused great anguish among pious Muslims, who considered the hat an infidel execration, the brim rightly hiding the shameful pagan face from the sight of God. There were riots and defiance. Atatürk declared the wearing of the fez a criminal offence. Within three weeks, with thousands of Turks hung, beaten or imprisoned, this reform was complete. Besides the more Western appearance it produced, perhaps he hoped that a head under a European hat would think European thoughts. The hat, furthermore, might in an insidious way discourage prayer, as the brim made it difficult to touch the forehead to the ground. But the people got around this by adopting the visored cap, which could be swiveled front to back so the wearer, his head still covered, could easily touch his forehead to the ground while performing the ritual prayer.

> **Edict enforced with violence; a determined heavy resistance to change that threatens religion**

> **Atatürk attempts to break cultural links**

> **People resourceful and stubborn**

Turkey had come so far. Much of the population after the First World War had been lost through battle, disease and starvation. No proper roads existed, only one railway from Istanbul with a few dead-end branches into Anatolia. Malaria and typhoid still broke out. There were no industries, no technicians or skilled workmen, in a country ninety per cent illiterate, with no established government. The heaviest liability, however, of Atatürk's derelict legacy from the Ottoman Empire was the great mass of benighted peasants, rooted in lethargy, living in remote poverty – stricken villages untouched by the outside world. Atatürk was determined to loosen the hold of Islam on the people, which he believed was the greatest obstacle to modernisation, and to awaken a sense of Turkish national pride. He fought fiercely for the emancipation of women, denouncing the veil, giving them the right to vote and divorce. He had a consuming faith in the qualities and the character of the peasants. The élite of the cities should turn to the people, he said, as the living museums of Turkey's cultural heritage. The élite possessed civilisation, the people culture.

> **Massive task for Atatürk; a broken and backward country**

> **Social, political, economic, psychological defeat after the First World War**

> **Atatürk saw Islam as an obstacle to modernisation**

> **Atatürk supported women's rights**

> **Atatürk aimed to unite a divided country**

'Atatürk understood our country,' Kâmuran always said. 'He was a peasant himself.'

> **Atatürk's humble roots**

Whenever I quoted facts about how much had been accomplished or still needed to be done, Kâmuran grew impatient. That there were only two taxis and one private car in the entire enormous province of Bingöl in 1963, and that in 1962, only 5,000 out of 60,000 religious leaders

> **It took many years to start to make any progress**

could write the Latin alphabet, that now nearly six million students were registered instead of the 380,000 when his father was his age, that the GNP was rising at a steady seven per cent a year, did not interest him.

'I do not understand numbers like that, they are not important for us now, maybe later. Only the things that keep these people's minds closed are important now.'

> Message got through to some people

Stage 1: Planning and preparation (continued)

4 Organisation of response

- Establish documentary setting/provide authentic context/voice
- Link to viewer's own experience
- Outline aim of programme
- Atatürk's plans/beginnings/condition of country/the challenge
- His vision/need to create national identity/problem of religion
- Attitude to women/the fez/the battle still being waged

Stage 2: Student A's response

The opening paragraph successfully picks up the context and links the topic to areas the viewer will be familiar with, and then goes on to make a connection with Atatürk and his task, stating clearly the aim of the programme. There is some minor but essential invention at the beginning in order to provide an appropriate imaginative context, but, other than that the material is clearly adapted from the source.

The second paragraph contains the essential information detailing the scale of the problems Atatürk had to face and his variable success in dealing with them. The sentences are often short to enable them to be spoken or read from an autocue by the presenter.

Hello. I'm Jeremy Vine and I'm speaking to you today from inside Turkey, the closest and largest Islamic country to the EEC. Many of us have been to Turkey for our holidays and have enjoyed its sunshine and the hospitality of the Turkish people. But how many of us know that less than 100 years ago Turkey was a backward and broken country, part of the ruins of the once great Ottoman Empire? The changes that have been brought about during the 20th century have been massive, and owe their origin to the fierce determination of just one man, Kemal Atatürk, who began the movement to modernisation and the creation of the new Turkish state. This programme aims to explain a little about Atatürk and the problems he faced in trying to turn Turkey into a modern secular state.

When Atatürk came to power in 1923, after the end of the First World War, he found a country that was socially, politically and economically in ruins. The population had been decimated by war, disease and starvation. The transport system lacked functioning roads and railways. There was no established system of government, no industries, no skilled workmen, and a population 90 per cent of whom were illiterate. The challenge was enormous. Atatürk felt that the first thing he had to do was to change the people's attitudes. Turkey's rural population was psychologically crippled, he felt, by poverty and lack of a sense of purpose, and in order to kick-start his revolution he had to create a new sense of national pride. He felt particularly that the hold religion had over the people was a major obstacle to modernisation, and so he set about a programme of reforms designed to break the power of Islam over the minds of the people and turn Turkey into a secular state. He passed laws which gave women the power to vote, to divorce and to not wear the veil. His most significant early battle with Islam, however, was over the wearing of the fez, which he saw as a symbol of Muslim fanaticism. He ordered that it should be replaced by Western-style hats with brims that made it more difficult for the head to touch the ground in prayer. He met heavy resistance and eventually had to enforce the law with violence, and thousands of Turks were hanged, beaten or imprisoned before it finally took effect. However, he never really succeeded in his aim, because the resourceful people adopted a visored cap which could be swivelled round to enable the forehead to touch the ground. Even by the 1960s Islam still had a strong hold over the people, and despite the progress to modernisation made in the cities, the countryside is still backward and ready for modernisation.

Examiner's comments

This is a fluent response which incorporates plenty of important information. It clearly addresses the imaginative context of the task, and does enough to make it convincing without spending too long on the introduction. It is accurately spelled and punctuated and the expression seems appropriate for the audience and context. Although it is a little over the recommended word count (by about 50 words), it would be difficult to reduce without losing either some important information or the sense of context and audience. If we measure it against the mark scheme for this question we can see that it meets many of the criteria in the top band. The Assessment Objective for this question is AO4, which states that candidates need to 'demonstrate expertise and creativity in using language appropriately for a variety of purposes and audiences, drawing on insights from linguistic and literary sources.' Appropriateness of language for purpose, context and audience is central, and this, of course, includes the ability to use accurate written expression.

	Marks out of 25	Demonstrate expertise and creativity in using language appropriately for a variety of purposes and audiences, drawing on insights from linguistic and literary studies. AO4
Band 4	22–25	Responds confidently and at top of band originality and flair. Skilfully handled writing which is completely fit for purpose. Sophisticated use of language at top end. Cohesive writing that works at bottom end. Engaging style with very clear and convincing ideas of audience and purpose. Firm control of technical aspects.
	19–21	Confident adaptation. Sustained use of appropriate style. Approaching fulfilment of aim. Content and style confidently selected for audience. Convincing use of form with sustained evidence of audience and purpose being addressed. Technically accurate.

Task two: the commentary

Examination-style questions

Write a commentary which explains the choices you have made when writing your introduction, commenting on the following:

- how language and form have been used to suit audience and purpose
- how vocabulary and other stylistic features have been used to shape meaning and achieve particular effects.

You should aim to write about 150–250 words in this commentary.

(15 marks)

To write an effective commentary in so few words means that you must focus on the key ideas quickly and explore some aspects of the language in detail. Clearly you cannot cover a great range in the time you have left, but in order to ensure that you are awarded a mark in the top band you need to write in as much detail as you can. Address the three key questions: Who? What? How? But give the majority of your time to showing how your language choices have enabled you to address your audience, create the appropriate context and fulfil your aim. You will need to quote briefly from your text in order to analyse your language effectively, and this really means that most good commentaries will be in the 230–250 word range.

Student A's response

My aim in this piece was to produce an authentic introduction to a TV documentary programme for the general public. I tried to convey the sense of the spoken mode by the use of direct address: 'Hello. I'm Jeremy Vine and I'm speaking to you today from inside Turkey'. Here I have used both the first and second person personal pronouns together with contractions to give a semi-informal tenor. The use of the name of a genuine broadcaster adds authenticity and the adverbial phrase at the end fixes the context clearly. I wanted to move from the familiar to the unfamiliar so followed the declarative ('Many of us have been to Turkey ...') with the inclusive first person plural pronoun and determiner ('us' and 'our'), and with a rhetorical question implying that there is something important that may be missing from our knowledge ('How many of us know ... ?'). This enabled me to introduce the key figure and begin to sketch his character with the adjective plus noun combination 'fierce determination'. This connotes a strong sense of purpose, and the use of the adverb 'just' in the phrase 'just one man' evokes admiration for him as an individual who achieved so much on his own. In the second paragraph I tried to continue the semi-formal register of the broadcast by the use of a series of short, simple sentences that identified the scale of the problem Atatürk faced: 'The population had been decimated by war, disease and starvation'; 'The challenge was enormous.' The use of the list reinforces the problems the country faced, as does the noun 'challenge' and the adjective 'enormous'. I continue the idea that Atatürk was waging a war with various reactionary forces by using battle imagery. He had a 'battle' with Islam, the 'battle to open people's minds is still being waged', he met 'heavy resistance' and his reforms were designed to 'break the power of Islam'.

Examiner's comments

This commentary is successful in that it identifies audience, aim and context and links language use to all three, using appropriate framework terminology. It attempts to cover word choice, imagery and sentence structure and link all three to the communication of meaning in the text. Quotations are brief but apt, and enable the student to focus on detail.

The Assessment Objective for this question is AO1 which states that candidates must 'select and apply relevant concepts and approaches from integrated linguistic study, using appropriate terminology and accurate coherent written expression', and if we apply the mark scheme to the response we can see that it fulfils many of the criteria for the top band:

	Marks out of 15	Select and apply relevant concepts and approaches from integrated linguistic study, using appropriate terminology and accurate coherent written expression. AO1
Band 4	13–15	Use of framework(s) enhances and illuminates textual interpretation. Has a possible overview of the text through the framework(s). Engages closely with the purpose, audience and meaning of the text; patterns fully appreciated. Possibly conceptual in use of framework(s). Fluent, cohesive writing.
	11–12	Coherent use of framework(s); some thoughtful probing of features and patterns. Thoughtful engagement with the text through framework(s) and details. Clear awareness of crafting evident through approach taken, framework(s) used. Fluent writing.

This chapter covers:

- looking at an example of an examination question on *Cupcakes and Kalashnikovs*

- exploring a strong student response with examiner comments

- exploring a weak student response with examiner comments.

Let us now look at a different task on the alternative set text, and two responses from different students.

The question for text B

Examination-style questions

Cupcakes and Kalashnikovs – Eleanor Mills (ed.)

Text B is from a report by Ann Leslie written for the *Daily Mail* at the time of the fall of the Berlin Wall in 1989.

a   Imagine you are the East German border guard who was on duty on the night described by Ann Leslie. Write a letter to your brother in which you describe the events and your thoughts and feelings about what happened.

   You should use and adapt the source material using your own words as far as possible. Your letter should be approximately 300–400 words in length.

   In your adaptation you should:
   - use language appropriately to address purpose and audience
   - write accurately and coherently, applying relevant ideas.

(25 marks)

b   Write a commentary which explains the choices you have made when writing your letter commenting on the following:
   - how language and form have been used to suit audience and purpose
   - how vocabulary and other stylistic features have been used to shape meaning and achieve particular effects.

   You should aim to write about 150–250 words in this commentary.

(15 marks)

Text B: 'Report on the fall of the Berlin Wall' from *Cupcakes and Kalashnikovs*, taken from the *Daily Mail*, Eleanor Mills (ed.)

1989, *Daily Mail*

Checkpoints at the Berlin Wall erupted into a huge carnival last night.

Thousands of East Germans flooded through, brandishing the champagne and beer bottles.

Many danced on top of the wall near Checkpoint Charlie* with good humoured border guards making no attempt to remove them or break up the bedlam.

Hours earlier, the Wall had been consigned to the history books as the infamous symbol of a divided Europe. East Germany's new leaders said their citizens could now emigrate freely and directly to West Germany.

On both sides of the Wall there was celebration that Checkpoint Charlie – dramatic backdrop of countless spy films and novels – was now nothing more than a tourists' turnstile. Crowds of East

Germans hurried through the no man's land where, hours earlier, they would have been shot at by guards. Thousands more crossed at other checkpoints, simply by showing their identity cards.

The developments surprised the West as much as the East. When in June 1987, Ronald Reagan stood at the wall built by Erich Honecker and called out: 'Mr. Gorbachev, tear this Wall down' no one imagined that within two years it would be defunct. Mr. Reagan's successor, President Bush[†] said of the news: 'I feel good about it.' He advised East Germans to stay on and 'participate in the reforms that are taking place.'

At first, a trickle of citizens arrived at the border in East Berlin. It soon became a deluge. In Bornholmer Strasse, border police gave up and let everybody through without checking, and first-aid teams were on hand to help some people who fainted with emotion.

On the West Berlin side, crowds shot off fireworks and clapped as the East Berliners surged through.

At one o'clock this morning, I spoke to Uta Ruhrdanz and four student friends at Friedrichstrasse checkpoint in East Berlin. 'We've just been to the West – for 20 minutes!' cried Uta. 'It's unbelievable! Still we can't understand how this happened and why, but for the moment we are just so excited and happy that we can't think much further!

'As soon as we heard the news we thought, "Can this be true – let's go and see." When we arrived the border guards said, "OK you can go across tonight and come back if you want. But tomorrow morning you should go and get your police stamp." There were lots of us crowding on to the train to West Berlin and we were all singing and laughing and some were trying to dance.

'And some people were still a little bit scared: they were saying "Perhaps it's all a trick, perhaps they won't let us come back again." We, too, felt a little bit frightened and so when we were in West Berlin we rushed out into the Kurfustendamm and bought souvenirs and then rushed back again. I think we were not believing completely that all this is true – but here we are. We are back and there has been no problem. It is so wonderful!'

As I returned to my hotel cars were honking, people were shouting greetings and a middle-aged couple came up to me and embraced me, beaming with excitement.

It had taken several hours since the historic announcement before East Berliners really began to believe what was now possible. Half-an-hour after the announcement I had gone to Checkpoint Charlie where I interviewed a border guard.

A fine drizzle fell, draping his cap with diamonds of light from the floodlights at the Wall: the scene was straight out of a spy thriller. But this border guard with his huge greatcoat had suddenly been transformed from a creature of totalitarian nightmare into an affable East German bloke clearly delighted to know that the more murderous part of his role was, as of half-an-hour earlier, effectively over.

Around me people were gathering, some toasting the great news with champagne. The guard looked up the road where foreign cars were lined up already.

'Isn't it great?' an East German friend with me asked him. 'Wouldn't it have been wonderful if they'd announced this four months ago?' 'Yes – it is wonderful but I don't think it's too late now. I think now there is hope for the country!' he replied. 'Oh, but you know that 43,000 people have left since the weekend?' my friend informed him. The border guard looked aghast. 'As many as that? I didn't realise.'

I asked him whether he was happy with the developments. He smiled ruefully. 'Personally, no – because it's going to mean I have to work much harder coping with the enormous queues that will be coming.'

The queue at the Friedrichstrasse checkpoint was growing by the minute. The people – young, old, middle-aged – were laughing, crying, embracing and all were telling each other (and me) exactly how and where they heard the news.

It had been yet another astonishing day in the city. Even yesterday I found that East Germans, for so long terrorized by the state security – the hated Stasi – would hesitate before speaking to me. They had developed a fear that even the walls in the streets were listening to them. But last night that fear seemed finally to have gone. In the queue at the Friedrichstrasse one woman said: 'They are still spying on us – look at that man listening over there. He is Stasi!'

In fact he turned out to be a harmless Swedish reporter, and even though people in the queue had looked at him you could tell that they suddenly didn't care whether he was Stasi or not.

The Wall still exists physically but in effect it has been destroyed. The psychological symbol of the Wall with its watch towers and its terrible no man's land had entered deeply into every East Berliner's soul. Now that the symbol, if not the physical presence, had been removed I found East Berliners looking on it as a simple border marker.

'I don't think they should pull the wall down yet,' said my East German friend. 'After all every country marks its border. But of course people on both sides should be able to pass to and fro – and now, at last, that is happening. This has been the most exciting day of my life.'

When we parted she flung her arms around me and kissed me, crying: 'Who would ever have believed that this would happen today!'

* Checkpoint Charlie: The most famous of the border crossing points between East and West Berlin.

† President Bush (American president from 1989 to 1993), the father of President George W. Bush (President from 2000 to January 2009)

[Note that such footnotes are unlikely to appear in an examination paper as it will be assumed you have done the necessary background research.]

Stage 1: Planning and preparation

This is an imaginative task, based on factual content. The letter is clearly informal as it is to a family member, but the content needs to be carefully selected to reveal a response to the events. This response will reflect the character of the guard. It could be emotional, cynical, enthusiastic, concerned, etc. It is also likely to include an awareness of the political context and the wider significance of the events. The letter form should present no problems, as long as the dates and names are credible. The material selected will tend to dictate the tone, and the structure is likely to be largely chronological, following the key events of the night.

Stage 2: Student B's response

Friedrichstrasse Barracks

November 10th '89

Dear Fritz,

Well, the impossible has happened. The wall came down last night after all these years. We had been told to let the people through if they showed their identity cards, and as soon as it was announced one or two turned up to see if it was true. It was as if they couldn't believe their ears, but once the news had filtered through, we were overwhelmed by crowds of excited people dancing on top of the wall, waving bottles of beer and champagne. It was <u>chaos</u>, but there was no point in trying to break up the celebrations. People fainted and first-aid teams had to be drafted in to cope with the casualties! We could hear the crowds on the other side clapping and setting off fireworks. At first there were just a few people coming through, but soon the crowds grew and grew. We tried to check all the ID cards, but it soon became impossible and we gave up trying! Crowds of people filled the trains to West Berlin, many of them drunk, but probably as much with excitement as with beer.

All the guards were caught up in the excitement too. It was truly fantastic but it was hard to understand how this had happened and why. It was great just to realise that I wouldn't have to shoot our countrymen as they rushed across no-man's land to the West. To be ordered to do that was always the part of the job I hated. But what was even more surprising, was those who had gone across were coming back!

Now I've had a bit more time to think about it, I am not looking forward to all the queues of people I am going to have to deal with. The job is going to get so much harder, but still I'm glad it has happened. The wall still exists but to all intents and purposes it has been destroyed. We have to keep it to mark the border, but the people should now be able to go backwards and forwards freely. We are living in exciting times!

Give my love to Eva and the children. I'll be over to see you as soon as I get some leave – but heaven knows when that will be now.

All the best,

Erich.

Examiner's comments

This is a good attempt at a friendly letter which uses convincing names, dates and references with only very minor invention of material to fix the context. This suggests that the source text has been thoroughly studied. It gets across a positive, optimistic tone, while conveying the range of feelings experienced by the guard, but without distorting the character as presented by Ann Leslie. It selects key information from the source text and recasts it in accurate English. (See marking scheme on p63.)

Student B's commentary

In my letter I tried to convey that the German guard was an ordinary soldier with similar feelings to everyone else. I tried to achieve a friendly, informal address to the brother by using features of speech, such as the monitoring feature 'well' in the opening sentence. The number (4) of exclamatory sentences such as 'it soon became impossible and we gave up trying!' helps to suggest the varied intonations of the spoken voice in the written mode. They suggest a number of emotions from astonishment to incredulity. The emphasis given to specific words by the spoken voice is conveyed through underlining ('it was <u>chaos</u>') where the emphasis helps to indicate the lack of order and the sense of helplessness the guard felt. Words and phrases such as 'the impossible' and 'couldn't believe their ears' carry connotations of incredulity and help convey the world-changing nature of the experience. I conveyed the ambivalent feelings of the guard in relation to his own life by using verbal phrases such as 'not looking forward to' and 'the job is going to get so much harder' while trying to maintain his overall positive view of events by the use of the adjectives 'glad' and 'great'. The sense of helplessness he felt at having to kill fellow Germans is conveyed through the use of the passive verb 'to be ordered to do that' and his dislike of doing that in the verb 'hated'. This reinforces the feeling that the guard is an ordinary man who can now admit his feelings. The simple sentence at the end 'We are living in exciting times' sums up his positive feelings.

Examiner's comments

This commentary, like the previous one, is about 260 words in length. It covers the three areas of whom, what and how. It addresses how language is used to address the audience and establish the character of the writer and his feelings in an appropriate imaginative context. It explores the language of the friendly, personal letter in some detail and considers the way in which spoken language features are used in the written mode. A number of examples from the text are quoted and analysed to demonstrate in detail how effects are achieved. This is a good response which does what is required in the words and time available. (See marking scheme on p65.)

Student C's response

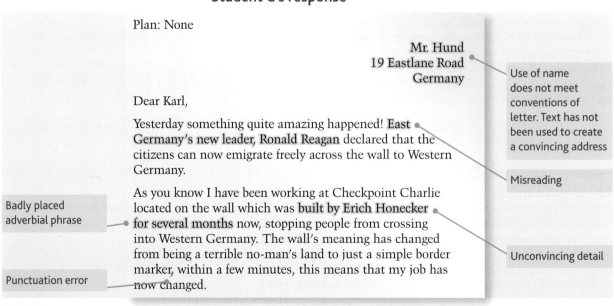

Plan: None

Mr. Hund
19 Eastlane Road
Germany

Use of name does not meet conventions of letter. Text has not been used to create a convincing address

Dear Karl,

Yesterday something quite amazing happened! <u>East Germany's new leader, Ronald Reagan</u> declared that the citizens can now emigrate freely across the wall to Western Germany.

Misreading

As you know I have been working at Checkpoint Charlie located on the wall which was <u>built by Erich Honecker for several months</u> now, stopping people from crossing into Western Germany. The wall's meaning has changed from being a terrible no-man's land to just a simple border marker, within a few minutes, this means that my job has now changed.

Badly placed adverbial phrase

Unconvincing detail

Punctuation error

I am delighted that the killing part of my job has now ended but ever since the announcement from Ronald Reagan stating to tear the wall down my job has become more complicated.

Poor expression — stating to tear the wall down

Half an hour after the announcement thousands of people crossed to my checkpoint including border police, first aid teams and fellow officers. They flooded through brandishing champagne and beer bottles, and many danced on top of the wall, the good humoured guards making no attempt to remove them. People were crying, shouting and fainting with excitement. Some of the girls flung their arms round our necks and tried to dance with us. They had really gone wild! Some showed ID cards others did not. Have you ever tried checking ID badges in a mass of people? Sorry, I forgot to tell you, only people with valid ID cards or police stamps can pass across into western Germany.

Copied from the text — They flooded through brandishing champagne and beer bottles, and many danced on top of the wall, the good humoured guards making no attempt to remove them.

Suggests lack of plan — Sorry, I forgot to tell you

This is a muddle: see below

Grammatical error — only people with valid ID cards or police stamps

Anyway, after about an hour only me and Hans (you remember Hans, he worked with me because Markus was ill, remained at checkpoint Charlie, well us and about 10 thousand people. We realised that stamps could be collected from the other side of the wall so we let people enter western Germany, explaining that they can cross but they have to get a stamp to cross back again. This means I need to work alot harder to cope with all of the ques but I believe that it's worth it, every country should be able to cross to and fro freely without getting shot by tired Border guard's

Punctuation error — me and Hans (

Muddle – see above

Spelling error — alot

Punctuation error

Spelling error — they can cross but they have to get a stamp to cross back again

Punctuation error — Border guard's

Well at least my job is more interesting now, I am off duty next friday so I will visit you then. Look forward to seeing you!

Wrong word

Needs capital letter

Punctuation error — now, I am off duty

Wrong part of verb — Look

Love Fritz

Examiner's comments

This response includes some important information, and there is a clear attempt to communicate the feelings of the border guard, but there is some evidence of misreading and muddle, and some inconsistency which suggests a lack of planning. There are also some problems with expression and a few fairly basic technical errors, although the control of language is generally sound. There is some attempt to place it in an imaginative context but this is only partly successful. It seems to fit the 13–15 descriptors of the lower band 3 category, which would be a pass, but would probably not get a mark of more than 14.

	Marks out of 25	Demonstrate expertise and creativity in using language appropriately for a variety of purposes and audiences, drawing on insights from linguistic and literary studies. AO4
Band 3	13–15	Expression generally clear and controlled. Definite if inconsistent use of register. Suitable style adopted for task/genre. Some minor technical flaws. Awareness of audience and purpose but may not be totally consistent. Some stylistic lapses occur.

Student C's commentary

Identifies aim, audience and genre

Uses framework terms correctly and an example to make a simple point

Explores use of three types of sentence

Point acceptable, but expression weak and example poor

Framework terms used but explanation vague

Acceptable point on tenor

The subject of my text is the Berlin Wall and the purpose is to explain, describe and inform on what events have happened, and the guard's thoughts and feelings about the events. The audience is the brother Karl who is recieving the letter. The genre is a letter.

Declaratives, for example, 'East Germany's new leader, Ronald Reagan ....' have been used in order to provide information to the audience so that they are aware of what the letter is about. Interrogatives 'Have you ever tried ...?' have been used to express opinions. Exclamatives – 'Look forward to seeing you!' – have been used to express the excitement of the guard.

The register of this text is quite informal, for example, 'to and fro' to relate to the audience in a describing yet talkative way. Side sequences 'you remember Hans ...' have been used in order to fit the friendly letter genre, this has been done to give the idea that the letter is not totally planned and that Fritz is writing ideas as soon as he thinks of them.

Adjectives and nouns, for example, 'interesting' and 'excitement' have been used to express the thoughts and feelings. Negative lexis 'murderous' has been used to express how Fritz's job and opinion/feelings have changed. Opinions have been used to express the writer's thoughts and feelings towards the events mentioned in the text 'my job has become more complicated.'

The text is written in a letter structure and format. The letter ends 'Look forward to seeing you! Love Fritz' to suit the informal friendly letter style to his brother who he misses and loves.

Spelling error

Factual error not penalised here

Acceptable mode point

Again vague

Unclear

To be grammatically correct, this should be 'whom'.

Examiner's comments

The expression is not always accurate and clear, but that is perhaps because it is the last response in a long and tiring paper. Framework terms are used accurately on the whole, and there is a clear structure to the commentary which deals with the three key ideas: what, who and how. There is some vagueness at times in the analysis, but there is a clear underlying understanding. This is a sound answer on the whole, and would be a clear pass probably getting a mark in the Upper Band 3 range (9–10):

	Marks out of 15	Select and apply relevant concepts and approaches from integrated linguistic study, using appropriate terminology and accurate coherent written expression. AO1
Band 3	9–10	Uses framework(s) to highlight reading. Describes significant features/patterns. Awareness of stylistic and linguistic features. Engages with text through explanation of features; possibly undeveloped in places. Clear and appropriate writing.

8   Advice on how to prepare for Section B

What is the best way to prepare for this part of the paper?

Here are some suggestions of ways to prepare for Section B:

- Know your chosen text well.
- Understand the contexts of the extracts.
- Practise different forms of recasting tasks by creating your own.

What texts could I be asked to produce?

Possible tasks in written mode

As discussed on p54, you could be asked to produce one of the following:

- entry for an encyclopaedia (for adults or children)
- editorial or article for tabloid or broadsheet newspaper
- leaflet
- report
- advertisement
- review
- letter
- magazine article
- newspaper article.

Possible tasks in oral mode

Because this paper is synoptic it is intended to test the skills that have been covered in the other three units. This means that as well as being asked to produce a written text, such as a letter or article, you could be asked to write the script for one of the following:

- broadcast (for radio, film or television)
- speech
- talk.

Remember that if you are asked to write the text for a speech or talk, your spelling and punctuation will still be taken into account.

Comparative analysis through independent study (coursework)

Introduction to Unit 4

This unit covers:

■ **AO1** Select and apply relevant concepts and approaches from integrated linguistic study using appropriate terminology and accurate coherent written expression.

■ **AO3** Use integrated approaches to explore relationships between texts, analysing and evaluating the significance of contextual factors in their production and reception.

Link

Look back to *AQA Language and Literature A AS* if you feel you need to refresh any of the skills you have already learned in ELLA1 or ELLA2.

▨ The coursework unit

What you have already learned

This is the coursework unit of your A Level and counts for 20 per cent of the overall mark. It continues the principles of integrated literary and linguistic study that is present in all four units. This means that, in previous units, you will already have developed:

■ an ability to use literary and linguistic terminology
■ an understanding of how to make comparisons
■ an awareness of what frameworks are and how to use them appropriately
■ some experience of literary texts and how they can be analysed.

What this unit will cover

Armed with these skills, you will be in a very good position to put them into action on the coursework unit. But preparation for the coursework unit needs careful planning so, to help your preparation, this unit is divided into the following areas:

■ The task
  – what you have to do
  – Assessment Objectives you must consider.
■ How to choose appropriate texts.
■ How to choose an appropriate theme.
■ How to apply frameworks to the texts.
■ How to make comparisons between texts.
■ Drafting and the final essay.

Your coursework

The inclusion of coursework within the qualification is intended to encourage the skills of personal study and to allow you to formulate a considered and focused argument on a theme of your choice. Your essay will be word-processed, though hand-written versions are permitted, and go through at least one previous drafting, so it is expected that the finished product will be of a higher standard than that possible in the limited time allowances of the exam room. This is very much the process you are likely to encounter at university level when you will be largely left to your own devices in the preparation of a finished essay. It is important that you show you can work largely on your own after an initial period in which your teacher will introduce you to the studied texts, help you to consider the ways in which you might choose a theme to write about, and ensure that you have chosen a manageable selection of poems or extracts to write about in a detailed and critical way.

9 Your coursework task

Texts

Your task is to write an essay comparing two texts thematically. The first of your texts *must* be a poetry text selected from the 12 available in List A. The second text may also be chosen from the poetry texts (List A) *or* you may select a second text from List B. This second choice allows you to study a novel, a set of short stories or a play alongside your poetry text. Your tutor must approve your choice of texts and question before you begin writing. The two lists are:

List A (poetry)

Ariel, Sylvia Plath

The Whitsun Weddings, Philip Larkin

The Wife of Bath's Tale, Geoffrey Chaucer

Selected Poetry, D. H. Lawrence

Taking Off Emily Dickinson's Clothes, Billy Collins

Selected Poems, Robert Frost

Songs of Innocence and Experience, William Blake

Selected Poems 1965–87, Seamus Heaney

Selected Poems, William Wordsworth

Mean Time, Carol Ann Duffy

Selected Poems, Emily Dickinson

Selected Poems, Elizabeth Jennings

List B (other genres)

A Handmaid's Tale, Margaret Atwood

Hamlet, William Shakespeare

As You Like It, William Shakespeare

Modern British Short Stories, ed. Malcolm Bradbury

Small Island, Andrea Levy

The Accidental Tourist, Anne Tyler

Waterland, Graham Swift

A Prayer for Owen Meany, John Irving

Dubliners, James Joyce

Hotel World, Ali Smith

Death of a Salesman, Arthur Miller

Translations, Brian Friel

Length

You need to write between *2,000* and *2,500 words* in your coursework essay. Once you get going you will find that this is not a great deal of writing and will run to only about *8 to 10 pages* of word-processed work. It is very important, therefore, to be clear that this is not a 'project' in which large quantities of background information are assembled. You are required to apply your skills for close analysis to short sections of text, which you have selected from your two chosen books, and to compare those sections of texts in terms of the theme that you have picked out for the essay.

Assessment Objectives

There are two equally weighted specific Assessment Objectives to concentrate on: AO1 and AO3. The specific requirements are:

Assessment Objective 1 (AO1)

Select and apply relevant concepts and approaches from integrated linguistic and literary study, using appropriate terminology and accurate, coherent written expression.

Look carefully at the highlighted phrases:

- concepts and approaches
- integrated linguistic and literary study
- appropriate terminology
- accurate, coherent written expression.

You have already been asked to concentrate on these features in both AS units but it is in Unit 1 and Unit 4 where this objective is given the highest loading of marks. There are different ways to analyse a text. Some candidates are very good at identifying **metaphor** and so write about the **imagery** in the text – the pictures that the words create and the associations attached to the meanings of those words. Others might be more at home with a grammatical analysis where the sentence structures (**syntax**) reveal a lot about the text being studied. Is there a pattern of short sentences? Are there multiple clauses? What do they contribute to the writer's meanings?

Both approaches use a particular **framework** for investigation. The best students know that they must select different frameworks for different tasks and it is the way in which they use their background in integrated linguistic and literary study to apply these concepts and approaches that enables them to write well. Identifying the individual features of a text and applying labels (metaphor, verb, alliteration, etc.) to these features is the skill of selecting appropriate terminology.

But accurate labelling itself is only the first step; your task is to identify what effect the selection of a particular literary or linguistic device has upon the overall text. This is not always easy and frequently the devices combine to create an overall effect without each device necessarily having that same immediate effect. We may become aware gradually, for instance, that the text is intended to be ironically humorous as the images become more and more exaggerated.

Finally, accurate, coherent written expression will always be important in your writing. Since you can spell-check your coursework on the computer before submission, spelling and grammar mistakes ought not to be a worry for you but the way in which you develop and structure an argument, and your ability to express yourself clearly and use regular examples of what you mean, will be judged as part of this Assessment Objective.

Assessment Objective 3 (AO3)

Use integrated approaches to explore relationships between texts, analysing and evaluating the significance of contextual factors in their production and reception. The key elements here are:

- integrated approaches
- exploring relationships between texts
- contextual factors.

Key terms

Metaphor: a direct comparison drawn between two different things as if the subject really is the thing it is being compared to; for example, 'her hands were ice-blocks' or 'he was a bear of a man'.

Imagery: in literary terms, imagery refers to the pictures created by a writer's choice of language, for example, their use of metaphor or personification.

Syntax: the study of the way words are combined to form sentences.

Framework: in the study of language and literature, this refers to structures around which you build your analysis. Individual frameworks may be: metaphor, lexis, grammar, etc.

Exploring relationships between texts

The central feature of this Assessment Objective is the skill of comparison. This skill will be considered in detail later on, but the process needs to be explained briefly here. Ideally, your essay will integrate the two texts in a comparative manner as fully as possible.

You might:

■ apply frameworks in turn to each of the two texts, paragraph by paragraph

■ develop one idea on one text at greater length before considering the other text

■ deal with one text completely and then move on to the other to make your comparative points. But, be warned that this approach needs careful attention to maintain the comparative emphasis, or comparison will be implicit rather than stated and your analysis will not be as successful.

Of course, a comparison that is too tightly and mechanically developed might limit the effectiveness of your answer. An example of this might be, 'Neither poet uses similes'. 'Both poets write about what they know'.

Contextual factors

Another aspect of AO3 is context. Of course it is important to know about the world in which the text was written and then consider the world in which it is being read and how different the two may be ('factors in their production and reception'). However, in a short essay of 2,000–2,500 words, there is very little space to explore these aspects fully and so only the most immediate contextual details ought to be considered. Important contextual details to note are where a passage is taken from in relation to the events and character development in a text or how the lexis in a poem may have shifted in its meaning since it was written. Such contextual information as the world in which the writer lived or prevailing attitudes of the time might well inform what you write about the texts but should never become the main focus of your essay.

There are a number of ways of looking at context. A short list might help to clarify exactly what context is.

■ *The relation of the extract to the wider text*. Particularly with longer texts like novels and plays, what you have to say about the extract you are looking at will inevitably be conditioned by the events that take place before and after the extract, and the ways in which characters behave in relation to those events in the chosen extract. Clearly, this placing of events is less important in poetry where a poem's context is generally complete in itself.

■ *The historical and cultural background against which the extract is taking place*. In modern critical writing this aspect often replaces the text rather than informs it because scholars are so eager to find new areas of research. The context of **pantheism** for Wordsworth, or contemporary attitudes to the supernatural in *Hamlet*, for instance, often explain why writers take a particular stance in their work. Since such background is often very interesting in itself, you must be disciplined in deciding how much of it can usefully be included in your essay so that it does not overwhelm your analysis.

■ *Audience and personal response* are contextual factors since you will have grown up in a world that is quite different from Shakespeare's or Wordsworth's. This may well colour your attitude to character and event and that background will inform the opinions you express.

Key terms

Pantheism: the belief that God is everything and everything is God. Descriptions of nature by some poets will reflect this philosophy.

AQA Examiner's tip

Be sure to concentrate on the 'How?' part of the question. This means writing about literary and linguistic devices and their effects rather than paraphrasing the meaning, or writing too much about context.

- *The writer's purpose.* It has been common in recent times to consider a text to be measurable only by the reader's response. Such an argument might run as follows: 'whatever the writer may have intended is irrelevant. All that matters is what readers can deduce from the text in front of them'. However, the attitudes of Arthur Miller towards consumerism in *Death of a Salesman*, for instance, or Chaucer's satirical purpose in *The Wife of Bath's Tale* clearly affect the writing. Are those writers' purposes superfluous to our analysis or do we take them into account as part of the historical and cultural context?

- *Structure is a context by which texts can be assessed.* In poetry, the shaping of the text, such as stanza division and setting out on the page are relevant as is the structuring of a novel or a play.

- *Genre* is another contextual factor. The demands and tactics of a novel, play or poem are different in kind from one another and those differences are important as part of a wider comparison.

- *Style and form* influence the impact of the text's message. Like structure, style and form create a contextual overview by which the ideas in the text can be judged.

This chapter covers:

- how to choose suitable texts for study

- whether you should study two poetry texts **or** one poetry text with a text of another genre

- different ways of approaching these choices.

AQA Examiner's tip

Context is only a small part of your area of study. The context of a writer's life or the times in which the writer lived should not be central to your essay but merely a contextualisation of your close comparative analysis. For instance, a writer's religious or political views or, indeed, the religious and political views of the time the writer was writing can be very interesting. Doubtless, they may influence the writer's thinking but you should avoid beginning with those details. Make your priority the close analysis of the literary and linguistic devices used by the writer to express that point of view rather than the origin of the views themselves.

If you choose a poetry text, you should not aim to write about any more than three or four poems from that text. If you choose a different genre to complement your poetry text, you should select a similar number of short passages to make your analysis. Covering a fuller range of poems or passages is likely to dilute the effectiveness of your technical analysis and so it would be very unwise to do so.

The first question you should consider is this: Should I choose two poetry texts **or** one poetry text and one text from another genre?

Two poetry texts

The advantage of choosing two poetry texts is that, in comparing like with like, your task of selecting suitable frameworks is likely to be more straightforward. The approach you use to write about poetry will be different from your approach to prose or drama. Close analysis of language is generally much more in evidence when a candidate writes about a poem than when writing about prose. Since one of the main demands of this coursework essay is to **analyse**, choosing two poetry texts may well be to your advantage.

One poetry and one other text

On the other hand, writing about two different genres gives you the opportunity to point out the different approaches that are appropriate for each. Writing about **context** is one part of AO3 and it is often helpful to mention stage directions in a play, or the crucial events that surround a particular passage you may have chosen in a prose text. This kind of context is not so relevant to poetry.

11 How to choose an appropriate theme

Your title

Your essay must be concerned with the question of *how/in what ways* writers create their effects in order to focus on a particular theme. Then, you must make a comparison of the methods of your two chosen writers. For that reason, your choice of a title must reflect this formula:

Compare the ways in which X and Y write about loneliness/death/the countryside, etc.

Your comparative essay should not have a title like 'Is X better than Y?' or 'How typical are X and Y of the periods in which they were writing?'

Just to be clear about how this formula is applied, here are some appropriate question titles that will enable you to demonstrate the close comparative analysis required:

Comparing poetry texts from List A

- *Selected Poems*, Robert Frost and *Selected Poems*, William Wordsworth

Compare the ways in which Frost and Wordsworth write about friendship.

- *Taking Off Emily Dickinson's Clothes*, Billy Collins and *Mean Time*, Carol Ann Duffy

Compare the ways in which Collins and Duffy use irony.

- *Selected Poetry*, D. H. Lawrence and *Selected Poems*, Emily Dickinson

Compare the ways in which Lawrence and Dickinson write about the natural world.

- *The Wife of Bath's Tale*, Geoffrey Chaucer and *The Whitsun Weddings*, Philip Larkin

Compare the ways in which Chaucer and Larkin write about marriage.

- *Songs of Innocence and Experience*, William Blake and *Selected Poems*, Elizabeth Jennings

Compare the ways in which Blake and Jennings view human justice.

- *Ariel*, Sylvia Plath and *Selected Poems 1965–87*, Seamus Heaney

Compare the ways in which Plath and Heaney explore childhood memories.

Comparing a poetry text (List A) with a text of a different genre (List B)

- *The Whitsun Weddings*, Philip Larkin and *Dubliners*, James Joyce

Compare the ways in which Larkin and Joyce portray family relationships.

- *Mean Time*, Carol Ann Duffy and *Hotel World*, Ali Smith

Compare the ways in which Duffy and Smith use different narrative points of view.

■ *Taking Off Emily Dickinson's Clothes*, Billy Collins and *The Accidental Tourist*, Anne Tyler

Compare the ways in which Collins and Tyler present ideas about travel.

■ *Selected Poems*, Elizabeth Jennings and *As You Like It*, William Shakespeare

Compare the ways in which Jennings and Shakespeare explore ideas about illusion and reality.

■ *Songs of Innocence and Experience*, William Blake and *A Handmaid's Tale*, Margaret Atwood

Compare the ways in which Blake and Atwood present the idea of social evil.

■ *Selected Poems*, Emily Dickinson and *A Prayer for Owen Meany*, John Irving

Compare the ways in which Dickinson and Irving explore religion.

■ *Selected Poems*, William Wordsworth and *Waterland*, Graham Swift

Compare the ways in which Wordsworth and Swift portray landscape.

■ *Selected Poems 1965–87*, Seamus Heaney and *Translations*, Brian Friel

Compare the ways in which Heaney and Friel explore the past.

■ *Selected Poetry*, D. H. Lawrence and *Death of a Salesman*, Arthur Miller

Compare the ways in which Lawrence and Miller present individual liberty.

■ *Ariel*, Sylvia Plath and *Hamlet*, William Shakespeare

Compare the ways in which Plath and Shakespeare present mental suffering.

■ *The Wife of Bath's Tale*, Geoffrey Chaucer and *Small Island*, Andrea Levy

Compare the ways in which Chaucer and Levy explore marital relationships.

■ *Selected Poems*, Robert Frost and *Modern British Short Stories*, ed. Malcolm Bradbury

Compare the ways in which Frost and the short story writers create a sense of place.

■ Different approaches to choosing a theme

There are a number of possible approaches that you might take in your selection of a theme.

Here are two markedly different approaches you might use.

Reading with a theme in mind

At one extreme, you might try to find two texts that would appear to share themes. For instance, suppose you were to choose the following title from the list above:

■ *The Whitsun Weddings*, Philip Larkin and *Dubliners*, James Joyce

Compare the ways in which Larkin and Joyce portray family relationships.

If you look at Larkin's poems, you will quickly find that *Self's the Man* is an obvious starting point for the struggles of family relationships from a father's point of view. *Take One Home for the Kiddies* is about another gloomy learning experience for family members. *The Whitsun Weddings* gives us the perspective of married life from a variety of people at different stages of the process and *An Arundel Tomb* suggests a view of marriage from an historical perspective. Both *Love Songs in Age* and *Reference Back* are about the poets' relationship with his mother. Even *Mr Bleaney* tells us something about a life without family connections and several other poems touch on the perspectives of family life. Most importantly, Larkin's views and emotions as writer are largely detached and different from those family members he is writing about. Three or four of these poems will give ample material to write a close analysis focusing on this theme.

Dubliners is a series of short stories and so choosing appropriate passages for comparison is relatively easy. 'The Sisters' and 'Araby' both give a clear view of a child's experience of oppressive older relations. The final section of 'A Little Cloud' is a sharp portrait of Chandler's frustration with his child and shame at his wife's scolding and would link with Larkin's 'Self's the Man' very effectively. The final story, 'The Dead' says a great deal about the pressures that exist in a marriage. A close analysis of just two or three passages from the whole text would be quite enough to match and compare with the three or four poems you have chosen from *The Whitsun Weddings*.

Below, you will find a long list of themes that have been successfully used in past years. You are certainly not restricted to choosing from this list but it may give you some helpful ideas for developing your own selection of a theme:

- Advertising
- Appeals to the senses
- Appearance and reality
- Attitudes about sex
- Attitudes and values of characters
- Attitudes of narrators
- Attitudes to the law
- Beauty
- British ways of life
- Character contrast
- Conflict
- Contentment
- Conversation
- Countryside
- Cultural difference
- Death
- Descriptive details
- Details of everyday life
- Disappointment
- Disasters
- Dishonesty
- Dramatic techniques
- Dreams
- Endings
- Enthusiasm for life
- Everyday experiences from an unusual point of view
- Everyday language
- Experience of suffering
- Failure
- Fame and success
- Family relationships
- Fantasy
- Fear and anxiety
- Flashback techniques
- Humour
- Hypocrisy
- Illustrative detail
- Imagination
- Imprisonment
- Innocence
- Jobs
- Journeys
- Language
- Loneliness and isolation

- Love and passion
- Love of money
- Marriage
- Memories
- Mental suffering
- Moral issues through narrative
- Narrative structure
- Narrative voice
- Nature and natural world
- Nature of good and evil
- Old age
- Openings
- Opposing points of view
- Ordinary people and their values
- Passage of time
- Past
- Power of nature
- Process of writing
- Relationships
- Religion
- Sea
- Selling
- Sense of menace
- Sense of place and setting
- Sense of tension
- Specific locations
- Storytelling skills
- Strong emotions
- Superstition
- Suspense
- Tension in relationships
- Unreal worlds
- Use of dialogue
- Use of imagery
- Use of irony
- Violence
- Wealth and status
- Women
- Youth

Remember that even if you feel that the two texts you have chosen appear to have very little in common, you can always make a technical comparison your theme. It is perfectly acceptable to concentrate on a particular framework (metaphor, lexis, grammar, phonology, etc.) for the purposes of your comparison and to make that your theme, using the following formula:

Compare the ways in which X and Y use metaphor in order to present their ideas.

Preparing your texts without a theme in mind

The problem with the theme-based approach is that, in reading texts with only one theme in mind, you may well stifle the pleasure of reading the texts for their own sake. In the A2 phase of the qualification, you have the opportunity to explore the skills you have mastered in the AS phase. This means that you will be much more confident about how to read a text technically. It might be limiting, therefore, to take the short cut of a pre-selected theme applied to two pre-selected texts.

This second approach to selecting your theme is radically different. It is more ambitious but might prove to be a more enjoyable process. The alternative approach is this: Choose two texts regardless of any similarities they may have. Get to know the texts gradually and discuss them in class without worrying too much about themes. How do their styles compare? Are there any poems or passages you particularly like? It is only once you are well acquainted with both texts that you start to consider themes. At this other extreme of selecting a theme, you can begin, if you wish, by reading as many texts as you can manage to try to find something you really enjoy and want to write about. This is a slower but more satisfying process and will certainly prepare you well for later university work. Of course, the selection of a theme will be at the back of your mind but will emerge organically from your own thinking.

The themeless process

In order to illustrate how this process might work, let's go through the stages it might contain. We will begin with a very well-known and popular text from List B, *Death of a Salesman*. At this stage, there is no need to consider a second text for comparison. That second text will, in any case, have to come from the poetry texts (List A). Poets rarely write consistently about a single theme in their work so we have to keep a very open mind about the way in which we might make comparisons with *Death of a Salesman* later on. List B texts are rather easier to write about as far as themes are concerned; for instance, *Translations* is very much about 'language and power' while *Waterland* could be said to be about 'curiosity and history'. Poetry texts rarely provide such straightforward, overall 'handles' for analysis.

Stage 1: Ideas (Death of a Salesman)

1 Metaphor

As you begin reading *Death of a Salesman*, one of the first things you notice is the extent of symbolic representation in the opening stage directions. The sound of the flute is 'telling of grass and trees and the horizon' in a play in which the set is 'towering, angular' surrounding the house 'on all sides' in 'an angry glow of orange'. So, the dreams of a country life (suggested by Ben, Biff's work in Texas, and Willy's father later on) are in direct conflict with the oppressive, cluttered city life, which the Lomans lead. The lesser symbols (the 'silver athletic trophy' and the raising of the boys' bedroom) both testify to the importance of Willy's investment in his sons' early life. Miller's initial plan was for the play to be called *The Inside of His Head*. Luckily, he changed his mind and selected a better title but the first choice gives us an insight into Miller's attempt to convey the machinations of Willy's mind against the events of the play. Clearly, then, there are two levels to the play, the realistic and the metaphorical. Immediately, this metaphorical level strikes us as something akin to the style of poetry and might be a theme to consider later on. 'Metaphor' is a wide field: it encompasses themes like appearance and reality, symbolism, unreal worlds, surrealism, etc. Consequently, it might be very appropriate to match it with a poetry text.

2 Human relationships

The next big area of interest in the play is probably the human relationships within it. These are varied: Willy's relationship with his wife, Linda; the relationship of the two brothers, Happy and Biff; the boys' relationship with their father; Willy's relationship with his older brother, Ben, or with his own father; the contrasting relationship of Charley and his son, Bernard. There is always something to be said about family relationships and this is a very fruitful area in which to make comparisons within the play as well as with relationships in the poetry text you will go on to study.

3 Abstract nouns

The third and greatest thematic area is endless and rich. That is the range of abstract nouns that describe the world of human emotion. Consider this list: love, death, happiness, misery, guilt, envy, despair, youth, old age. This is the stuff of literature and you will never be short of a theme if you think along these lines.

Stage 2: Reading a poetry text (Selected Poems of Robert Frost)

By now, you will know *Death of a Salesman* well and be able to recall specific passages with little difficulty. Until you've selected some poems for comparison you will not know which passages you are going to use or which theme you will choose to write about. At this stage, it is time to look for suitable poems.

One poet who is often anthologised in GCSE courses and whom, therefore, you may have come across is Robert Frost. Although the *Selected Poems* on this syllabus covers poems from his entire works, you will notice that the 'famous' poems like *Mending Wall*. *After Apple-Picking*, *The Road Not Taken*, and *Out, Out*, all come from quite early collections that cover only a short period (1914–1916). The other interesting thing about Frost's poetry is that, broadly speaking, his poems use two quite different styles. The first is the formal lyrical style of the poems already mentioned but the second is found in the anecdotal, conversational poems that tend to be much longer and are less well known. The conversational style is, however, very much in keeping with Miller's dramatic style in *Death of Salesman*. Making a comparison between Miller and Frost is helped by this comparison of style, and contrasts may be enhanced by considering the more lyrical style of one or two of Frost's other poems. Another point of comparison is that they are both American writers who share a concern for how people exist in their own particular environments, whether it is the city or the countryside.

Remember that your coursework essay will be most successful if you limit your selection of poems to three or four and then match them with two or three passages from *Death of a Salesman*. If you begin by looking at Frost's most famous collection, *North of Boston* (1914), you will be struck by how the themes of the first two poems leap out in their similarity to Miller's concerns. *Mending Wall* is about the relationship between the poet (or the persona of the poem) and his neighbour. Even though neither keeps cows, the neighbour is insistent that *Good fences make good neighbors*, a wisdom he has unquestioningly inherited from his father. The poet seeks to challenge that wisdom. This challenging of established values is one of the themes of *Death of A Salesman* in which Willy's insistence on the values of a salesman are challenged by his son, Biff, and, more kindly, by his neighbour Charley. The longer second poem, *The Death of the Hired Man* tells the tale of an old and unreliable temporary worker whom the poet and his wife are obliged to care for. The poem also reveals that this hired man has had disputes with a younger and better-educated fellow worker over how things should be done. The parallels here with Charley's relationship with Willy in *Death of a Salesman* again are very obvious and would make an interesting point of comparison.

■ Link

To read *Mending Wall* and *The Death of the Hired Man*, turn to pp127–9.

As you read through the rest of the poems in *North of Boston*, you will notice a number of long poems. Since we already have a long poem in *The Death of the Hired Man*, we must be careful not to attempt too much in our 2,000–2,500 word essay. Since the first two poems provide plenty of comparative ammunition, a quick summary of themes in the other poems in this selection might help us to select one or two more at the most. The *Mountain* is an exchange between two men about the local mountain which seems to represent human ambition. Oddly, the local man who has worked the slopes all his life has never been to the top of the mountain and seen the spring there. *A Hundred Collars* brings two men with different social backgrounds together. The poem undermines the notion that those with different backgrounds have nothing in common. *Home Burial* shows the tensions between a husband and wife whose child has died. *A Servant to Servants* is a wonderful monologue by a lonely woman who talks to visitors about her life. *After Apple-Picking* is a famous poem about work and human ambition. Its rhythms are repetitive and sleepy. This poem provides plenty of opportunities for close analysis if we can link it to an appropriate theme. *The Fear* tells of that apprehension that underlies the human psyche, in this case the belief of a woman when returning home with her husband that someone is watching them through the dark. Finally, *The Wood-Pile* shows characteristically Frost-like concerns. The poet (or persona) wonders at a neglected wood-pile and how it came to be that way.

Stage 3: Choosing the theme

Like Miller, Frost seems to be concerned with the big issues of how people survive in their different environments. Some of the key themes that link these poems might be: conflict in human relationships, ambition, fear, and social concern for others. Any of these would provide you with a good basis for an essay and the list is a long way from complete. How human beings interact is the real concern of all our lives and it is not surprising that it is the basis of all art. Choosing one of these big issues as a theme for your coursework is not a disadvantage as long as you remember that it is the *how* and not the *what* that matters most in your essay. A good essay will focus on the literary and linguistic techniques that a writer uses (the 'how') in order to convey ideas about a subject or theme (the 'what'). You should not, therefore, use the essay to demonstrate how wide your reading has been. Rather, it is your skill in condensing and focusing that wide reading into a relatively short analytical essay that matters. So, let us suppose that we choose the following title:

Compare the ways in which Miller and Frost explore conflict in human relationships.

Stage 4: Drafting the coursework essay

The requirement for drafting is intended to help you formulate your ideas so that your teacher can assist you in the process towards the final version. The approach to drafting will vary enormously. At a basic level, it will ensure you are on course for completing the task to the satisfaction of the teachers and examiners who want to see you perform at your best. It is certainly not intended to force you to prepare multiple drafts with minor adjustments at each stage. You will probably benefit, however, from preparing a short preliminary draft before you start writing. This should contain:

1   Your title.

2   A list of the passages or poems on which you intend to concentrate.

3   A brief outline of your plan which might include a few of the literary and linguistic devices in the passages/poems you intend to compare.

4   The preliminary draft for the projected Miller and Frost titles above would look like this:

   –   Title: **Compare the ways in which Miller and Frost explore conflict in human relationships.**

   –   Passages/poems chosen:

   Miller (the page references are from the Penguin Modern Classics Plays edition)

   a   Initial stage directions pp7–8

   b   Willy and Charley playing cards pp32–6

   c   At Charley's office pp68–71

   d   Requiem pp110–12

   Frost (the page references are from the Penguin edition)

   a   *Mending Wall* p43

   b   *The Death of the Hired Man* p44

   c   *Home Burial* p59

   d   *After Apple-Picking* p68.

■ Link

A complete version of this essay can be found later in the text in the chapter 'Writing your coursework essay' on pp131–5.

5 Plan.

Probably (b) and (c) in the Miller list will be enough for analysis of the characteristics of spoken dialogue. Some of the ideas from ELLA2 about dialogue form studied last year will help here. Sections (a) and (d) are for contextualisation of character although the metaphorical ideas in (a) are too good to overlook! They have to link to the theme chosen, though.

With Frost, the dialogue style in (b) and (c) are obvious areas for comparison. It would be useful, too, to look at the way Frost changes his style to accommodate dialogue in a more lyrical setting in (a). (d) is very tempting for its phonological repetitions but, as with Miller (a), it must be related to the theme. Man's conflict with his own ambition in work is a fair link in (d) to the overall idea of the essay, though.

Writing about poetry texts

■ Applying frameworks

You will know what frameworks are already because the work you did in the AS units will have required a knowledge of frameworks and how they are applied. Perhaps it is easiest to think of frameworks as tools for analysis. If you look at the seven frameworks proposed below for studying literature, you will see that they are grouped by areas of study: grammar, metaphor, lexis and so forth. Each of these areas of study is called a framework. You can write about them one by one or you can integrate them if you prefer. There are two good rules to remember when applying frameworks:

1 Write a lot about a little and not a little about a lot.
2 Be flexible.

The first of these rules draws your attention to the importance of close analysis. In the coursework unit you must avoid the temptation to range widely across the poems and passages you choose and concentrate instead on making the most of a small number of extracts by analysing them very closely.

The second rule is intended to remind you that not all frameworks will be equally valuable in analysing every poem or passage. While audience and purpose are important elements for analysing a production piece or some spontaneous speech, they are not as helpful in analysing a poem.

Because at least one of your texts must be a poetry text, we need to consider how to apply these two rules to the particular qualities of a poem.

Here is a grid that presents seven frameworks that are suitable for analysing poetry. Apart from the first, 'Beginnings', they can be considered in any order. They are not all-encompassing and there may be other aspects of the poem that you might look at but, for the purposes of the coursework that you are preparing for ELLA4, you would be wise to employ this grid.

1 Beginnings	a	Subject/plot
	b	Theme
	c	Point of view/persona
	d	Context
	e	Audience
2 Manner	a	Tone
	b	Mood
	c	Register
3 Lexis	a	Semantic field
	b	Connotations
	c	Word classes
4 Metaphor	a	Imagery
	b	Metaphor/simile
	c	Symbolism
	d	Personification/apostrophe
	e	Oxymoron

5 Rhetoric		
Phonological patterning:	a	Alliteration/assonance
	b	Onomatopoeia
	c	Rhyme
	d	Caesura/enjambement
Structural patterning:	a	Repetition/listing
	b	Parallelism/antithesis
	c	Formal rhetoric
6 Grammar	a	Levels of formality
	b	Syntax/sentence structure
	c	Tense/verb mood
	d	Punctuation
7 Form	a	Poetic form/structure
	b	Metre/rhythm
	c	Layout/graphology

■ Link

An explanation of the different literary and linguistic devices and how they are used was provided in your study of the AS units. In case you need a reminder, there is a glossary at the back of this book on pp160–3.

Remember to be flexible. If you work through the frameworks mechanically like a check-list, you may end up driving all the life out of the poem. You are not taking part in a vivisection in which the constituent parts of a poem are left in a big mess of sinew and unrecognisable offal on the dissecting table. On the contrary, you want to draw attention to the living qualities of the poem so that others reading your essay might be persuaded to read it and enjoy it. This requires careful close analysis but it does not mean you have to mention everything listed in the framework. A thorough job using elements from two or three frameworks is more than enough to write well. What matters is how well you select from the frameworks in order to draw out the particular qualities of the poem.

The object of this section of the guide to coursework is not to reintroduce each of the literary and linguistic terms from the framework one by one but to try and integrate them all in every approach to each section of text. In this way, you will begin to understand how selectivity works and how you have to be prepared to leave out much of what you already know as you develop a more disciplined and flexible approach to analysing texts.

With every poem you look at, the first question is 'What is it about?' Once that is established, you can start to consider other questions:

■ What kind of feelings does the poem create?
■ What kinds of patterns in the poem create those feelings?
■ Whose point of view is being expressed?

By this stage, you will be looking for *how* the poet has made you feel the way you do.

■ What do the words mean and why choose those words in particular?
■ What kinds of sound patterns are there?
■ What pictures/images are created?

The first question is essential; the other questions attempt to explain the methods used by the poet to create meaning but if we do not begin by explaining what the poem is about, there is no meaning.

Of course, the meaning may not be straightforward. Sometimes a mood is created without any clear sense of the poem having a story or a plot. It is perfectly acceptable to recognise this aspect of poetry. Avoid a narrow reading in which the poem can only be about one thing. It is a healthy critical approach to acknowledge that the language of the poem may lend itself to alternative readings. That does not mean that anything goes. Your explanation of meaning will be supported with evidence from the poem and will not be a wild assertion based on something you might have read about the poet's life (such as 'she committed suicide', 'he took drugs', etc.).

💡 Close reading – writing about poetry

In this section we are going to look closely at three short poems of increasing difficulty. By setting you ten questions on each poem, it is hoped that you will begin to deal with *how* questions as a preface to considering the more important *why* questions. To help you apply different approaches depending on the circumstances of the poem concerned, the questions will not be the same for each poem. The answers will follow and will go beyond the straightforward brief answer to exploring how the literary and linguistic devices used in the poems contribute to meaning. It is in writing about these effects that the real business of critical analysis will really start.

ℹ️ Poem 1: *The Rainbow* by William Wordsworth

Let's begin by looking closely at this very famous short poem by William Wordsworth. It's usually called *The Rainbow* although it was actually never given a title by Wordsworth himself.

> My heart leaps up when I behold
> A rainbow in the sky:
> So was it when my life began;
> So is it now I am a Man;
> So be it when I shall grow old,
> Or let me die!
> The Child is father of the Man;
> And I could wish my days to be
> Bound each to each by natural piety.

Critical response activity

Answer the following questions about the text. A commentary is provided to help you to measure your responses against the type of responses that will gain you high marks.

1 What is the poem about? (maximum of three words)

2 Give one example of a metaphor in the poem.

3 Can the poem be split into different parts? If so, where would you put the dividing line?

4 How many syllables do most of the words have?

5 List all the verbs that are used.

6 Which is the shortest line?

7 Which is the longest line?

8 How many different types of punctuation are used?

9 Are there any repetitions in the poem?

10 What does 'piety' mean?

AQA Examiner's tip

Notice that none of these questions ask you why yet. As you become more skilful in your analysis, you will go beyond the mere identification of parts of the poem and start to consider what effects these parts have in enabling you to understand the poem. It is the combination of these effects that is important to your analysis. Begin with *what*, then ask *why*?

AQA Examiner's tip

One very useful additional question to ask is *so what*? This final question is the one you ask yourself for every point you have made. If you note, for instance, that the poem rhymes, and then go on to explain the structure of that rhyming pattern, you then must ask yourself *so what*? In other words, *does it make any contribution to the meaning of the poem*? If the answer is no, you have to be brave enough to leave out that information in favour of something more relevant.

■ Key terms

Argument: a connected series of ideas, backed up by relevant facts, that tries to make a case, and convince us of its truth and validity.

Coda: a musical term which describes a completion or rounding off.

Commentary

For each of the answers below, the answer to the question, *so what*? is implied at the end. You can see very quickly that the answer to the question has very little importance if there is no attempt to answer the, *so what*? question.

1 What is the poem about? (maximum of three words)

The poem is about 'a rainbow' or 'love of nature'. The first answer, 'a rainbow', is the **subject** of the poem and it is useful to focus on this but 'love of nature' is really the **theme** of the poem. When making the distinction between the subject and the theme, you are distinguishing between two ways of looking at the poem. The subject of a poem is very often a **metaphorical** expression of an abstract idea. By creating pictures that represent feelings in order to communicate the idea of the poem, Wordsworth is following a long tradition. His theme is an abstraction – the love of nature – and he expresses it by choosing a symbol or metaphor that creates a picture to represent that feeling (the rainbow).

2 Give one example of a metaphor in the poem.

We have already seen that the 'rainbow' is a metaphor for an abstract idea but in this poem it is actually there in the sky so it is literal rather than figurative. But it also represents much more than itself in the poem; it becomes a metaphor, too. Another example of a metaphor in the first line is a more traditional metaphor: 'My heart leaps up'. Clearly the heart stays in one place in the human body but by giving it this leaping quality, Wordsworth is communicating that sudden jolt of excitement he feels when he sees a rainbow. Because the heart itself is not an independent human entity, he is using **personification** here. By giving the heart independent life, he creates the sense of it being a living independent personality. This is a **figurative** device that is also metaphorical because it gives the heart representational qualities beyond its literal ability.

3 Can the poem be split into different parts? If so, where is the dividing line?

There is only one **stanza** to the poem but the division of the **argument** is debateable. One interpretation is that the poem could be divided after the first six lines so that the final three lines are a comment or **coda** to the description of feeling in the first six lines. This would divide the argument into two parts. The gap between the two is emphasised by the very short line (the only one in the poem), 'Or let me die!' (line 6). This pause is heightened by the use of an exclamation mark which creates a hiatus. Additionally, despite the use of other punctuation marks (colon and semi-colons), the poem is in two sentences, one six lines long and the other three lines long, and each of the suggested parts is one sentence. If you have a different interpretation of how the poem can be split, make sure that you can justify your opinion. For example, you might look at how many independent clauses there are in the poem, or the purpose of various lines. It might, for instance, be justified to say that there are three parts to the poem (the first two lines, then the next four, then the final three). In this version, the opening couplet states the fact on which the poem is based, the second section corroborates the feeling expressed in the opening couplet through reference to other occasions, and the third section acts as the philosophical coda.

4 How many syllables do most of the words have?

Amazingly, 56 of the 61 words in the poem are **monosyllabic**. What does that tell us? It suggests simplicity but the variety of verbal constructions ('was it', 'is it', 'be it', 'could wish') in the poem and the use of **lexis** like 'piety' modifies that simplicity. Wordsworth is communicating a sense of humility and awe in the face of the wonders of nature and the monosyllables express the grandeur and weight of that feeling. This is an observation about **phonology** in that there is a pattern of **long-vowelled** syllables in the opening of the poem ('h<u>ea</u>rt', 'l<u>ea</u>ps', 'I', 'beh<u>o</u>ld', 'r<u>ai</u>nbow', 'sky') and perhaps contrast with the rush of 'was it', 'is it', and 'be it' as the enthusiasm grows. Also, the poet has felt these emotions since he was a child, so he wants to recreate that innocent intensity in his adult response to the rainbow. The language is not childish but it represents the idea that 'The child is father of the Man', and so has something to teach mankind about loving nature.

Key terms

Phonology: a study of the qualities and effects of different sounds and patterns of sounds in language.

5 List all the verbs that are used

The verbs used are:

leaps up, behold, was, is, be, grow, let, die, is, could wish, and *be bound*.

The pattern of the verbs is important here because they combine to create a sense of the poet in thrall to the power of nature. The only **dynamic verb** is 'leaps up' and that is the action of his untameable heart although 'grow' also suggests a certain slow dynamism. The other verbs suggest a state of existence rather than action. The verbs 'was', 'is' and 'be' are **stative** forms of the verb 'to be'. This pattern of appearing to be at the mercy of a greater power is heightened by the **imperative** 'let (me) die' which grants nature further power over him, and the passive 'be bound' with its sense of being enslaved to a higher master has an additional meaning of solidarity in the idea of the days being bound together. Even his own expression of desire, 'wish', is modified almost apologetically with the **modal** 'could'.

6 Which is the shortest line?

'Or let me die!' is the shortest line. It indicates a dramatic conclusion to the rush of feeling of the previous lines. This hiatus or **caesura** created by a two-beat line (iambic dimeter) is made more striking by the four-beat lines (iambic tetrameter) that surround it.

7 Which is the longest line?

The longest line is the final line, 'Bound each to each by natural piety'. It is the only **iambic pentameter** in the poem and is elongated further if you consider 'natural' a three syllable word. However, most of us would pronounce it with two syllables. Structure is often something that appears clear-cut to students of poetry. As with biography where the dates of a poet's life are fixed, so the structure of a poem appears to offer some certainty in a confusing storm of options. It is quite difficult, however, to extract some real significance from the structure of a poem. Philip Larkin famously argued that when writing a poem, 'The first few lines come of a piece and the rest must follow'. In other words, the structure is often quite accidental and does not signify meaning. In Wordsworth's poem, however, what begins as a ballad form (an iambic tetrameter followed by a **trimeter**) is quickly overwhelmed by the intensity of feeling that the poet has so that the next three lines are all repetitive tetrameters that culminate and expire with the gasp at the end of the two-beat line ('Or let me die!'). As the feeling becomes more meditative in the second part of the poem, it begins to offer some explanation for this rush of feeling. The lines lengthen again and the final line is a culmination of that settling from excitement into humbled awe.

8 How many different types of punctuation are used?

The punctuation consists of a colon, two semi-colons, a comma, an exclamation mark, another semi-colon and a full stop. Looking at punctuation is another way of trying to deduce a **structure** in the poem. We have already established that the argument of the poem is divided into two sentences. Within those sentences, the punctuation further divides the stages of the argument. The opening two lines consist of a statement; the colon at the end of that statement begins an illustration of that statement in three stages in the form of a list, which is appropriately separated by semi-colons. The exclamation mark at the end of the first sentence shows us the strength of feeling that the sentence expresses. **Rhetorically**, he is addressing Nature here so this exclamation is also called an **apostrophe**. The more balanced and considered sentiment of the second sentence uses the semi-colon differently; as a way of indicating the two parts of the final sentence's argument.

9 Are there any repetitions in the poem?

Apart from the articles 'a' and 'the', the repeated words are:

my, when, I, so, it, is, Man, be, and each.

There is also the sequence 'So was it' 'So is it' and 'So be it'. which is an example of **rhetorical parallelism**, a series of repetitions often used in poetry. It is a technique that originated in **oral poetry** since it is a device that helps the listener to remember it in the absence of a written text. Among the repeated words, 'Man' is interesting because it is capitalised, an example of a **graphological** effect. It indicates more than the individual man that the child became. It is mankind itself that is represented here. The line, 'The Child is father of the Man' probably means that adults could learn something from the simple enthusiasm of the child. This would explain the **paradoxical** idea that the child is the 'father' (teacher) of the adult man.

10 What does 'piety' mean?

'Piety' means reverence for and obedience to God. Here, however, because of Wordsworth's **pantheistic** beliefs (that God is represented in all elements of Nature), it is an expression of reverence and awe in the face of Nature's wonder. The word 'piety' has religious **connotations** and so makes a fitting **lexical choice** to conclude a poem about a state of reverence and awe begun in childhood and continued throughout life. The **register** of the final sentence creates a tone of dignified humility, which effectively supersedes the joyfully enthusiastic **tone** of the first part of the poem.

Ten relatively simple questions have enabled us to cover all seven of the frameworks suggested for dealing with poetry. It is not necessary to work methodically in sequence through the frameworks, although you can do that if you wish. You can see that even a very short poem of nine lines offers many clues about the ways in which a writer creates effects. If you were to now choose a theme for your coursework essay based on this analysis, an obvious one would be:

Compare the ways in which Wordsworth and … express their enthusiasm for nature.

All we need now is another writer from the list to fill the gap.

Poem 2: *Lizard* by D. H. Lawrence

D. H. Lawrence is better known for his novels than his poetry but he wrote many poems. Although you would be wise to resist too much **contextual** information, in the introduction to the Penguin *Selected Poems of D. H. Lawrence*, W. E. Williams writes that Lawrence's poems

---

■ **Key terms**

Graphology: the layout of a text, with use of such features as typeface

Paradox: an apparently self-contradictory statement which is true.

were 'detonated rather than composed', which gives us some idea of
the explosive intensity of his writing. Williams also quotes Lawrence
as saying, 'I have always tried to get an emotion out in its own course,
without altering it. It needs the finest instinct imaginable, much finer
than the skill of a craftsman.' This might strike us as an odd thing for a
poet to say but Lawrence clearly valued 'instinct' over craftsmanship and
that might explain the affection for nature and frequent contempt for
mankind that he shows in so many of his poems.

Having considered an approach for analysing poetry, let us look at one
of those Lawrence poems that express enthusiasm for nature. It is called
Lizard and, again, is a very short poem. Like Wordsworth's poem, *The
Rainbow*, *Lizard* is also relatively straightforward in meaning.

> A lizard ran out on a rock and looked up, listening
> no doubt to the sounding of the spheres.
> And what a dandy fellow! the right toss of a chin for you
> and swirl of a tail!
> If men were as much men as lizards are lizards
> they'd be worth looking at.

Critical response activity

Answer the following questions about the text. A commentary is provided to
help you measure your responses against the type of responses that will gain
you high marks.

1 Which words indicate the lizard's movement?
2 What is the lizard listening to?
3 What does 'dandy' mean?
4 What examples of punctuation are there?
5 Are there any patterns to be found in the sentence structure?
6 What does 'right' mean in this poem?
7 The poem doesn't rhyme but are there any other patterns of sound?
8 Who is the 'you' in the poem?
9 What repetitions can you find in the poem?
10 The argument of the poem is in two parts. Where is the division?

This is a slightly more difficult poem to write about because, unlike *The
Rainbow*, *Lizard* is not structured in any rhyming pattern at all. In fact,
it appears to deliberately defy such structural patterning in order to retain
the freshness of its observation. The subject matter, however, is quite
straightforward – an admiration for the lizard and the kind of nobility it
has, which in the opinion of Lawrence, mankind lacks. The following
answers attempt to show how you can make many analytical points
about a poem despite its apparent lack of form.

Commentary

1 Which words indicate the lizard's movement?

'Ran out', 'looked up', 'listening', 'toss of a chin' and 'swirl of a tail' all
indicate the lizard's movement. The movements suggest eagerness ('ran
out'), alertness ('looked up', 'listening') and a certain elegant arrogance
('toss of a chin', 'swirl of a tail') that is consistent with the description
of the lizard as a 'dandy'. By using **enjambement** at the end of the first

line, Lawrence creates an effect that prompts the reader to hesitate after 'listening'. This heightens the sense of anticipation. It is only as we read on into the second line that we realise the verb 'listening' is followed by 'to' and the **object,** 'the sounding of the spheres'. We cannot help but hear, incidentally, the distant hissing that the lizard perceives in the **sibilance** of 'li<u>s</u>tening/<u>s</u>ounding/<u>s</u>phere<u>s</u>'.

2 What is the lizard listening to?

It is listening to the 'sounding of the spheres'. It was a belief of the Ancient Greek mathematician, Pythagoras, that the planets emitted a vibrational sound which was dependent on the distance of each planet from the earth. The combination of the sounds emitted by different planets created a harmony. The effect of this image is to suggest that the lizard has an intelligent sensitivity to the universe. The lizard is attuned to the universe in a way that mankind cannot achieve. The fact that this **phrase** is prefaced with the **discourse marker** 'no doubt' intensifies the poet's admiration and also a conversational tone.

3 What does 'dandy' mean?

A 'dandy' is someone who dresses fashionably and has an elegant arrogance about him. It is a rather dated word but for Lawrence it enables him to create an image of the lizard as proud of the way he looks and of his essential 'lizard-like' qualities. The use of the lexis 'dandy' would normally be applied to men rather than animals. The usage here humanises the lizard and sets up the contrasting argument of the final lines of the poem in which mankind is berated for lacking the confidence and pride which all human beings should exhibit – the pride of their species.

4 What examples of punctuation are there?

There are three sentences. In the first, the comma before 'listening' heightens the intensity of that listening by creating a brief stillness. The second sentence ought strictly to be two sentences since there is an exclamation mark in the middle as well as at the end. Lawrence chooses to begin the second part of this sentence with a lower case letter. The effect of this double exclamation mark is to give greater power to his enthusiasm for the lizard. The final sentence is a pronouncement on that enthusiasm and an opportunity to make a moral point, so it is allowed to run on without interruption. It is also worth noting the apostrophe in 'they'd' which gives a slightly **colloquial** feel to the moral pronouncement after having voiced it in **subjunctive** terms ('If men were as much men as lizards are lizards ...').

5 Are there any patterns to be found in the sentence structure?

As already mentioned, the poem is in three sentences, each making up two lines of the poem. The first sentence is narrative in style. It uses the **past tense** to establish some distance and to describe the lizard in a context ('on a rock'). It enables the poet to create an atmosphere of anticipation for what is to come and to familiarise the reader with the subject matter. This is a novelistic device which prepares the way for what is to come. The only intrusion on the events here is the poet's use of 'no doubt' which draws our attention to his opinion, which will be developed in the rest of the poem. The two **exclamations** of the second sentence express admiration. The first almost humanises the lizard ('dandy fellow!') and the second gives two details to justify that human admiration. The final sentence is an expression of opinion that partly exhorts men to show the same pride in their human qualities as the lizard does in celebrating 'lizardness' but suggests, too, a disappointment

■ Key terms

Subjunctive: A verbal form or mood expressing hypothesis, for example, 'if I were rich I would buy a house'.

in what man has lost from his primitive self. This attitude can be found in many other poems by Lawrence (*Pansies, Give Us Gods*, etc.). Lawrence's view is that modern mechanised mankind has lost much of its primitive power.

6 *What does 'right' mean in this poem?*

'Right' means correctly executed to win admiration but 'right' also implies correctly consistent with what you might expect of a lizard. There is an implication that man, by contrast, is 'wrong' in the way he carries himself in the modern age.

7 *The poem doesn't rhyme but are there any other patterns of sound?*

Lawrence makes use of a number of phonological devices. The use of the 'l' echoes the lizard's movement in 'lizard', 'looked', 'listening' and later in 'swirl' and 'tail'. The liquid sound of 'l' creates a light padding sound such as the lizard's movements might make on the rock. 'Liquid' is a phonetic term to describe the effects of the 'l' and the 'r' sounds where the tip of the tongue touches lightly on the upper palate in a gliding way. (Try it for yourself!) The sibilant hiss of 'sounding of the spheres' has already been mentioned. These are all examples of **alliteration**, as is 'ran out on a rock'. These elements of sound combine to create the swift, light movement of the lizard emerging into the sun.

8 *Who is the 'you' in the poem?*

'You' partly addresses the reader but it has a more colloquial idiomatic effect here, too, which is consistent with the admiration expressed. The expression 'for you' is similar to the use of 'you' in the modern expressions 'there you go' or 'there you are', which imply a sharing of experience which is exactly what Lawrence wants to do with his poem.

9 *What repetitions can you find in the poem?*

Apart from the alliteration effects already mentioned (see 7) and the syntactical structuring (see 4 and 5), there is a neat, rhetorical elegance to the pairing of 'men were … men' with 'lizards are lizards'. The contrast of the subjunctive ('If (men) were') with the **declarative present tense** ('lizards are lizards') also emphasises how mankind has fallen short of his true capacity but might still remedy it.

10 *The argument' of the poem is in two parts. Where is the division?*

The division falls after line 4. As with Wordsworth's poem *The Rainbow*, Lawrence uses the final lines as a comment or coda on what has gone before. It marks a change in tone from admiration to regret.

Poem 3: *The Hanging Man* by Sylvia Plath

A reminder about context

Before we consider the final poem in this sequence of three, it is very important to say something more about context. You have already been discouraged from concerning yourself with too many biographical details in writing about a poem. Keep in mind that your coursework essay is only 2,000–2,500 words long. For most candidates the challenge will be to cut it down to this number rather than struggle to find enough to say. You have to be ruthless with yourself and confine yourself only to contextual detail that directly enhances what you say about devices used in a poem. For example, Wordsworth's views on pantheism are interesting and would link usefully to writing about the ways in which he celebrates nature but your overwhelming priority is to write about literary and linguistic effects

(AO1). Context forms a part of AO3 and will doubtless inform your judgements, but comparison is the main requirement of AO3, so balance must be maintained.

Similarly, Lawrence's attitudes to the plight of modern man are also interesting. You will notice that there are some introductory remarks used to contextualise these attitudes in order to help us to understand the poem but they are brief and pertinent. A contextual point is used, also, to explain the expression 'sounding of the spheres' but an understanding of that is not absolutely essential to an understanding of the poem.

The problem of context is mentioned here because the final poem we will look at is *The Hanging Man* by Sylvia Plath. Plath is often regarded as a difficult poet and that often leads critics to be more concerned about her relationship with the poet, Ted Hughes, and her suicide than with her poems. In effect, context completely replaces the poetry. Avoid this strategy – it is often a response to struggling with the poetry. We are all interested, as human beings, in the details of other human lives and there is no point in denying this trait.

> **AQA Examiner's tip**
>
> Let this be your motto: My knowledge of context may inform my analysis but never replace it.

> By the roots of my hair some god got hold of me. I sizzled in his blue
> volts like a desert prophet.
> The nights snapped out of sight like a lizard's eyelid:
> A world of bald white days in a shadeless socket.
> A vulturous boredom pinned me in this tree.
> If he were I, he would do what I did.

It is more difficult to establish what this kind of poem is specifically about than it is with the previous two poems. Don't be discouraged. Try not to think of a poem as a set of crossword puzzle clues that have to be decoded. Also, don't race to the internet to get it decoded for you because other 'experts' may well distract you with contextual background. An additional reading of this poem at the end of the analysis will show you how misleading an approach this might be. With very short poems, such as the three presented here, there is a possibility that you can learn them by heart, carry them around in your head and think about them for a few days. Incidentally, there is actually very little help available with *The Hanging Man* either on the internet or in critical studies, so trust your powers of judgement instead.

First of all, a quick glance at the poem will show you that there is not a single word that is completely strange to you. Even a word like 'vulturous' which seems to be a **neologism** (a made-up word) can easily be guessed at. 'In the manner of a vulture' seems a likely meaning.

Secondly, if the meaning of a poem is not immediately apparent, settle for establishing the more general emotional mood of the poem. Is this poem about a happy state? Is the persona in control of emotions or dependent on something or somebody else? Poems that express concern or unhappiness about relationships of all kinds may not speak directly. Sometimes poets are struggling to express an emotion they are unsure about and the poem acts as a kind of therapeutic process.

Critical response activity

Answer the following questions about *The Hanging Man*. A commentary is provided to help you measure your responses against the type of responses that will gain you high marks.

1 What verbs are there in the poem?

2 What abstract nouns would you use to describe the mood of the persona?

3   What is unusual about the syntax of the first sentence?

4   How many sentences are there?

5   What adjectives are there?

6   What religious images can you find?

7   Are there any sound patterns in the poem?

8   What are the qualities of 'a lizard's eyelid' that are brought out in the poem?

9   What idea does 'sizzled in his blue volts' suggest?

10 Who is the 'he' of the final line?

Commentary

1 What verbs are there in the poem?

The verbs are 'got hold', 'sizzled' and 'pinned' 'were', 'do', 'did'. The verbs 'got hold', 'sizzled' and 'pinned' are all used to show that the persona is the victim of a greater power. The victim is the object of the action in the verbal relationship. It is as if the persona is aware of what is happening to her but has no control over the process. It could be that the 'vulturous boredom' she feels is a product of that victimisation. They all contribute to a **semantic field** of helplessness in the face of violence.

2 What abstract nouns would you use to describe the mood of the persona?

Abstract nouns about the mood here might include 'powerlessness' and 'boredom'. Where do we get these ideas from? There is a stillness to the poem despite the verbs of action. Days and nights are marked by the 'snapping' open and closed of a lizard's eye. The descriptive imagery suggests a barren waste ('desert', 'shadeless') and that is clearly a metaphor for the way the persona feels. The build-up of monosyllables ('the roots of my hair', 'world of bald white days') in which long vowels dominate enhances this feeling of slow, undeviating tedium.

3 What is unusual about the syntax of the first sentence?

The syntax delays the important **subject**-verb-object ('some god', 'got hold', 'me') by beginning with an **adverbial phrase** ('by the roots of my hair'), which would normally come after the main clause. This shift of emphasis draws the reader's attention to the point of pain as the hair is 'got hold of' 'by the roots'.

4 How many sentences are there?

There are five sentences. They follow a simple pattern of statements and even the middle sentence, which is divided by a colon, could easily have been made consistent with the pattern by adding 'It was' after the colon. This repetitious formula emphasises the unrelenting boredom of the events.

5 What adjectives are there?

The adjectives are *'blue'*, *'desert'*, *'bald'*, *'white'*, *'shadeless'*, *'vulturous'*. Considering the mood of indifference that permeates the poem, this is quite a high incidence of descriptive language. However, rather than energising the imagery with the added detail, the effect is actually to intensify the world over which the persona has no control and thus increase its power. There are two **similes** in the poem – 'like a desert prophet' and 'like a lizard's eye' – which increase the descriptive repertoire of the poem to heighten the effect already described.

6 *What religious images can you find?*

The religious images are 'god' and 'desert prophet'. These images are consistent with the potent **allusion** to the desert in which Jesus spent forty days and forty nights (perhaps echoed in the image of nights and days in the central sentence). The fact that it is 'some god' rather than a capitalised 'God' is sinister because such vagueness suggests that there are other malevolent 'gods' and the violence in the poem is somehow made more random by the generalised 'some' god. A 'prophet' is someone who is a messenger or a cipher for God's word through which he has the capacity for predicting events in the future. Perhaps in the desert the prophet lacks an audience and therefore the poet is suggesting an inability to communicate what is felt to the world.

7 *Are there any sound patterns in the poem?*

The sound patterns in the poem are complex and, we gradually realise, carefully developed. Firstly, there is the hollow echo of long vowels found in the many monosyllables – 'roots', 'hair', 'hold', 'blue', 'volts', etc. These contrast with the rapid short-vowelled movement of 'snapped' and 'socket'. That latter device creates a sinister watching quality that implies the persona's movements are restricted to the simple open-shut action of the lizard's eyelid. There is a sibilant alliteration in 'snapped out of sight' and 'shadeless socket' that suggests the hiss of a silent desert in which distance and openness heighten that stillness. There is **onomatopoeia** in the verb 'sizzled' and a warm and lazy kind of **assonance** in 'days' and 'shadeless', which is added to by the **half-rhyme** 'world'/'bald'.

8 *What are the qualities of 'a lizard's eyelid' that are brought out in the poem?*

The lizard's eyelid has the simple reflex quality of a camera lens. It lacks the quality of expression that a human eyelid might have. It is a 'shadeless socket' lacking eyebrow or jutting forehead and this exposed sensation is heightened by the arid setting of the desert. The lizard's eyelid controls what is seen by the persona even though she wishes to communicate more to us than the world which is limited to the 'bald white days'. It is as if her head is held in a vice and she cannot move her own eyes to take in any more than the 'lizard' allows. In this way, the lizard is linked with 'some god' as a controller of her destiny.

9 *What idea does 'sizzled in his blue volts' suggest?*

'Sizzled in his blue volts' is clearly an image of electricity. We sense the involuntary tremors and the complete control of another's power. Because the 'blue volts' are 'his' we are aware that any energising that the electricity creates seems to increase his power and diminish hers. She is the victim here. Is this poem about a relationship between two people? It's a possibility. An electric charge is sometimes an image that describes a feeling of being in love, although here it is more likely to suggest that one is in the 'power' of somebody else and therefore not free to act independently.

10 *Who is the 'he' of the final line?*

This is perhaps the hardest question to answer. 'He' could refer to 'some god', and doing 'what I did' might mean 'he would respond to this treatment in the same way as 'I did'. It is possible that this final line refers to something completely outside the imagery of the rest of the poem, something that we cannot be sure of knowing. We are left, in that case, with a poem that concentrates on feelings rather than on explanations. If this is so, do not 101be afraid to give emphasis to a more emotional response to the language in the poem. There is never a single right answer to a question about a poem's meaning and the important thing is that you build up some evidence from the poem to justify what you say about its possible meanings.

A warning about contextual distractions

Sylvia Plath's husband, Ted Hughes, edited her poems after her suicide and, in recent years, wrote his own poems about their relationship. The book is called *Birthday Letters* and in it he uses similar imagery to Plath's in *The Hanging Man* to try to echo her mood in his own poem. Biography tells us that the poem is Plath's attempt to write about an experience she had years before when, after a suicide attempt, she had electroconvulsive therapy as part of her treatment. The important question to ask yourself at this stage is 'How much does that knowledge help my analysis of the language of the poem?' Perhaps now we can dismiss ideas that the poem is about a relationship but, by looking closely at the language and trying to build a picture, we have got very close to the emotions that Plath is recreating – the helplessness, the sense of being in the power of someone else. Probably, too, the boredom described may emanate from depression. Working towards an understanding from close scrutiny of the poem will always be a more effective form of analysis rather than allowing contextual knowledge to substitute for this close scrutiny. Only those who see a poem as a puzzle to be solved will be satisfied with the biographical explanation.

Another misleading aspect of context might be found in the fact that, if you look at a pack of Tarot cards, you will notice that the Hanged Man is portrayed as 'pinned ... in this tree' and his hanging head appears to be 'sizzl(ing) in ... blue volts'. Is the poet really writing her poem about the man in the Tarot card? The card, apparently, represents a 'suspension in affairs followed by a turning point in the Questioner's life. This card may show up when a destructive relationship is coming to an end.' Those eager to see all Plath's poems as about her troubled relationship with Ted Hughes will have a field day with this reading of the poem! All this information is interesting; it appeals to the detective in all of us but it is, in the end, a distraction to analysis. Hughes tells us that the poem was actually written on 27 June 1960, long before their troubles began and just after Plath had given birth to her first child. Plath, like all poets, may well have drawn on biographical experience but in a poem it is transmuted into something else. Perhaps only the mood remains and we, as readers, must focus on what is there on the page rather than the biographical details that surround the poem.

Poem 4: *London* by William Blake

The following poem and multiple-choice questions will help you apply what you have learnt from your analysis of poems 1–3. The poem is by another well-known poet, William Blake, from a collection of his poems entitled *Songs of Innocence and Experience*. The poem is called *London*.

> I wander thro' each charter'd street,
> Near where the charter'd Thames does flow
> And mark in every face I meet
> Marks of weakness, marks of woe.
>
> In every cry of every Man,
> In every Infants cry of fear,
> In every voice: in every ban,
> The mind-forg'd manacles I hear

How the Chimney-sweepers cry
Every blackning Church appalls,
And the hapless Soldiers sigh
Runs in blood down Palace walls.

But most thro' midnight streets I hear
How the youthful Harlots curse
Blasts the new-born Infants tear,
And blights with plagues the Marriage hearse.

■ Critical response activity

This multiple choice quiz will help you to evaluate how well you can identify the notable features in this poem.

1 The poet's tone can best be described as:

a surprised

b shocked

c disinterested

d despairing.

2 The poem is written in:

a iambic pentameters

b trochaic pentameters

c iambic tetrameters

d trochaic trimeters.

3 'mind-forged' is an example of:

a a dynamic verb

b a compound adjective

c a proper noun

d an adverb.

4 The use of 'mark' to mean 'to notice' as well as 'stain or distinguishing feature' is an example of:

a a metaphor

b a pun

c a personification

d a simile.

5 The repetition of 'every' best suggests:

a amazement at the volume of noise

b the weariness of those who suffer

c the injustice of the political system

d the church's lack of concern.

6 An example of synaesthesia (the mixing of sensations) is:

a 'blights with plagues'

b 'Chimney-sweepers cry'

c 'every cry of every Man'

d 'Soldiers sigh'/'Runs in blood'.

7 'midnight' is used here as:

a a verb

b a noun

c an adjective

d a compound noun.

8 'The Marriage hearse' means:

a divorce

b the unhappy marriage of the couple

c the death of the married couple from disease

d the end of romantic love.

9 'Church' and 'Palace' are used in the poem as symbols of:

a those who have caused the suffering

b the only institutions that we can still look up to

c the start and finish points for the Marriage hearse's journey

d the places that the poor can still go to find comfort.

10 In which of the following do repeated long vowels indicate weariness?

a 'Every blackning'

b 'of every Man'

c 'in every ban'

d 'marks of woe'.

One person's answers are:

1	d	**6**	d
2	c	**7**	c
3	b	**8**	c
4	b	**9**	a
5	b	**10**	d

Of course, everyone will not have the same interpretation. If you can make a convincing case for another answer then it may be just as valid.

Developing ideas about poetry

I felt a Funeral by Emily Dickinson

As we have already discovered, there is more to writing about poetry than merely identifying features. In order to see how a good candidate writes about poetry, it's important to look closely at the following essay which is an answer to the question:

How does Dickinson express her thoughts and feelings in *I felt a Funeral*?

In order to get the most out of the essay and the comments that follow each paragraph, you need to acquaint yourself with the poem first. To help you focus, there are some questions on the poem which preface the essay and are answered in what follows. Read the poem below and then make a list of your own responses to the questions that follow it before reading the essay.

I felt a Funeral, in my Brain,
And Mourners to and fro,
Kept treading – treading – till it seemed
That Sense was breaking through –

And when they all were seated,   5
A Service, like a Drum –
Kept beating – beating – till I thought
My Mind was going numb –

And then I heard them lift a Box,
And creak across my Soul   10
With those same Boots of Lead, again.
Then Space – began to toll,

As all the Heavens were a Bell,
And Being, but an Ear,
And I, and Silence, some strange Race,   15
Wrecked, solitary, here –

And then a Plank in Reason, broke
And I dropped down, and down –
And hit a World, at every plunge,
And Finished knowing – then –   20

Critical response activity

Consider *I felt a Funeral* and answer the following questions, which will help you to think about your own response to the poem before you read the sample essay which follows.

1 Which of these best describes the subject of the poem: 'death', 'descent into madness' or 'depression'?

2 What is the metrical pattern?

3 Choose three words from the poem that have connotations of death.

4 What is the effect of the repetition of the words 'treading' and 'beating' in the poem?

5 Why is 'Brain' a better lexical choice in the first line than 'mind' or 'head'?

6 Find three dynamic verbs in the poem.

7 What effect is created by the sibilance in line 15?

8 Choose a phrase from the poem that suggests the sound of falling.

9 What does 'Being, but an Ear' mean?

10 Why does the poem end with a dash?

Link

You will find an explanation of how to use a thesis at the beginning of the comparative writing section on p106.

Sample answer

Now that you have some opinions of your own about the poem, read the following essay, which is an excellent example of how to order observations intelligently.

- Some words and phrases are in highlighted blue to show us the language of analysis in this student's response.
- Terminology used is highlighted pink so that frameworks can be identified.

We are never left wondering which part of the poem the writer is referring to – it's always stated. The analytical language is used flexibly and moves the argument along logically.

This candidate begins with a strong **thesis** and works efficiently through the lines and argument of the poem, drawing on frameworks as they are appropriate rather than processing them in a mechanical way. The argument is clear and persuasive and the essay is neatly rounded off with a conclusion that brings us back to the central thesis but which widens its implication.

[1] One of Dickinson's darker, more gothic poems, *I felt a Funeral* is a hugely ambitious dramatic monologue. The poem could perhaps show a literal death in which – typical of Dickinson – she takes the reader to the brink of death and then ends, unwilling to take us beyond the grave due to her uncertainty in the Calvinist faith. The poem could also be showing someone's descent into total madness but Dickinson is possibly implying depression rather than a complete mental breakdown.

[2] Dickinson explores the idea of the death of the rational or social mind in order to see clearly and that it is a painful experience to gain revelation and understanding. In general the metre remains steady, which contrasts with what is evidently a 'rough journey' within the poem. The simple rhyme scheme also tends to remain constant, only breaking in the final stanza when the reader must question whether this really is 'the end'.

Paragraph 1: The candidate allows for three possible readings of the poem: it could be about a literal death, a descent into total madness or depression. The tone of the poem does not clash with any of these readings and it is good to keep your interpretation open and not be too dogmatic about a single possible meaning. The form (dramatic monologue) is noted, as is the genre (Gothic) and already there is an awareness of audience response. A very good start.

Paragraph 2: The theme is enlarged to consider more difficult ideas (the death of the rational or social mind) and there is an attempt to consider the form (metre and rhyme scheme) and its impact on the mood of the poem.

[3] The capitalised 'Funeral' in the first line provides immediate connotations of death and establishes the darker mood. The use of the word 'Brain' rather than 'mind' (or similar) and 'a Funeral' rather than a possessive 'my Funeral' gives a detached unemotional tone in the poem suggesting a sense of powerlessness.

[4] The repetition of the word 'treading' in the third line of the first stanza creates a sense of weight. The word 'treading' itself has a very heavy sound heightening the sense of monotony.

[5] The dynamic verb 'breaking' suggests pain and that to gain 'Sense' – knowledge and understanding – you must suffer. Dickinson is implying that pain is the price you must pay to see clearly.

[6] The formal, social ceremony of a funeral is described at the beginning of the second stanza: 'when they all were seated, / A service'. Dickinson, by describing that the 'service, like a drum / Kept beating', shows herself to be outside normal social formalities. By undermining the religious and social importance of a funeral, Dickinson is hinting that she can see past the pious exterior of faith – perhaps a reason why she never committed herself to the Calvinist church.

[7] Dickinson goes on to repeat the word 'beating', highlighting the relentless pounding by placing it between dashes. Dickinson continues the sound imagery into the third stanza with the word 'creak'.

[8] In the third stanza Dickinson implies that this has happened before: 'those same Boots of Lead, again' which is perhaps more suggestive of depression than any other interpretation. The noun 'Lead' enhances this theme of heaviness, a sense of all-consuming weight that is unbearable.

[9] The last line of stanza three, 'Then Space – began to toll,' makes the reader question what is 'out there' – what is this empty unknown place? The word 'toll' continues the sound imagery and is connotative of a church bell ringing a death toll, and harks back to the idea of a funeral.

[10] Dickinson creates a bleak view of faith with 'All the Heavens were a Bell' – reducing the whole idea of paradise to a bell in church. By reducing the 'Heavens' to a sound, Dickinson is maybe implying that faith is simply a noisy gong with nothing beyond the sound: that there may be nothing after death. In the second line of this stanza, Dickinson uses synecdoche to reduce humanity to one sense, creating a sense of isolation: 'And Being, but an Ear'. This may be Dickinson suggesting that people have blind faith – they hear the 'Heavens' but can do nothing but listen. This sense of being reduced, though, also creates a disorientating image and a sense of loss.

[11] The last line of the third stanza, 'Wrecked, solitary, here – ', further adds to the isolation and desolation felt by the narrative voice. Dickinson also uses sibilance in this stanza. By using sibilance – 'Silence', 'some', 'strange' and 'solitary' – she creates a whispering effect which is reflective of the silent emptiness she describes.

[12] The final stanza is full of violence, reflected in the semantic field: 'broke', 'dropped', 'hit' and 'plunge', reinforcing the idea that revelation is a painful experience. A 'Plank in reason, broke' suggests that all rationality is being lost and that it is painful.

[13] The repetition of 'down' in 'I dropped down, and down' creates an image of a figure falling into nothing, a vast blackness, highlighting the emptiness and isolation she feels.

Paragraph 3: Now the candidate begins a logical analysis of the poem in chronological order. Frameworks are drawn upon according to their usefulness. There is attention to lexis ('Brain'), graphology (capitalised), and grammar (possessive) here.

Paragraph 4: A phonological point (repetition) is developed here with good focus on its effect (this sense of monotony) and the implication that that is consistent with the mood of the poem.

Paragraph 5: A lexical explanation together with a grammar point (dynamic verb) to support it.

Paragraph 6: A further thematic development with some contextual support. Note that the candidate always lets us know precisely which part of the poem (the beginning of the second stanza) is being examined.

Paragraph 7: More phonological support for the tone analysis which is already established.

Paragraph 8: There is support for one of the suggested themes (depression) with useful lexical evidence.

Paragraph 9: Imagery is noted with the link to phonology and lexical analysis included. A reminder of 'us' as the audience ('makes the reader question').

Paragraph 10: A development of more complex ideas in the poem with synecdoche (a figurative device whereby a part represents the whole – in this case, a bell representing paradise) mood and imagery noted.

Paragraph 11: Mood, point of view, and phonology are all linked neatly together.

Paragraph 12: Two more lexical points linked with a clear sense of the mood of the poem.

Paragraph 13: Imagery and mood are sustained through a phonological effect (repetition).

Paragraph 14: A further explanation of the theme of the poem firmly rooted in lexical detail.

Paragraph 15: A lot is included here. The candidate has concentrated on mood throughout but engages the reader here on the rational interpretation. The questions show engagement with the ideas in the poem without any need to come up with a definitive answer. There is a strong sense of the persona's mood (the narrative voice) and lexical and punctuation points are also made.

Paragraph 16: The idea of paradox enlarges what has already been said about the emotional focus of the poem. It's a neat conclusion to an impressive argument.

[14] In the third line of the final stanza, 'hit a World, at every plunge' gives a more cosmic scale to the poem. The experience is completely outside every society and, as a result, the narrator is now able to see the 'bigger picture'. This provides a sense of enlightenment. Through the loss of a social world, revelation has been found.

[15] The final line is perhaps the most ambiguous. 'Finished knowing' could have many meanings. Is it death? Is it the end of the depression? Despite this pain the narrative voice has endured – has the 'revelation' simply stopped? Dickinson finishes the poem with the word '– then –' between dashes – a 'trademark' ending suggesting that something happens after. Is this the end? Perhaps this is the point of death and Dickinson, as ever, simply refuses to take the reader past what she knows to be true.

[16] *I felt a Funeral* is a dramatic monologue which has many interpretations. It shows the paradox of losing the mind, life or rationality in order to gain insight into what is beyond normal society. Through a range of techniques, Dickinson takes the reader on a violent journey of which the destination is unclear.

Lessons to be learned from this essay

1 Begin with a clear thesis.

2 Use frameworks flexibly as and when they present themselves as useful.

3 Working through the poem chronologically allows you to explain the theme and draw on frameworks appropriately.

4 Try to develop some of the language of analysis (seen in the phrases highlighted pink). This will allow you to structure your argument and reinforce the points you have made so that there is a clear cumulative effect.

5 Don't be afraid to allow for several possible meanings.

■ How to make comparisons between poetry texts

Now that we have established an approach to looking at poetry, we need to focus on the requirements of the coursework essay. Perhaps we might best start by comparing two poems which we have already discussed and which are therefore already familiar: *The Rainbow* and *Lizard*. Having analysed these texts separately, we now have to organise the observations we have made into a comparative essay based around a theme. We have already considered a possible theme for this comparison so let's follow it up.

Our title will be:

Compare the ways in which Wordsworth and Lawrence express their enthusiasm for nature.

Admittedly, our comparison will be based on only one poem by each poet but, having got our ideas clear about the theme in this comparison, it will be not be so hard to find other material from the poetry collections to corroborate and enhance what we have to say about these two poems. Since Lawrence also wrote a poem entitled *The Rainbow*, it might be worth including that in a wider comparison later on.

 Link

To reread these poems, look back to p91 (*The Rainbow*) and p95 (*Lizard*).

■ Writing a good thesis

Establish a thesis that will be the basis of your whole essay and which will help you to focus your argument logically. The world 'thesis' as used here means 'a proposition which you intend to prove'. The plural of thesis is theses. A good essay will have a thesis in the first paragraph, which will enable the reader to follow the argument of the essay and the writer to be clear about where the essay is going.

Opening paragraphs often give the examiner a very good idea as to whether the essay is going to be successful or not. There are, of course, candidates who write their way into an essay gradually and eventually end up making valid points but they will have robbed themselves of the opportunity to do even better by such an unfocused approach to the task.

Here, for example, are some weak opening sentences to an essay:

1   Stating the obvious:

'Wordsworth and Lawrence share a number of similarities in the way they express their love of nature but there are also differences.'

We can assume that a comparative essay will inevitably draw our attention to similarities and differences. It is not necessary to repeat this. This regurgitation of the task is superfluous.

2   The biographical detour:

'William Wordsworth was born …'

There is no need for a biographical introduction. Begin immediately with a thesis.

3   Making plans:

'In this essay, I intend to show the differences between Wordsworth and Lawrence by looking at all the frameworks in turn and then coming to a conclusion.'

This strategy should be obvious from the evidence in the essay. Don't say what you are going to do. Just do it.

Better by far is to have thought about the evidence in advance and decided the direction your essay will take. Here are three good theses with which to begin such an essay:

- 'Both Wordsworth and Lawrence have an obvious enthusiasm for nature. Wordsworth, the pantheist, sees wonder in all God's creations, mankind included. Lawrence, however, sees mankind as having fallen short of his potential and this colours his writing.'

- 'Though both are lovers of nature, Wordsworth and Lawrence express this love quite differently. Wordsworth makes the artificial rhythm of the line central to his expression of enthusiasm while Lawrence sees free verse as the only honest way to convey such charged emotion.'

- 'Though their styles may be different, both Wordsworth and Lawrence share an enthusiasm for nature that delights in spontaneous natural beauty, and contempt for the ways in which mankind has become removed from that.'

Each of these theses makes it perfectly clear how the essay will be argued. If you believe there is a philosophical difference in the way the two poets write, you can choose the first opening. If you want to concentrate on stylistic differences rather than differences of attitude you might choose the second opening. Or you might choose a compromise version like the third, whereby you begin with a stylistic difference but use it to show a similarity of attitude between the two poets. These are not, of course, the only possible openings for dealing with the title we have chosen but, unlike the earlier poorer openings, they do show the way the essay will develop. You should make your argument as easy to follow as you can and a strong opening thesis will do just that.

Planning the essay: making framework notes

There are two important tasks before writing begins. One of them is to plan how to use the information accumulated so far in a comparative essay. You can do this by making a two-column list considering the material from both poems side by side. By working through the frameworks, you can draw up potential comparative paragraphs. Your paragraphing by frameworks is only one potential approach to the problem but it is sufficiently structured to make sense of the material you want to use in the essay.

If you now look at the answers to the questions on the two poems that we discussed earlier in the chapter, you can draw up an approach to your essay which is based on frameworks. Here is an outline of the points made which have been transferred into a grid.

	The Rainbow (Wordsworth)	*Lizard* (D. H. Lawrence)
Beginnings	Rainbow – love of nature Child 'father of Man' Pantheism	Admiration of lizard/nobility Mankind falling short Narrative style
Manner	Tone shift – enthusiastic awe to humility	Atmosphere of anticipation Conversational tone – 'they'd', 'you' – idiomatic use Tone shift – admiration to regret
Lexis	Monosyllables + 'piety'	'Dandy' – archaic 'sounding of spheres' 'right'
Metaphor	Rainbow/heart leaps up	
Rhetoric (Phonological patterning and structural patterning)	Long vowels – heart, leaps, I, behold, rainbow, sky Apostrophe Parallelism: 'so was …'	Sibilance – listening/sounding/spheres Liquid 'l' – looked /swirl/ tail – alliteration Rhetorical style – men were men v. 'lizards are lizards'
Grammar	Punctuation – exclamation mark/colon/semi-colon Stative verbs v. leaps up Imperative – let me die Modal – could wish	Verbs of movement – looked up, listening Movement noun – toss, swirl Sentence structure – exclamation marks Subjunctive – 'if men were' v. declarative present tense
Form	1 stanza/2 parts – see punctuation 4 beat lines v. 2 beat – why? 'Man' capitalised	Verb/object line break – listening Use of coda/comment

■ Link

For a more detailed, blank version of this framework, see pp89–90.

It is not necessary to follow the frameworks slavishly. For example, in writing about the structures of the poem (the logical argument, the verse pattern, the sentence divisions, the punctuation) you will inevitably combine some of the points made from several frameworks. Additionally, you need to give yourself room to develop arguments that you think are central to the thesis you have presented in the opening paragraph.

Evaluating the effectiveness of openings

Your opening to the essay we have discussed might begin like this (the language of comparison is highlighted in **blue**):

Compare the ways in which Wordsworth and Lawrence express their enthusiasm for nature.

Though their styles may be different, both Wordsworth and Lawrence share an enthusiasm for nature that delights in spontaneous natural beauty and feels contempt for the ways in which mankind has become removed from that. Both writers imply that mankind has lost some of the nobility he once had in a more natural state. While Lawrence makes it clear through his conclusion, 'If men were as much men as lizards are lizards/they'd be worth looking at', that he is expressing his contempt for what man has become, Wordsworth is kinder. His only sense of mankind falling short is in the idea that, 'The Child is father of the Man'. He suggests that mankind has lost his natural wonder and might learn it again if he returns to the innocent state of awe that he once had.

There are shifts of tone in both poems. They both begin with expressions of awe and admiration for the subjects of their poem but both poems also use a sentence structure that moves the argument from image to comment by the conclusion. Wordsworth's initial overflow of emotion results in giving up the ballad form of the first two lines and replacing it with three tetrameters of similar structure ('So was it / is it / will be,,,'). This parallelism gives the poem a rising intensity, which explodes in the two-beat 'Or let me die!' This short line, ending in an exclamation and expression of commitment, marks the end of the first stage of the poem. The second part or coda is a more considered expression of ideas in which the tone becomes one of humility. Lawrence, by contrast, moves from a narrative strategy in which we are invited to watch the appearance of the lizard with anticipation. The subtle movements of the lizard are reflected in the verb choice 'looked up' and 'listening' and, as with Wordsworth, it is only when we have been invited to share his enthusiasm ('the right toss of a chin for you') that his tone changes to express a sense of disgust at mankind's shortfall in the coda. Both poets, then, adopt a similar structural strategy to combine expressions of enthusiasm with comment.

You will see from the highlighted parts in the two paragraphs above how clearly the language of comparison is used. But you must not allow this process to make your essay mechanical and repetitive. Do not be afraid to develop a point that needs developing without worrying too much about the slight loss of direct comparison. You will see that there are several lines in paragraph 2 above where there are no highlighted phrases. This is because, in order to explain Wordsworth's rhyming structure adequately, it is necessary to become more detailed. Because you have already stated your thesis and have made it clear that you are in the process of comparing structural style at this point, the reader will not lose the thread of your argument and will be happy to see this seeming detour develop. Also, a good essay will need to integrate frameworks from time to time. You will see from these two opening paragraphs that the process of the argument has been established and, as long as the reader can see where you are going, it is perfectly acceptable not to follow the individual frameworks paragraph by paragraph.

Link

If you are not yet familiar with Larkin or Plath's poetry, there is a poem by each of them in this chapter, on pp111–12.

One textual pairing with which many candidates may be familiar is Philip Larkin's *The Whitsun Weddings* and Sylvia Plath's *Ariel*. We will begin by comparing the opening paragraphs of two very successful essays on the following thematic title:

Compare the ways in which Larkin and Plath write about death.

Critical response activity

Remember that we are looking for two particular features in the opening of the essay:

- a clear thesis
- a clear focus on comparison.

Which of the two essays (X and Y) does this job most successfully in your opinion?

Candidate X

Both poets explore death in different ways. In *Lady Lazarus*, Plath explores how death has affected her. The poem is much more personal to her as it addresses her attempts to take her own life. The title *Lady Lazarus* suggests humour and instils a religious image in the mind of the reader. This is because, in the Bible, Lazarus rose from the dead. I feel the humorous title sets the tone throughout the poem. I will compare this with *Ambulances* by Larkin. This poem isn't personal to Larkin as death affects us all. The title *Ambulances* sets a dark tone in the poem, which is continued through each stanza.

Candidate Y

Both poets, Philip Larkin and Sylvia Plath explore the idea of death in their poetry. Larkin has a more reflective view on death in comparison to the world and life. This is seen in poems such as *Ambulances* and *An Arundel Tomb*, whereas in contrast Plath takes a more humorous view on death yet is almost ironic and savage.

Examiner's commentary

There is no doubt that both candidates use comparative language ('both', 'different', 'more', 'in comparison to', 'in contrast') but how useful as a thesis is the opening?

Candidate X begins with a general statement of difference and then becomes distracted with contextual background on *Lady Lazarus*, which would be best left until a later paragraph. There are, however, two clear theses. One is about style ('humorous' v. 'dark') and the second is about relationship to death ('personal' v. 'impersonal'). We will naturally be expecting some detailed justification of both these ideas later in the essay but we at least have some idea of where the essay is going.

Candidate Y's opening is briefer but does express the thesis that the styles will be contrasted by a 'reflective' approach on the one hand, with an 'ironic and savage' humour on the other. Is it necessary at this stage to state the poems you will be looking at? No, it isn't. It will be obvious once you begin your analysis. Remember: don't say what you're going to do, just do it.

Both candidates' openings are focused and they largely restrain themselves from moving into detail straight away. A fairly brief opening thesis will set up the contrasted argument clearly enough. You then have the choice of alternating comparative paragraphs between the two writers you are studying or trying to sustain an integrated comparison throughout.

A sample of a full comparative essay on poetry

Finally, here is a full comparative essay on the Larkin and Plath texts with comments after each paragraph. Although it is a comparison of two poems without a particular thematic focus, it is an excellent example of how tightly comparative an essay can be.

The essay focuses on one poem from each text and is prefaced with the text of the two poems discussed. Read them and consider them carefully before reading the essay that follows.

Poems

Mr Bleaney by Philip Larkin

'This was Mr Bleaney's room. He stayed
The whole time he was at the Bodies, till
They moved him.' Flowered curtains, thin and frayed,
Fall to within five inches of the sill,

Whose window shows a strip of building land,
Tussocky, littered. 'Mr Bleaney took
My bit of garden properly in hand'
Bed, upright chair, sixty-watt bulb, no hook

Behind the door, no room for books or bags –
'I'll take it.' So it happens that I lie
Where Mr Bleaney lay, and stub my fags
On the same saucer-souvenir, and try

Stuffing my ears with cotton-wool, to drown
The jabbering set he egged her on to buy.
I know his habits – what time he came down,
His preference for sauce to gravy, why

He kept on plugging at the four aways –
Likewise their yearly frame: the Frinton folk
Who put him up for summer holidays,
And Christmas at his sister's house in Stoke.

But if he stood and watched the frigid wind
Tousling the clouds, lay on the fusty bed
Telling himself that this was home, and grinned,
And shivered, without shaking off the dread

That how we live measures our own nature,
And at his age having no more to show
Than one hired box should make him pretty sure
He warranted no better, I don't know.

Wintering by Sylvia Plath

This is the easy time, there is nothing doing.
I have whirled the midwife's extractor,
I have my honey,
Six jars of it,
Six cat's eyes in the wine cellar,

Wintering in a dark without window
At the heart of the house
Next to the last tenant's rancid jam
and the bottles of empty glitters –
Sir So-and-so's gin.

This is the room I have never been in
This is the room I could never breathe in.
The black bunched in there like a bat,
No light
But the torch and its faint

Chinese yellow on appalling objects –
Black asininity. Decay.
Possession.
It is they who own me.
Neither cruel nor indifferent,

Only ignorant.
This is the time of hanging on for the bees – the bees
So slow I hardly know them,
Filing like soldiers
To the syrup tin

To make up for the honey I've taken.
Tate and Lyle keeps them going,
The refined snow.
It is Tate and Lyle they live on, instead of flowers.
They take it. The cold sets in.

Wintering by Sylvia Plath *continued*

Now they ball in a mass,
Black
Mind against all that white.
The smile of the snow is white.
It spreads itself out, a mile-long body of Meissen,

Into which, on warm days,
They can only carry their dead.
The bees are all women,
Maids and the long royal lady.
They have got rid of the men,

The blunt, clumsy stumblers, the boors.
Winter is for women –
The woman, still at her knitting,
At the cradle of Spanish walnut,
Her body a bulb in the cold and too dumb to think.

Will the hive survive, will the gladiolas
Succeed in banking their fires
To enter another year?
What will they taste of, the Christmas roses?
The bees are flying. They taste the spring

Essay

Compare Larkin's *Mr Bleaney* with Plath's *Wintering*

Paragraph 1: Quite a generalised thesis to begin, without any real sense of contrast.

[1] Within Larkin's *Mr Bleaney* and Plath's *Wintering*, both poets create a strong sense of mood through their descriptions of their surroundings. However, both poets differ between optimism and uncertainty in the assumptions they draw from their observations.

Paragraph 2: The lexical detail here clarifies what was missing from the opening paragraph. Now we can see a comparison of tone is developed.

[2] The semantic fields used by both poets are similar in terms of their negativism. Within *Mr Bleaney*, Larkin uses language such as 'thin … frayed … no room … frigid … fusty' to create a sense of blandness and squalor within his description. Similarly, Plath in *Wintering* utilises the words 'nothing … wintering … dark … black … decay … cruel' to similar effect. This highlights a very drab and dour mood created within both poems through the poets' descriptions of their surroundings.

Paragraph 3: Some sensible explanation of a distinction between Larkin's distanced view with Plath's more emotional response. There is brief evidence to support each view.

[3] However, both poets differ in their focus within the poem. Larkin focuses upon very mundane and ordinary objects within *Mr Bleaney*, such as 'Bed, upright chair, sixty-watt light bulb, no hook / behind the door' which contrasts with Plath's focus upon more emotional responses: 'appalling … possession … ignorant … clumsy'. The differing approaches undertaken by both poets highlight a contrasting theme: Larkin distances himself from Mr Bleaney by the very fact he is mainly unresponsive in the first section of his poem to his own thoughts and feelings about this room and prefers to highlight the ordinariness of the place: 'I know his habits'. This is a conscious contrast with Plath's more emotional and direct response to the 'bees' she observes: 'It is they who own me'. This in turn highlights Larkin's fear that maybe he glimpses something of himself within Bleaney; his overeagerness to rent the room – 'I'll take it' – for example, and so wishes to distance himself.

[4] Both poems also appear to exist within the same mood or season – winter. Within Plath's *Wintering*, she highlights the lethargy of the time through using words such as 'hanging on ... so slow ... clumsy stumblers ... boors' to create a very slow and melancholic mood within the poem. This coincides with Larkin in *Mr Bleaney* who includes 'whose windows shows a strip of building land ... Frinton folk ... shivered ... fusty bed ... tussocky' to create a very similar slumbering mood. The word 'Bleaney' itself highlights the blandness and boredom through the sound of the 'b' complemented by the 'y' sound at the end, which highlights the simplicity and common nature of this man.

[5] Whereas Larkin decides to use a male character, 'Bleaney', for the focus of his poem, Plath adopts a much more feminine focus and perspective. The phrases 'They have got rid of the men' and 'Winter is for women' emphasise that female focus and viewpoint which underpins the poem. Perhaps Plath associates winter with a sort of security and warmth – evidence such as 'ball in a mass', 'at her knitting' and 'the cradle' suggests this. This closeness is similarly found in *Mr Bleaney* where Larkin, like Plath, highlights the almost claustrophobic nature of the room, 'no room ... no hook ... lay on the fusty bed.' Both poets endeavour to create a closeness within the poem, something Plath describes as 'the room I could never breathe in'.

[6] Plath makes use of colour within *Wintering* to create a more potent image: 'Chinese yellow on appalling objects/Black asininity ... black bunched ... smile of the snow is white.' This in turn adds to the prevailing mood of the poem. White for Plath is usually associated with nothingness and emptiness, reflecting the emotions she feels within winter. In contrast, black is placed with words such as 'mass' and 'asininity' to create a much harsher image through collocation. Colours, however, are completely absent from *Mr Bleaney* which highlights the blandness of the surroundings. Where Larkin does describe 'flowered curtains' which suggest some character, he uses words such as 'thin and frayed' to dirty the image and make them appear neglected.

[7] A definite sense of loneliness and isolation are created within the two poems. Within Larkin's *Mr Bleaney* images such as 'the Frinton folk ... for summer holidays' and 'Christmas at his sister's house' emphasise a certain regularity and structure to this man's life – without variation. Within *Wintering* the same effect is created – 'wintering ... a dark without window ... no light ... heart of the house' which adds to the typical associations of coldness and isolation we attribute to winter. The effect this creates is that both poets feel a loneliness within themselves and seek to attach themselves to either 'Bleaney' or the 'bees' to distract themselves from monotony and isolation.

[8] Both poets endeavour within the latter halves of their poems to create a sense of sympathy. Larkin uses words like 'telling himself that this was home ... grinned ... shivered ... dread ... having no more to show' to create sympathy whereas Plath shows concern within the line 'Will the hive survive ... to enter another year?' Both Larkin and Plath demonstrate an emotional response to their surroundings within the two poems which highlights the sympathetic natures they wish to demonstrate, if only to describe the humanity of the situation.

Paragraph 4: A lexical and phonological contrast accurately made.

Paragraph 5: Several contrasts made – male/female; closeness/claustrophobia; attitudes to winter.

Paragraph 6: A contrast of imagery which is consistent with the idea of tone already developed earlier.

Paragraph 7: Lexical support for the shared mood of loneliness and islation.

Paragraph 8: An interesting variation on the theme focuses on audience response. Should the 'sense of sympathy' be more fully explained here? The textual support suggests we might pity Bleaney and the implied comparison is that we are on the side of the bees' struggle to survive, too.

Paragraph 9: A straightforward contrast of pessimistic and optimistic conclusions. The modified stance of 'I don't know' at the end of the Larkin poem surely deserves comment here, too.

Paragraph 10: This is a very successful structural and *syntactical* comparison. Note the way in which each point made at this stage of the essay is intended to support the thesis about a difference of tone and not random comparisons that occur as afterthoughts.

Paragraph 11: More structural support here though the absence of direct reference to lines in the poems diminishes the power of the assertions.

Paragraph 12: Sound, supported syntactical points.

Paragraph 13: This concludes a sequence of paragraphs in which structural devices are shown to support the initial thesis. Again, some evidence of the rhyming features discussed ought to be incorporated here.

Paragraph 14: A sound conclusion that reiterates the initial thesis having developed detailed support for it in the body of the essay.

[9] At the end of *Mr Bleaney* Larkin expresses uncertainty which addresses his rather negative assumption 'how we live measures our own nature … he warranted no better, I don't know.' This conclusion is almost critical of Bleaney, suggested by the 'warranted', which highlights how Bleaney had a hand in his own fate and chose this life. The pessimistic conclusion is rather different by comparison with Plath's ending. The images of 'Christmas roses … the bees are flying … they taste the spring' create an optimistic and bright ending, which contrasts with much of the negativism that precedes it where 'the cold sets in.'

[10] Another comparison between the two conclusions of the poems is the way they are structured by the poets. Larkin's final sentence comprises the last two stanzas which serve to draw the reader in by not placing a full stop anywhere. The last three lines of the poem contain no punctuation at all except for the comma used to highlight the uncertainty of the last three words, 'I don't know'. This pause before Larkin's final conclusion almost creates an anti-climax, ensuring that the uncertainty is highlighted. In contrast, Plath's syntax of the last line – a division into two separate sentences – forces an even greater pause within the conclusion. However, these pauses are different from Larkin's; his emphasise uncertainty while Plath's suggest clarity. The last line sounds very much like an assured and successive evaluation, contrasting with Larkin's doubtfulness.

[11] The stanzas of both poems are also similarly structured to emphasise a shift in mood. *Mr Bleaney* and *Wintering* both utilise stanzas as a form of progression within mood. In Larkin's poem, he is rather disdainful of Bleaney within the earlier stages and then moves on towards an almost compassionate ending. Similarly, Plath uses her stanzas to move away from a morose and sombre description towards a fresher and brighter final stanza. Larkin and Plath both wish to highlight a shift in mood and opinion by structuring their stanzas in such a way as to emulate a progression of thought.

[12] In general, Plath's sentences are rather shorter than Larkin's, including some sentences comprising only a single word – 'Decay./ Possession.' This contrasts with Larkin's longer and almost rambling sentences – 'Where Mr Bleaney lay … he egged her on to buy'. Through syntax, Plath sounds much more assured and clear than Larkin does in his longer sentences, which reaffirm his meditative and uncertain approach.

[13] Finally, Larkin makes use of a rhyme scheme (a/b/a/b) whereas Plath does not. This flowing and simple rhyme format reflects the monotonous and somewhat boring existence that Mr Bleaney led. However, a rhyme does serve to amalgamate and galvanise the thoughts of Larkin into a structure. Plath pays no attention to rhyme and adopts a more free-flowing approach, emphasising her more emotional response in relation to Larkin's rigidity.

[14] Larkin's *Mr Bleaney* and Plath's *Wintering* are similar in their creations of mood within the two poems but differ in the approaches and conclusions both poets adopt in order to finalise their poems, ensuring themes of isolation, boredom, sadness, optimism, uncertainty and assuredness are present within both.

Practical activity

Choose a theme of your own through which to compare the two poems *Mr Bleaney* and *Wintering* and write an opening paragraph which sets up a clear and interesting thesis that you could build on.

13 Writing about other genres

The principles developed in work on ELLA1 and ELLA2 are entirely relevant here so it should not be necessary to explain again the range of terminology that can be applied to extracts from novels, plays and short stories. There are general contextual differences that apply to different genres but these should emerge in the specific comparison of the textual extracts which you choose. For example, we may well get a considerable amount of character information in the stage directions of a play but we are more likely to judge characters by what they say, what is said to them, and what others say about them in the course of a play. Similarly, a novel, if, for instance, it is written in the first person, may appear to develop a limited and controlled view of the world from just one character's point of view but we, the readers, will still form our judgement of the characters in that novel independent of the narrator's attitudes. The point is that the genre does not dictate our response but it may use different means to provide it with information.

The framework grid we used to analyse poetry is still largely applicable to studying prose and drama but needs expanding here and there. Here's a slightly extended version for literature in general.

1	Beginnings	a	Subject/plot
		b	Theme
		c	Point of view/persona
		d	Narrative voice
		e	Context
		f	Audience
2	Manner	a	Tone
		b	Mood
		c	Register
3	Lexis	a	Semantic field
		b	Connotations
		c	Word classes
		d	Speech – direct/indirect
4	Metaphor	a	Imagery
		b	Metaphor/simile
		c	Symbolism
		d	Personification/apostrophe
		e	Oxymoron
5	Rhetoric		
	Phonological patterning:	a	Alliteration/assonance
		b	Onomatopoeia
		c	Rhyme
		d	Caesura/enjambement
	Structural patterning:	a	Repetition/listing
		b	Parallelism/antithesis
		c	Formal rhetoric

6 Grammar	a Levels of formality
	b Syntax/sentence structure
	c Tense/verb mood
	d Punctuation
7 Form	a Poetic form/structure
	b Metre/rhythm
	c Layout/graphology

💡 Close reading: writing about prose

Once again, you are presented here with excerpts from the set texts and invited to consider ways into analysis that might differ from the approaches we used in looking at poems. For the purposes of this section, we will not make comparisons but the techniques of comparing poetry with other genres will follow this section.

Let's begin by looking at the opening paragraphs of a modern novel. For all readers, the first task is always to try and work out what is going on. Will we get information about a central character in these opening lines? Will the events be chronological or are there time-lapses? What is happening to characters involved in these opening lines?

Extract 1: from *Hotel World* by Ali Smith

> Wooooooooo –
> hooooooo what a fall what a soar what a plummet
> what a dash into dark into light what a plunge what a
> glide thud crash what a drop what a rush what a swoop
> what a fright what a mad hushed skirl what a smash
> mush mash-up broke and gashed what a heart in my
> mouth what an end.
> What a life.
> What a time.
> What I felt. Then. Gone.
>
> Here's the story; it starts at the end. It was the height of
> the summer when I fell; the leaves were on the trees. Now
> it's the deep of the winter (the leaves fell off long ago) and
> this is it, my last night, and tonight what I want more
> than anything in the world is to have a stone in my shoe.
> To be walking along the pavement here outside the hotel
> and to feel a stone rattling about in my shoe as I walk, a
> small sharp stone, so that it jags into different parts of the
> sole and hurts just enough to be pleasure, like scratching
> an itch. Imagine an itch. Imagine a foot, and a pavement
> beneath it, and a stone, and pressing the stone with my
> whole weight hard into the skin of the sole, or against the
> bones of the bigger toes, or the smaller toes, or the inside
> curve of the foot, or the heel, or the small ball of muscle
> that keeps a body upright and balanced and moving
> across the breathtaking still-hard surface of the world.

Critical response activity

Answer the following questions to get yourself familiar with the passage from *Hotel World*. The answers to these questions might also form the basis to a commentary on the passage:

1 What contextual factors might you want to highlight since the passage is the opening section of the whole novel?

2 What sound qualities can you find in the first paragraph and what effects do they create?

3 What details about the narrator can you find in this extract?

4 What does 'Here's the story; it starts at the end.' tell us about the chronology of the novel?

5 Why does the narrator want to feel the pain of a stone in the shoe?

6 What is the effect of the detail about leaves falling from the trees?

7 Why is there so much close detail about the foot in the final paragraph?

8 Why is the imperative used in 'Imagine an itch.'

9 There are two meanings to 'what I want more than anything in the world'. What are they?

10 Comment on Smith's use of syntax in order to create a style.

Commentary

1 What contextual factors might you want to highlight since the passage is the opening section of the whole novel?

Obviously, all novelists attach a great deal of importance to the opening paragraphs of their novels in which they 'set the scene', but approaches vary greatly. They may, for instance, set the historical background or introduce a central character or create an atmosphere of suspense. Try not to generalise about narrative beginnings but refer specifically to the features of the text you are examining. Also, although you will have read this opening for the first time with some bewilderment, by the time you come to write about it, you will know what happens next (or in this case, before) and can explain the context. The opening here describes a fall by the narrator in which she climbed inside a dumb waiter (a hoist for moving food from the kitchen up to the top of the building) at the hotel in which she worked. The fall resulted in her death. However, we don't know all this yet and so are caught up in the immediacy of the fall itself. There are two peculiarities that need explaining. Firstly, the narrator is dead and recalling events that culminated in her death. Secondly, she appears to have been allowed a certain time in 'transit', as it were, in order to tell the story. It is as if both the body and the soul have separate voices. This situation allows for all kinds of surreal experiences but Smith decides to concentrate on getting the reader to share the intensity of her own experience as a preface to inviting us to continue the patterns of thought and feelings that her characters are experiencing throughout the novel.

2 What sound qualities can you find in the first paragraph and what effects do they create?

The first paragraph begins with a shriek that suggests the excitement of a roller coaster ride rather than panic. There follow all kinds of phonological effects that suggest the tumbling free fall motion of the plummeting dumb waiter. There is no punctuation to stem the flow and the repetition of 'what a ...' mimics the clattering sound of the falling dumb waiter. There is a great deal of onomatopoeia in this paragraph which includes the alliterative effects of the plosives in 'dash into dark' and the sibilants in 'smash mush mash-up'. The tumbling comes to a deafening halt and is replaced by temporary silences between the run of brief sentences which slow to single words:

> What a life.
> What a time.
> What I felt. Then. Gone.

3 What details about the narrator can you find in this extract?

This opening passage gives virtually no evidence at all about the narrator. Instead we are invited to feel the falling motion which, in turn, is an inducement to continue to sense the longings of the narrator in the paragraph about feet. The narrator is easing us into an appreciation of the sensations of life itself with such intense physical scrutiny in order to replicate a sense of what death might deprive us of.

4 What does 'Here's the story; it starts at the end.' tell us about the chronology of the novel?

By starting with the event that ends her life, the narrator establishes a framework in which all the experience of the novel is seen in flashback. It is a novel of causation in which the suspense is initially created by a need to know what this opening is describing and how it will affect what we read thereafter.

5 Why does the narrator want to feel the pain of a stone in the shoe?

Since the writer is deprived of life, she is also deprived of all the minutiae of feeling that life allows us. By choosing something that might be regarded as a minor irritation to most of us, she creates the sense that any feeling is valuable in that it means that we are alive. This establishes an atmosphere of hope and optimism in the face of what would be described as a great tragedy.

6 What is the effect of the detail about leaves falling from the trees?

The metaphor of leaves falling from the tree parallels the narrator's fall in the dumb waiter but also allows us to see the passing of time from the tragic event at the height of summer to the point at which the story is being told, which is in winter when all the leaves have fallen. The traditional symbolism of the seasons is given a new twist in order to create this unusual notion of the capacity for telling stories after death having a finite time (until the soul passes) and to give a sense of urgency ('my last night') in completing the tale.

7 Why is there so much close detail about the foot in the final paragraph?

As well as drawing our attention to the importance of the most minute details of feeling, the constant repetitions help to create an atmosphere of frustration which the audience is eager to have explained.

8 Why is the imperative used in 'Imagine an itch'?

The use of the imperative here encourages us to feel exactly the same emotions she might feel if she had feeling. The audience thus becomes a surrogate provider of that missing experience. It is a neat way to draw us further into the atmosphere established.

9 There are two meanings to 'what I want more than anything in the world'. What are they?

'I want more than anything in the world' is an idiomatic expression used to express desire. It is usually used hyperbolically, that is, in an exaggerated rhetorical way. A second sense, however, is that the narrator is literally deprived of 'anything in the world' since she is dead and this heightens the sense of longing for everyday emotions and feelings.

10 *Comment on Smith's use of syntax in order to create a style.*

There is a great variety of punctuation used here. After the unpunctuated rush of the first falling sentence, Smith uses elliptical brevity ('Then. Gone'). She has created a parallelism with three expressions ('What a life. What a time. What I felt.') that could equally have been left unpunctuated in the previous sentence. She does this in order to create a sound shift, a halting, but also to move from the present tense into the past (What I felt.'). This tactic is to prepare us for an explanation of this main event as an event in the past even though it has so far been expressed as a present event. It is a paradox that all the subsequent events in the novel combine to bring us towards this present moment. Even in the description of sensations about the feet there are elliptical sentences and full stops used where grammatically they ought not to be found ('To be walking ...') together with sentences with multiple clauses exploring the variety of potential experience in the feeling of a foot. The effect of this is to draw us in to the stream of consciousness mode of the narrator and allow us to be close to the movement of that thought process.

Extract 2: from *The Accidental Tourist* by Anne Tyler

> As much as he hated the travel, he loved the writing – the virtuous delights of organizing a disorganized country, stripping away the inessential and the second-rate, classifying all that remained in neat, terse paragraphs. He cribbed from other guidebooks, retrieving small kernels of value and discarding the rest. He spent pleasurable hours dithering over questions of punctuation. Righteously, mercilessly, he weeded out the passive voice. The effort of typing made the corners of his mouth turn down, so that no one could have guessed how much he was enjoying himself. I am happy to say, he pecked out, but his face remained glum and intense. *I am happy to say that it's possible now to buy Kentucky Fried Chicken in Stockholm*. Pita bread, too, he added as an afterthought. He wasn't sure how it had happened, but lately pita had grown to seem as American as hot dogs.

(Please note that the original US spelling has been retained in this extract)

Context

This paragraph serves as part of a character description of Macon Leary, the central character of the novel and introduces us to his job as a travel guide writer for businessmen who, like Macon, hate to travel. Since the paragraph occurs after we have learned two significant facts about him – that his wife has left him and his young son has been murdered – we are less disposed to laugh at him for his fussy habits. We are more prepared to see this essentially comic description as a device for inducing us to try and understand how his obsessive desire for control may have some advantages in enabling him to survive the trauma of recent events.

Note, first of all, that this contextualisation is essential to our reading. If this paragraph had appeared at the beginning of the novel, as the Ali Smith extract does, our reading of Macon's character might be harsher. We would be wondering what bearing his job had on the events that followed and we would not yet be clear how we are supposed to respond to Macon. Is his obsessive behaviour sinister, loveable or laughable? Is he more antagonist than protagonist? The novel's title *The Accidental*

Tourist might suggest a character who is accident-prone or thrown into an adventure against his will and our initial reading will be trying to establish which of these ideas is likely to be more true. Other events clearly have a bearing on the information given in this paragraph. By dipping into the novel elsewhere you will have noticed that Tyler's style might be described as 'affectionately satirical' or 'a mixture of comedy and tragedy in an everyday setting'. This general expectation might also influence our view of Macon.

■ Critical response activity

Here are some questions to assist your reading of the paragraph from *The Accidental Tourist*. The answers to these questions will form the basis of your commentary.

1 What is Tyler's purpose in including the list of activities that appear in the first sentence?

2 Why are these activities described as 'virtuous' rather than, say, 'essential'?

3 What is the effect of the phrase 'organizing a disorganized country'?

4 What clues to Macon's personality are shown in this pattern of verbs: 'organizing, stripping away, classifying, discarding, weeded out'?

5 What is the implication of contrasting lexis like 'cribbed' and 'dithering' with 'seizing small kernels of value' and 'righteously, mercilessly'?

6 Choose two other phrases in the paragraph that imply the same contrast.

7 Why would he 'weed out the passive voice'?

8 What is ironic about the inclusion of 'pita bread' as seeming 'American'?

9 The contrasts of the paragraph depend on the antithesis set up in the opening line. What is this contrast?

10 How do you feel about Macon by the end of the paragraph?

Commentary

1 What is Tyler's purpose in including the list of activities that appear in the first sentence?

The (**asyndetic**) listing serves to show how methodical and efficient Macon is. Had each activity been separated by 'and' (**syndetic** listing), the elongation and repetition of the pattern might have seemed more of a chore and less enjoyable to Macon.

2 Why are these activities described as 'virtuous' rather than, say, 'essential'?

The connotations of 'virtuous' imply a general good – that Macon is performing a service for humanity – and therefore considers himself above reproach. The irony is, of course, that Macon is involved in ripping all the curiosity and joy of travelling out of his guidebooks and replacing it with homogenous, unadventurous, Americanised pap. This is one of the central ironies of the whole novel. It is worth pointing out here that Macon's character is one who is unable to express emotions freely, who is anxious about change in his life and who takes no risks. It is a common expectation that the central character in a work of fiction will undergo change during the course of the novel and so this characterisation of Macon early on in the novel sets up the potential for his character's development and change. How will he learn to express his emotions and to take more risks in life? What or who will be the catalysts in this process?

3 *What is the effect of the phrase 'organizing a disorganized country'?*

It has a pleasing euphony (a smooth set of sounds) which suggests the busy hum of Macon's rather smug work habits. The contrast of the positive and negative versions of the same word (organise/disorganise) also reaffirms Macon's certainty that he is doing 'virtuous' work.

4 *What clues to Macon's personality are shown in this pattern of verbs: 'organizing, stripping away, classifying, discarding, weeded out'?*

There is a ruthless efficiency to these verbs that suggest Macon's power over his environment. Tyler very cleverly sets up a contrast between Macon's certainty he is doing worthwhile jobs and an alternative view that his attempts to control his world are laughable. We swing between seeing the world as he sees it through the use of these verbs and another view of a less impressive Macon in lexis like 'cribbed' and 'dithering'.

5 *What is the implication of contrasting lexis like 'cribbed' and 'dithering' with 'seizing small kernels of value' and 'righteously, mercilessly'?*

As shown above, 'cribbed' and 'dithering' describe an outsider's view of Macon's behaviour, whereas 'righteously, mercilessly' are of the same semantic field as 'organizing' and 'classifying' which give us Macon's version of his activities were he to articulate this view. His 'seizing small kernels of value' creates an image of him as a squirrel, carefully selecting good nuts from bad.

6 *Choose two other phrases in the paragraph that imply the same contrast.*

'The effort of typing made the corners of his mouth turn down' and 'no one could have guessed how much he was enjoying himself' imply the same contrast. There is a contrast here between the world's perception of Macon and an insight into his own view of the activity. This contrast works very well on many occasions in the novel as a description of a character whose emotional inwardness is often mistaken for a lack of humanity.

7 *Why would he 'weed out the passive voice'?*

The passive voice ('It was felt that') as opposed to the active voice ('I felt') is usually used to create a formal distance. It is the language of laws and instructions. Ironically, Macon thinks that by using expressions, such as 'I'm happy to say it's now possible', he is creating a personal touch to his writing, the purpose of which is actually to discourage personal involvement with other people when travelling.

8 *What is ironic about the inclusion of 'pita bread' as seeming 'American'?*

Another irony here is that the US is a nation formed of many nationalities all of whom bring their contributions to their new country. Pita bread is Greek in origin but more recently integrated into American culture than German hot dogs. Macon, however, is determined to steer American travellers away from any non-American experiences so it is amusing that he should accept pita bread as thoroughly American.

9 *The contrasts of the paragraph depend on the antithesis set up in the opening line. What is this contrast?*

The antithesis is 'he hated the travel, he loved the writing'. Throughout the paragraph there is a deliberate lexical contrast between Macon's pleasure at controlling his writing and his dislike for the uncontrollable experiences of travelling in foreign countries.

10 *How do you feel about Macon by the end of the paragraph?*

The answer to this question may be informed by how much of the novel you have read. It is hard to dislike Macon but already we may have learned to share the frustration of others who must deal with his reticence and emotional disengagement. Tyler is very careful not to allow too much sympathy for Macon at this stage so that we warm to him only gradually as we learn to appreciate his rather eccentric patterns of behaviour.

Extract 3: from 'The Invisible Japanese Gentlemen' by Graham Greene in *The Penguin Book of Modern British Short Stories*

She said, 'They are giving me an advance of five hundred pounds, and they've sold the paperback rights already.' The hard commercial declaration came as a shock to me; it was a shock too that she was one of my own profession. She couldn't have been more than twenty. She deserved better of life.

He said, 'But my uncle...'

'You know you don't get on with him. This way we shall be quite independent.'

'You will be independent,' he said grudgingly.

'The wine-trade wouldn't really suit you, would it? I spoke to my publisher about you and there's a very good chance...if you began with some reading...'

'But I don't know a thing about books.'

'I would help you at the start.'

'My mother says that writing is a good crutch...'

'Five hundred pounds and half the paperback rights is a pretty solid crutch,' she said.

'This Chablis* is good, isn't it?'

'I daresay.'

I began to change my opinion of him – he had not the Nelson touch. He was doomed to defeat. She came alongside and raked him fore and aft. 'Do you know what Mr Dwight said?'

'Who's Dwight?'

'Darling, you don't listen, do you? My publisher. He said he hadn't read a first novel in the last ten years which showed such powers of observation.'

'That's wonderful,' he said sadly, 'wonderful.'

*Chablis is a type of wine

This is an extract from a short story in which the writer, Graham Greene, eavesdrops on a young couple seated two tables away from him in a restaurant. Some Japanese diners are seated at the table, between the writer and the couple. The title, 'The Invisible Japanese Gentlemen', is an ironic reference by Greene to the fact that, despite being a writer (a profession which requires perceptiveness), the young woman about whom Greene is writing is so full of her own importance that she has failed to notice the presence of the Japanese gentlemen seated at the very next table to her. They are, therefore, 'invisible' to her.

Speech analysis

There is a good opportunity here to use the knowledge you have gained from your study of speech last year in ELLA2. Here's a reminder of some of the ways in which you can structure your approach to writing about speech:

■ Link

For more information on the analysis of speech in literary texts, look back at *English Language and Literature A AS*, Unit 2 Section A.

1 Beginnings	a Relationship	Who are the speakers and what is their relationship?
	b Formality	What is the context for the speech and how does it affect register and manner?
	c Topicality	Who controls the conversation? How does each speaker try to seize the 'topic'?
	d Structure	Is this just an excerpt of a longer conversation or is it complete? What is unresolved?
2 **Types of utterance (the purpose of speaking)** Note: It is possible for a conversation to show elements of all of these	a Phatic	Social chatter (remember that this can have an important function)
	b Expressive	Expressing feelings
	c Directive	Utterances that say 'Do this!'
	d Transactional	Getting something done
3 **Types of sentence (syntactic category)**	a Interrogative	Questions
	b Declarative	Statements
	c Exclamative	Exclaiming
	d Imperative	Sentences that give an instruction
4 **Structural devices (ways in which a conversation takes shape)**	a Adjacency pairs/ chaining	
	b Cooperation	
	c Deixis and referencing	
	d Discourse markers	
	e Back-channelling	
	f Emphasis	
	g Closing signals	
5 **Features of speaking (used in literary texts, too)**	a Contracted forms	
	b Ellipsis (omission of words)	
	c Elision/liaison/ juncture/contraction/ end-clipping (all phonological effects)	
	d Repetition	
	e Fillers	

In looking at this extract from the Graham Greene short story, begin with some of the key ideas: relationship, topicality and structure. These are all inter-related but modified by the fact that this is Greene's version of the conversation and he has the power to influence our perceptions of the characters with his occasional, interjected comments.

■ **Critical response activity**

Here are some questions to focus your ideas on the extract from *The Invisible Japanese Gentleman*, back on p122:

1 Who is in control of the topicality in this conversation?

2 Which two adverbs indicate the young man's defensive attitude to his girlfriend?

3 What structural evidence can you find of the young woman's influence over her boyfriend?

4 What syntactical evidence is there that this is a transactional exchange of utterances?

5 In Greene's comments about the young lady, what do you think he means by 'She deserved better of life'?

6 Greene uses a naval metaphor to describe the young man's weakness. What is it and why do you think Greene chooses it?

7 What is the purpose of the line 'This Chablis is good, isn't it?' in the passage?

8 What does the young man's reference to what his mother said about writing reveal to us about him?

9 What is your opinion of the young woman and on what in the passage is it based?

10 Although not mentioned in this passage, we are aware of the Japanese gentlemen seated between Greene and the young couple. What do you make of the positioning of this overheard conversation and how does it affect our view of the couple?

Commentary

1 Who is in control of the topicality in this conversation?

Clearly, the young woman is in charge of both the topic and the social interaction of the whole conversation. The topic on which she wishes to dwell is her future career and the benefits it will bring to both of them. Although we see a sequence of chained adjacency pairs, it is clear that the young man is uncomfortable with the picture her conversation paints of his future lack of independence in the relationship. Whenever he attempts to subvert her train of thought by trying to change the topicality ('But my uncle ...', 'My mother says ...', 'This Chablis is good ...'), she steps in to cut him short dismissively.

2 Which two adverbs indicate the young man's defensive attitude to his girlfriend?

They are 'grudgingly' and 'sadly'. These adverbs reveal his clear sense of failure to take control of the conversation and, indeed, the relationship.

3 What structural evidence can you find of the young woman's influence over her boyfriend?

It is important that the structure of the conversation begins with 'She said ...' By prefacing her 'hard commercial declaration' with 'She said' rather than ending her speech with it, Greene foregrounds her importance in the relationship. A glance at the passage shows that she says a good deal more than her boyfriend does and controls the topicality. Also, when ellipsis is indicated by three dots, in his case, it shows that she is cutting him off ('But my uncle ...' 'My mother ... a good crutch ...') and in her case, it indicates that the conclusion is self-evident and she does not consider she has to spell it out ('there's a very good chance ... if you began with some reading ...').

4 What syntactical evidence is there that this is a transactional exchange of utterances?

It is a transactional dialogue in the sense that the young woman wishes to achieve a business outcome from their conversation. Some of the syntactical constructions have been touched upon in the answer to question 3 above but you might also like to mention the use of tag questions. Because of the power difference in their relationship, when she adds 'would it?' or 'do you?' it is not to soften the preceding declarative but to reinforce it. By contrast, when he says' This Chablis is good, isn't it?' it is used as an appeal for agreement.

5 In Greene's comments about the young lady, what do you think he means by 'She deserved better of life'?

Greene's comments modify and influence the way we feel about the two characters. He has already indicated an unattractive materialist streak in the young woman, which is somehow made worse by the fact of her youth. He professes shock that she, like him, is a writer, presumably because it is not a profession in which material gain is the main motive. By saying 'She deserved better of life' he hints that she may be destined to suffer for her youthful confidence. To be a writer to Greene is to be a perpetual observer and recorder of life by instinct and, unlike many other professions, not to be concerned with material reward. The young woman, in her failure to observe the world around her, is likely to suffer as a writer in the future for this weakness.

6 Greene uses a naval metaphor to describe the young man's weakness. What is it and why do you think Greene chooses it?

The naval metaphor is 'She came alongside and raked him fore and aft'. It is prefaced by a reference to Nelson, the well-known naval hero. The young man is characterised as being attacked by a naval vessel because the conversation is clearly a kind of battle in which the outcome is extremely significant.

7 What is the purpose of the line 'This Chablis is good, isn't it?' in the passage?

'This Chablis is good, isn't it?' indicates an attempt by the young man to seize topicality in a conversation in which he is in danger of being obliterated. It might also indicate that he has a genuine interest in wine, something that she has been dismissive about because it counters her 'solution' to the problem of their future together. Her dismissive response, 'I daresay' also suggests that she has as little interest in wine as he does in books and this does not bode well for their future relationship.

8 What does the young man's reference to what his mother said about writing reveal to us about him?

We do not know exactly what he was going to say about writing but his girlfriend has naturally assumed it was derogatory. Perhaps he was about to say that writing might well support another career but not replace it for many people. Possibly, he knows so little about the world of writing that in quoting his mother he is at least able to express some kind of opinion. Perhaps the idea of his family creates security for him since he feels he is being undermined by his girlfriend's plans. All these possibilities combine to suggest a rather insecure personality which, in referring to the opinion of a member of his family, is looking for a refuge in a storm.

9 *What is your opinion of the young woman and on what in the passage is it based?*

Though Greene pretends to offer her sympathy in his comment, we are invited to dislike her for her aggressive materialism and for her dismissal of the young man's own potential. She has been seduced by the gushing praise of her publisher and will clearly stop at nothing to succeed. She assumes a false knowledge of her boyfriend ('You know you don't get on with him') and it is possible that all this bluster may exhibit a different approach to dealing with her own insecurity. Certainly, Greene emphasises the imbalance of the power struggle by declaring that the young man 'was doomed to defeat'.

10 *Although not mentioned in this passage, we are aware of the Japanese gentlemen seated between Greene and the young couple. What do you make of the positioning of this overheard conversation and how does it affect our view of the couple?*

At the very least it suggests Greene's remarkable powers of hearing and memory! It also indicates that the conversation of the young couple obliterated the conversation of the Japanese gentlemen and contrasts the coarseness and disregard of the young woman with the restraint and good manners of the Japanese gentlemen. This is heightened by the fact that the young woman, who has chosen a profession in which observation is central, has not even noticed her Japanese neighbours.

Writing your coursework essay

This chapter covers:

- how to compare two different modes of writing
- how to develop a finished essay
- a reminder of the key elements in a successful coursework essay.

This chapter contains the complete essay based on the earlier section in Chapter 11, How to choose an appropriate theme. In order to enable you to form your own opinions about the texts, all four sections discussed are provided here: the two poems by Robert Frost: *Mending Wall* and *The Death of the Hired Man*; and the two conversations between Willy Loman and his neighbour, Charley, from *Death of a Salesman*. Take your time reading through these extracts and poems, getting to know them and forming your own opinions BEFORE reading the essay that follows.

 Extracts

Poem 1: *Mending Wall* by Robert Frost

Something there is that doesn't love a wall,
That sends the frozen-ground-swell under it,
And spills the upper boulders in the sun;
And makes gaps even two can pass abreast.
The work of hunters is another thing
I have come after them and made repair
Where they have left not one stone on a stone
But they would have the rabbit out of hiding,
To please the yelping dogs. The gaps I mean,
No one has seen them made or heard them made
But at spring mending-time we find them there.
I let my neighbor know beyond the hill;
And on a day we meet to walk the line
And set the wall between us once again.
We keep the wall between us as we go.
To each the boulders that have fallen to each.
And some are loaves and some so nearly balls
We have to use a spell to make them balance:
'Stay where you are until our backs are turned!'
We wear our fingers rough with handling them.
Oh, just another kind of outdoor game,
One on a side. It comes to little more:
There where it is we do not need the wall:

He is all pine and I am apple orchard.
My apple trees will never get across
And eat the cones under his pines, I tell him.
He only says, 'Good fences make good neighbors.'
Spring is the mischief in me, and I wonder
If I could put a notion in his head:
'Why do they make good neighbors? Isn't it
Where there are cows? But here there are no cows.
Before I built a wall I'd ask to know
What I was walling in or walling out,
And to whom I was like to give offense.
Something there is that doesn't love a wall,
That wants it down.' I could say 'Elves' to him,
But it's not elves exactly, and I'd rather
He said it for himself. I see him there
Bringing a stone grasped firmly by the top
In each hand, like an old-stone savage armed.
He moves in darkness as it seems to me,
Not of woods only and the shade of trees.
He will not go behind his father's saying,
And he likes having thought of it so well
He says again, 'Good fences make good neighbors.'

Please note that the original US spelling has been retained in this poem

Poem 2: The Death Of The Hired Man by Robert Frost

Mary sat musing on the lamp-flame at the table
Waiting for Warren. When she heard his step,
She ran on tip-toe down the darkened passage
To meet him in the doorway with the news
And put him on his guard. "Silas is back."
She pushed him outward with her through the door
And shut it after her. "Be kind," she said.
She took the market things from Warren's arms
And set them on the porch, then drew him down
To sit beside her on the wooden steps.
"When was I ever anything but kind to him?
But I'll not have the fellow back," he said.
"I told him so last haying, didn't I?
'If he left then,' I said, 'that ended it.'
What good is he? Who else will harbour him
At his age for the little he can do?
What help he is there's no depending on.
Off he goes always when I need him most.
'He thinks he ought to earn a little pay,
Enough at least to buy tobacco with,
So he won't have to beg and be beholden.'
'All right,' I say, 'I can't afford to pay
Any fixed wages, though I wish I could.'
'Someone else can.' 'Then someone else will have to.'
I shouldn't mind his bettering himself
If that was what it was. You can be certain,
When he begins like that, there's someone at him
Trying to coax him off with pocket-money,—
In haying time, when any help is scarce.
In winter he comes back to us. I'm done."
"Sh! not so loud: he'll hear you," Mary said.
"I want him to: he'll have to soon or late."
"He's worn out. He's asleep beside the stove.
When I came up from Rowe's I found him here,
Huddled against the barn-door fast asleep,
A miserable sight, and frightening, too—
You needn't smile—I didn't recognise him—
I wasn't looking for him—and he's changed.
Wait till you see."
"Where did you say he'd been?"
"He didn't say. I dragged him to the house,
And gave him tea and tried to make him smoke.
I tried to make him talk about his travels.
Nothing would do: he just kept nodding off."
"What did he say? Did he say anything?"
"But little."
"Anything? Mary, confess
He said he'd come to ditch the meadow for me."
"Warren!"
"But did he? I just want to know."
"Of course he did. What would you have him say?
Surely you wouldn't grudge the poor old man
Some humble way to save his self-respect.
He added, if you really care to know,

He meant to clear the upper pasture, too.
That sounds like something you have heard before?
Warren, I wish you could have heard the way
He jumbled everything. I stopped to look
Two or three times—he made me feel so queer—
To see if he was talking in his sleep.
He ran on Harold Wilson—you remember—
The boy you had in haying four years since.
He's finished school, and teaching in his college.
Silas declares you'll have to get him back.
He says they two will make a team for work:
Between them they will lay this farm as smooth!
The way he mixed that in with other things.
He thinks young Wilson a likely lad, though daft
On education you know how they fought
All through July under the blazing sun,
Silas up on the cart to build the load,
Harold along beside to pitch it on."
"Yes, I took care to keep well out of earshot."
"Well, those days trouble Silas like a dream.
You wouldn't think they would. How some things linger!
Harold's young college boy's assurance piqued him.
After so many years he still keeps finding
Good arguments he sees he might have used.
I sympathise. I know just how it feels
To think of the right thing to say too late.
Harold's associated in his mind with Latin.
He asked me what I thought of Harold's saying
He studied Latin like the violin
Because he liked it—that an argument!
He said he couldn't make the boy believe
He could find water with a hazel prong—
Which showed how much good school had ever done him.
He wanted to go over that. But most of all
He thinks if he could have another chance
To teach him how to build a load of hay—"
"I know, that's Silas' one accomplishment.
He bundles every forkful in its place,
And tags and numbers it for future reference,
So he can find and easily dislodge it
In the unloading. Silas does that well.
He takes it out in bunches like big birds' nests.
You never see him standing on the hay
He's trying to lift, straining to lift himself."
"He thinks if he could teach him that, he'd be
Some good perhaps to someone in the world.
He hates to see a boy the fool of books.
Poor Silas, so concerned for other folk,
And nothing to look backward to with pride,
And nothing to look forward to with hope,
So now and never any different."
Part of a moon was falling down the west,
Dragging the whole sky with it to the hills.
Its light poured softly in her lap. She saw

And spread her apron to it. She put out her hand
Among the harp-like morning-glory strings,
Taut with the dew from garden bed to eaves,
As if she played unheard the tenderness
That wrought on him beside her in the night.
"Warren," she said, "he has come home to die:
You needn't be afraid he'll leave you this time."
"Home," he mocked gently.
"Yes, what else but home?
It all depends on what you mean by home.
Of course he's nothing to us, any more
Than was the hound that came a stranger to us
Out of the woods, worn out upon the trail."
"Home is the place where, when you have to go there,
They have to take you in."
"I should have called it
Something you somehow haven't to deserve."
Warren leaned out and took a step or two,
Picked up a little stick, and brought it back
And broke it in his hand and tossed it by.
"Silas has better claim on us you think
Than on his brother? Thirteen little miles
As the road winds would bring him to his door.
Silas has walked that far no doubt to-day.
Why didn't he go there? His brother's rich,
A somebody—director in the bank.
"He never told us that."
"We know it though."
"I think his brother ought to help, of course.
I'll see to that if there is need. He ought of right
To take him in, and might be willing to—
He may be better than appearances.
But have some pity on Silas. Do you think
If he'd had any pride in claiming kin

Or anything he looked for from his brother,
He'd keep so still about him all this time?"
"I wonder what's between them."
"I can tell you.
Silas is what he is—we wouldn't mind him—
But just the kind that kinsfolk can't abide.
He never did a thing so very bad.
He don't know why he isn't quite as good
As anyone. He won't be made ashamed
To please his brother, worthless though he is."
"I can't think Si ever hurt anyone."
"No, but he hurt my heart the way he lay
And rolled his old head on that sharp-edged chair-back.
He wouldn't let me put him on the lounge.
You must go in and see what you can do.
I made the bed up for him there to-night.
You'll be surprised at him—how much he's broken.
His working days are done; I'm sure of it."
"I'd not be in a hurry to say that."
"I haven't been. Go, look, see for yourself.
But, Warren, please remember how it is:
He's come to help you ditch the meadow.
He has a plan. You mustn't laugh at him.
He may not speak of it, and then he may.
I'll sit and see if that small sailing cloud
Will hit or miss the moon."
It hit the moon.
Then there were three there, making a dim row,
The moon, the little silver cloud, and she.
Warren returned—too soon, it seemed to her,
Slipped to her side, caught up her hand and waited.
"Warren," she questioned.
"Dead," was all he answered.

Please note that the original US spelling has been retained in this poem

First excerpt from *Death of a Salesman* by Arthur Miller (Act 1, pp32–4)

Charley: Everything all right?
Happy: Yeah, Charley, everything's...
Willy: What's the matter?
Charley: I heard some noise. I thought something happened. Can't we do something about the walls? You sneeze in here, and in my house hats blow off.
Happy: Let's go to bed, Dad. Come on.
(*Charley signals to Happy to go*)
Willy: You go ahead, I'm not tired at the moment.
Happy (*to Willy*): Take it easy, huh? (*He exits*)
Willy: What're you doin' up?
Charley (*sitting down at the kitchen table opposite Willy*): Couldn't sleep good. I had a heartburn.
Willy: Well, you don't know how to eat.
Charley: I eat with my mouth.
Willy: No, you're ignorant. You gotta know about vitamins and things like that.

Charley: Come on, let's shoot. Tire you out a little.
Willy (*hesitantly*): All right. You got cards?
Charley (*taking a deck from his pocket*): Yeah, I got them. Someplace. What is it with those vitamins?
Willy (*dealing*): They build up your bones. Chemistry.
Charley: Yeah, but there's no bones in heartburn.
Willy: What are you talkin' about? Do you know the first thing about it?
Charley: Don't get insulted.
Willy: Don't talk about something you don't know anything about. (*They are playing. Pause*)
Charley: What're you doin' home?
Willy: A little trouble with the car.
Charley: Oh. (*Pause*) I'd like to take a trip to California.
Willy: Don't say.
Charley: You want a job?
Willy: I got a job, I told you that. (*After a slight pause*) What the hell are you offering me a job for?
Charley: Don't get insulted.
Willy: Don't insult me.

Please note that the original US spelling has been retained in this extract

Second excerpt from *Death of a Salesman* by Arthur Miller (Act 2, pp68–71)

Willy: Let's go! (*He is starting out, with his arm around Biff, when Charley enters, as of old, in knickers*) I got no room for you, Charley.
Charley: Room? For what?
Willy: In the car.
Charley: You goin' for a ride? I wanted to shoot some casino.
Willy (*furiously*): Casino! (*Incredulously*) Don't you realize what today is?
Linda: Oh, he knows, Willy. He's just kidding you.
Willy: That's nothing to kid about!
Charley: No. Linda, what's going' on?
Linda: He's playing in Ebbets Field.
Charley: Baseball in this weather?
Willy: Don't talk to him. Come on, come on! (*He is pushing them out*)
Charley: Wait a minute, didn't you hear the news?
Willy: What?
Charley: Don't you listen to the radio? Ebbets Field just blew up.
Willy: You go to hell! (*Charley laughs*) (*Pushing them out*) Come on, come on! We're late.
Charley (*as they go*): Knock a homer, Biff, knock a homer!
Willy (*the last to leave, turning to Charley*): I don't think that was funny, Charley. This is the greatest day of his life.
Charley: Willy, when are you going to grow up?
Willy: Yeah, heh? When this game is over, Charley, you'll be laughing out of the other side of your face. They'll be calling him another Red Grange. Twenty-five thousand a year.
Charley (*kidding*): Is that so?
Willy: Yeah, that's so.
Charley: Well, then, I'm sorry, Willy. But tell me something.
Willy: What?
Charley: Who is Red Grange?
Willy: Put up your hands. Goddam you, put up your hands!

(Charley, chuckling, shakes his head and walks away, around the left corner of the stage. Willy follows him. The music rises to a mocking frenzy)

Willy: Who the hell do you think you are, better than everybody else? You don't know everything, you big, ignorant, stupid....put up your hands!

Please note that the original US spelling has been retained in this extract

Sample essay

Compare the ways in which Frost and Miller explore conflict in human relationships

[1] The main focus of this comparison is the relationship between neighbours and the ways in which those close social relationships demand compromise. In *Death of a Salesman*, the relationship between Willy and his neighbour Charley is fraught with conflict and two short passages from the play demonstrate this clearly. In Frost's *Mending Wall*, two neighbours with very different attitudes to life come into conflict and, in one of Frost's longer poems, *Death of the Hired Man*, conflicts exist between the husband and wife over their dealings with, Silas, the Hired Man and in Silas's conflict with a younger worker and with his own wealthy brother within the story of the poem.

Paragraph 1: This opening contextualises the focus of the essay. 'Conflict in human relationships' has been made more precise by the focus on how neighbours with different attitudes must compromise in order to resolve their differences.

[2] Metaphorically, walls play a major role in both poems and in the excerpts from *Death of a Salesman*. While Charley is attempting to break down the walls between himself and his neighbour by offering him a job, Willy is determined to block out Charley's overtures by creating walls. Charley says to Willy, when he is awakened by Willy's ranting, 'Can't we do something about the walls?' The symbolically oppressive 'solid vault of apartment houses' in which they live creates tensions that must be overcome. Both Frost and Miller convey these human conflicts through their manipulation of language and in the contrast of attitudes that is expressed through that manipulation.

Paragraph 2: The writer is aware of the metaphorical expression of these conflicts. We have a clear sense that some kind of comparison has been established but by the third paragraph we are hoping for something a little more precise.

[3] In *Mending Wall*, Frost sets up a binary opposition of attitudes between the persona of the poem and his neighbour. They meet each year to rebuild the wall between their two farms. The 'I' of the poem believes fiercely, 'Something there is that doesn't love a wall'. So much so that it is the opening line of the poem. He repeats this line later in the poem. It is a stance that allies him with some inexplicable supernatural force that is personified in the first few lines. This 'something' sends the 'frozen-ground-swell', 'spills the upper boulders' and 'makes gaps' in the wall – the dynamic verbs emphasising the presence of a kind of unseen mischief-maker. It is this sense of mischief that the persona takes on to goad his neighbour with. This neighbour believes equally strongly that 'Good fences make good neighbours'. He doesn't know why. He just knows that his father taught him this truth and he is charged with defending its wisdom. He, too, repeats this mantra later in the poem so the two attitudes are part of the antithetical structuring of the poem. The inability of each to see the other's point of view is symbolised by the line 'We keep the wall between us as we go' and the perfectly balanced syntax of the ensuing 'To each the boulders that have fallen to each'.

Paragraph 3: There is plenty of literary/linguistic analysis here. There is always a balance to be struck in such an essay between developing analytical points thoroughly and maintaining an integrated analysis at the same time. Has this writer got this balance right or are we spending too long on one text?

[4] Frost writes in a loose iambic pentameter here, an unrhymed blank verse. The need to retain the iambic feel of the metre partly explains some of the odd syntactical reversals ('something there is' rather than the more natural 'there is something' and 'like an old-

Paragraph 4: More pertinent analysis that is establishing a wide range of frameworks but we still haven't heard about *Death of a Salesman*.

stone savage armed' rather than 'armed like an old-stone savage') but it creates another effect, too. Frost wants us to accept the presence of a mischievous supernatural presence that is moving the walls and so this archaic sentence structure, in which the main verb 'is' is delayed and the adjective 'armed' is suspended beyond the simile of the 'old-stone savage', suggests a language of archaic syntax that is in keeping with a pre-civilised world of elves and savages. The presence of 'Elves' justifies the inexplicable chaos of the fallen stones and the likening of his neighbour to a prehistoric archetype, the 'old-stone savage', serves the same purpose.

Paragraph 5: Clearly the candidate has plenty to say about this poem and there is no doubt that it is related to 'human conflict' but the comparative element is now beginning to suffer.

[5] The narrator's argument is that walls are to keep cattle apart and since 'He is all pine and I am apple orchard' the wall has no useful purpose. Of course, the use of the first person pronoun 'I' throughout allows the persona an unfair advantage in the argument with his neighbour. We are privy to his inner monologue as well as the things he says to his neighbour, so he has the chance to justify his argument. This argument is essentially logical and anti-traditional but it is a feature of Frost's poetry that 'walls' are never just walls, they serve as a symbol for human difference, just as pines and apple trees are not just trees but representative of human types. The pine (his neighbour) is aloof, evergreen and, therefore, unchanging while the persona is 'apple orchard' – sociable, productive, deciduous and redolent of the passion of the Garden of Eden. The argument of the poem is that it is the persona who (a) instigates the rebuilding ('I let my neighbour know'); yet (b) doesn't regard the job as serious or necessary ('just another kind of outdoor game'); and (c) wants to tease his neighbour into recanting the need for walls ('Spring is the mischief in me'). He enlists the supernatural to support him in this. The supernatural is personified throughout the poem and this produces a contrastive argument leading to two polarised semantic fields. The first field is lively, mischievous and unseen ('something', 'sends', 'spills' 'spell', 'spring', 'mischief', 'elves' – note the playful whispering sibilance of the 's' here). The second is stodgily pragmatic, unchanging and defiant ('wall', 'repair', 'mending-time', 'rough' ,'cones', 'fences', 'stone', 'grasped firmly', 'darkness'). You can hear the stubborn digging sounds in the long vowels and scraping end consonants in this second list.

Paragraph 6: There is a comparison made at last. Perhaps the candidate might improve this essay simply by moving this paragraph more towards the beginning. In that way, the comparison is implied straightaway. The necessary contextualisation of this paragraph would then match that of *Mending Wall*.

[6] The relationship between Willy and his neighbour Charley is also based on a conflict. In this case, Willy's exhausted despair had heightened his aggression towards a man to whom he clearly feels inferior. It is Willy's credo that 'being well-liked' is everything to a salesman but he is incapable of following it through with his own neighbour. This is because Charley is everything Willy isn't. He is 'a large man' to whom Willy is constantly comparing himself and falling short. One telling stage direction reveals that Charley is 'in all he says, despite what he says, there is pity'. Charley wants to give Willy a job but Willy is too proud to be able to take it and concede this power to his neighbour. We see a similar pride in *The Death of the Hired Man*, in Silas' reticence to approach his brother who is 'rich,/A somebody – director in the bank'. Silas, says Warren, is 'just the kind that kinsfolk can't abide' and this is true of neighbours like Willy, too. The stubborn pride of those who are closest to us is always a block to successful relationships.

[7] Charley's first appearance comes early in the play when Willy has returned from a failed trip. Happy has unsuccessfully tried to calm his exhausted father and it is Charley who has to make the effort to settle him down in the middle of the night. This is a delicate manoeuvre. Willy is child-like in his self-absorption and failure to see the subtleties

in language. His greatest failing is his total lack of a sense of humour. Charley, by contrast, is a grown-up who must ride the insults that Willy throws at him and not take offence. Later in the play, Charley asks Willy 'when are you going to grow up?' Willy has locked himself into a cage of immature slogans about the life of a salesman, all of which have let him down.

[8] A close look at their first meeting reveals a sequence of exchanges in which Charley must use cunning and subterfuge to lull the 'baby' to sleep. He suggests that it was heartburn that kept him awake, thus shifting the responsibility for their sleeplessness away from Willy. The adjacency pairings suggest an old friendship in which seeming insults are sent back and forth without much offence being taken:

Charley: Don't get insulted.
Willy: Don't talk about something you don't know anything about.
and later:
Charley: Don't get insulted.
Willy: Don't insult me.

The neat parallelism of these constructions, all imperatives, shows a pattern of behaviour that is so often repeated that the insult implied has almost entirely lost its force.

[9] Charley's strategy is to subjugate himself to Willy's control so that he might be in a better position to launch his offer of a job on a more compliant Willy later on. But Willy is a hard nut to crack. Charley proposes a game of cards, complains about heartburn, asks about vitamins, expresses his wish to go to California, all as deflective devices to engage with Willy and to tire him out a little. His job offer, when it comes, is rebuffed, as it always is:

Charley: You want a job?
Willy: I got a job, I told you that … What the hell are you offering me a job for?

This final question, like many in their exchange, is not seeking information. The use of interrogatives here ('What are you talkin' about? Do you know the first thing about it?' 'What's the difference?' 'Then what the hell are you bothering me for?') allows Willy to disallow the value of anything Charley says to him and retain, as he sees it, the upper hand. Just occasionally, Willy will speak the truth ('I got nothin' to give him, Charley. I'm clean.') and when Charley's advice is dismissed ('That's easy enough for you to say'), Charley retorts with 'That ain't easy for me to say'. This antithetical structure contrasts Willy's dismissiveness with the serious understanding about life that Charley has and Willy lacks. Charley's son, Bernard, is 'gonna argue a case in front of the Supreme Court' while Willy's boys are likened to broken deposit bottles for which 'you don't get your nickel back'.

[10] In *The Death of the Hired Man*, Frost examines the obligations of a farming couple, Warren and Mary, to an old itinerant farmhand, Silas. There is conflict because, despite Warren's kindness, Silas has often let him down ('Off he goes always when I need him most') yet Mary pleads on Silas' behalf.

[11] The poem is like a short story in its narrative thrust. Although Frost employs his familiar loose unrhyming iambic pentameter throughout, the poem is essentially a conversation and so comparable to the exchanges between Willy and Charley in *Death of a Salesman*. Willy and Charley, in the Act 2 extract, may appear to converse in straightforward question and answer adjacency pairs:

Paragraphs 7–9: This is an effective analysis of conversation and takes advantage of the candidate's knowledge of Unit 2 frameworks. It is worth considering how you might best utilise the range of your knowledge in selecting your texts.

Paragraphs 10–11: This is a better integrated comparative passage, moving between Miller and Frost with relative ease.

Willy: I got no room for you, Charley.
Charley: Room? For what?
Willy: In the car.

However, there is a humorous goading of Willy by Charley who pretends to know nothing about football in order to expose Willy's excessive seriousness as laughable ('I don't think that was funny, Charley'). Though less humorous, Warren's response to Mary's pleading is a series of defensive questions:

"When was I ever anything but kind to him?
But I'll not have the fellow back," he said.
"I told him so last haying, didn't I?
'If he left then,' I said, 'that ended it.'
What good is he? Who else will harbour him
At his age for the little he can do?

This contrasts his practical reasoning with Mary's more emotional pleading on Silas' behalf ('He's worn out. He's asleep behind the stove.').

Paragraph 12: The candidate is making up now for some of the unspecified comparison of the early part of the essay. Although there are fewer literary/linguistic points made, the comparison is clear.

[12] The human conflict inherent in all relationships is explored in the mention of Silas' rich brother ('A somebody – director in the bank') whom Silas is too proud to approach for help. It's also there in the clash between Silas' old ways and the ways of the young student, Harold Wilson. This parallel is very similar to the neighbours' relationship in *Mending Wall* and to the wariness of the Willy/Charley relationship. Silas has skills ('He could find water with a hazel prong' and 'build a load of hay'). Harold, however, is 'daft on education' and has 'studied Latin'. Just as Willy thinks Charley has no respect for him, so Silas dwells on young Harold's refusal to acknowledge Silas' own wisdom. Mary says 'I know just how it feels/ To think of the right thing to say too late' as Silas has done, and this is a universal sentiment.

Paragraph 13: Clearly focused on the topic and perhaps giving a little more contextualisation to the relationship.

[13] Charley knows well that the football game in which Biff is playing is the biggest day in Willy's life and perhaps is showing poor timing by taking some of the pomp and ceremony out of the occasion. Even Linda can see it's a joke but, typically, Willy doesn't understand this ('That's nothing to kid about!'). Charley plays the scene like a comedy routine with Willy as the stooge and the source of the neighbours' tension is exposed in Willy's line – 'Who the hell do you think you are, better than everybody else?' This shows his inferiority complex and exposes the roots of the tension between Willy and Charley.

Paragraph 14: Further information about the relationships. This candidate feels the need to explain context in order to demonstrate an argument properly. Are we losing the balance between analysis, comparison and context here a little?

[14] There is a contrast between the hushed whispers of Warren and Mary and the loud, taunting exchanges between Willy and Charley. The former, a husband and wife, are considering difficult moral decisions. Silas has clearly designated them as 'home' and they do not want to hurt his feelings ('Sh! Not so loud: he'll hear you'). The conversation is a realistic mixture of short sentences, sometimes simulating the repetitions of spontaneous speech ('What did he say? Did he say anything?'), and elliptical responses ('He didn't say'/ 'But little.'). There is a tension that arises from the need to make rapid decisions so that the conversation is urgent and the topicality is dominated by Silas' state of health. Mary leads the topic in relating her findings to Warren ('Silas is back') but, after his initial defensiveness, he begins to mock Silas' ambitions ('Confess he said he'd come to ditch the meadow for me') and Mary shames Warren to a halt ('Warren!') after which they share their reminiscences of the man.

Paragraph 15: Some restoration of the comparative framework here.

[15] Willy and Charley, however, are old rivals. In a commercial world in which display is important, Willy is always sparring with

his neighbour. Unfortunately, Charley is too clever for him. On two occasions in the second extract, Willy responds to Charley's set-up by asking, 'What?' to questions that are only designed to make fun of his seriousness. It is a mark of Willy's failure to 'grow up' that he challenges Charley to a fight ('Put up your hands.') because he is incapable of matching Charley's wit or irreverence. Like the conversation in *The Death of the Hired Man*, there is a great seriousness underlying the relationship that has been established over many years. However, whilst the husband and wife relationship of Warren and Mary is conciliatory and sensitive to difficulties, the relationship between Willy and Charley is wary and defensive on Willy's part and full of subtle amelioration on Charley's.

[16] There is a symbolic use of light and dark in both texts. Frost begins with the contrast of Mary in the 'lamp-flame' and then in 'the darkened passage'. While Warren remembers Silas fighting 'under the blazing sun' and goes to make manly negotiations with Silas, Mary sits where:

> 'Part of a moon was falling down the west,
> Dragging the whole sky with it to the hills.
> Its light poured softly in her lap. She saw
> And spread her apron to it.'

The male qualities of action and physical work are embodied in the 'blazing sun', while the moon represents the imagination and nurturing of the feminine Mary. It is precisely the outcome of the traditional battle between these two forces that will settle their decision about Silas' future.

[17] Miller's stage directions make much of similar imagery. He contrasts 'the blue light of the sky' with 'the angry glow of orange' emanating from the 'solid vault' of apartment houses. The contrast between the natural possibility of the blue and the oppressive unnatural 'orange' of the compressed living spaces provides a background to the tensions that inevitably exist between neighbours in a crowded world. The echo of the past is always redolent of a world that was free and spacious whereas now it is cramped and hopeless. Much of this symbolism colours the tensions between Willy and his neighbour.

[18] Miller and Frost share an American background and are both concerned with the encroachment of city life on the traditions and freedom of the countryside. This is reflected in the contrast of attitudes: Ben's enterprise in Alaska with Willy's confined hopes in New York; Warren and Mary's traditional neighbourly obligations with the newer 'educated' attitudes of Harold Wilson (in *The Death of the Hired Man*) and the persona of *Mending Wall*; and Charley's kindly, sometimes playful, support of Willy with Willy's dogmatic commercial ambitions.

Paragraph 16: Analysis and comparison are better integrated here through the comments on symbolism.

Paragraph 17: The discussion of symbolism is extended to include Miller's stage directions.

Paragraph 18: Some final relationship contrasts in order to bring the discussion together.

Examiner's comments on the essay as a whole

There are times in this essay when the comparative framework is sacrificed in order to develop a closer analysis and fuller contextualisation. The close analysis here is of a varied kind but on occasions a more integrated comparative approach might have improved the final effect.

15 Mark band descriptors: understanding the way the examiner reads your coursework essay

This chapter covers:

- how to get inside the mind of the examiner

- how to differentiate between effective and ineffective writing

- how to show the qualities the examiner is looking for.

☑ Some understanding of the language of mark descriptors is often helpful in determining why an essay is not regarded more highly than it is. What follows is an explanation of the Assessment Criteria for coursework and, in a close analysis of a Grade E essay, how those band descriptors are used.

Mark band descriptors (AO1)

To be placed in a particular mark band, it is not necessary for a candidate to demonstrate achievement under every point. Internal assessment should therefore assess a candidate's work under the 'best fit' principle.

Band 5 (26–30)	■ Use of framework(s) enhances and illuminates textual interpretation ■ Has an overview of the text ■ Engages closely with the meaning of the texts; patterns analysed ■ Conceptualised analysis ■ Fluent, cogent writing
Upper band 4 (23–25)	■ Coherent analysis through the framework(s); some analytical probing of features and patterns ■ Thoughtful engagement with texts ■ Interpretation evident through approach taken ■ Fluent writing
Lower band 4 (20–22)	■ Uses framework(s) to highlight reading ■ Describes significant features/patterns ■ Awareness of stylistic and linguistic features ■ Engages with texts through explanation of features; possibly underdeveloped in places ■ Clear and appropriate writing
Upper band 3 (16–19)	■ Uses a suitable framework(s) ■ Evidence of some range ■ Sense of patterns may emerge in places; likely to be under-developed; may use different approaches for literary/linguistic study; able to distinguish between different features fairly accurately but may be unable to comment on effect of features ■ Clear, but straightforward, expression
Lower band 3 (12–15)	■ Identification through framework(s); shows some of writer's choices within the text ■ List-like but sound ideas ■ Broad comments on effects and stylistic points ■ Aware different modes need approaching in different ways but may do so in simplistic fashion ■ Straightforward expression with some errors

Upper band 2 (9–11)	■ Simplistic ■ Attempts to use framework(s) but likely to be limited ■ Identifies some points ■ Limited analysis occurs ■ Some awareness of the focus of a text ■ Common sense approach but does not discuss how language works ■ Underdeveloped writing
Lower band 2 (7–8)	■ Scattergun approach to analysis ■ Little apparent planning with probably no use of framework(s) ■ Implicit views of language use ■ Superficial ideas ■ Muddled expression with very few relevant ideas
Band 1 (1–6)	■ Little awareness ■ Possible framework misconceptions ■ Weak writing ■ No apparent direction ■ Very wayward ■ Persistent misuse of terms ■ Inaccuracies abound

■ Mark band descriptors (AO3)

To be placed in a particular mark band, it is not necessary for a candidate to demonstrate achievement under every point. Internal assessment should therefore assess a candidate's work under the 'best fit' principle.

Band 5 (26–30)	■ Assimilates and contextualises references with originality ■ Total overview that may offer observations on wider contexts ■ Exploratory ■ Significant similarities and differences are analysed and in an original, personal, or conceptual, manner ■ Texts effortlessly integrated
Upper band 4 (23–25)	■ Skilful and secure analysis and commentary ■ Clear sense of context/variation/contextual influences underpins reading ■ Close focus on texts ■ Coherently compares and contrasts writers' choices of form, structure, mode, language ■ Confident comparison
Lower band 4 (20–22)	■ Expresses clearly comparisons and contrasts between two texts ■ Clear interplay between text and context/sense of contextual variation ■ Comments clearly on a variety of points/areas ■ Analysis may be imbalanced; may use anchor text; possible imbalance in text coverage
Upper band 3 (16–19)	■ Context commented on ■ Points are made but not clearly developed ■ Analysis may show implicit meanings ■ Some comment on language use in texts ■ Imbalance in coverage

Lower band 3 (12–15)	■ Comparative framework(s) used but may be partial/simplistic ■ Develops a line of argument underpinned by comment on overall context ■ Probably list-like in construction ■ Imbalance in coverage of texts ■ Lacks evidence in places
Upper band 2 (9–11)	■ May see how context influences language use ■ General awareness of writers' techniques and impact on meaning ■ Responds to obvious or broad links or comparisons ■ Sometimes comments on less important links ■ May lack detail and evidence
Lower band 2 (7–8)	■ Superficial idea of context ■ Occasional insight but not sustained ■ One area of study noted, others are ignored ■ Lacks detail and probably little evidence used
Band 1 (1–6)	■ Very little awareness of context ■ Very limited ideas ■ Very superficial ■ Contextual features identified erroneously/misreads ■ Weak ideas

The descriptors above are crystallised in the following comments from a Principal Examiner's Report:

Candidates who score highly on AO1 will:

■ demonstrate a thoughtful *focus* on the theme selected
■ maintain a *close reading* of the texts through *careful illustration* of points
■ show a *clear and detailed knowledge* of the texts
■ use a *range of literary* and *linguistic terms* accurately
■ consider the *effects* of the language devices used
■ express their *ideas fluently* and with *technical accuracy*.

Candidates who score highly on AO3 will:

■ make an *integrated comparison* of the texts chosen
■ *use contextual detail unobtrusively*.

In order to understand the difference between an A, C and E grade in the A2 coursework paper it is necessary to:

1 have some idea of the relationship between bands and actual grades
2 be clear about some of the expressions used in the Band Descriptors.

Sample essay which may achieve grade E/U

So far, we have only considered A grade essays in the exemplar material. But what are the qualities of an E grade essay? What does it lack that prevents it from scoring higher? We need to begin by looking at the kind of essay that is right on the borderline of grades E and U. Typically, such an essay may have patches of good writing but will lack the consistency expected of an essay at a higher grade.

By looking at a borderline E/U essay, it will be possible to point out at the end of each paragraph how the language of the band descriptors is used to establish the overall quality of the essay and the ways in which it might be improved in order to get a better grade. Detailed examiner comments follow each of the paragraphs from the essay below. By looking at the comments and thinking about the ways in which you might improve the essay yourself, you will be in a good position to understand how the grading system works.

Compare the ways in which Larkin and Plath express their views on life

[1] Both Larkin and Plath express their views on life through describing a particular place. However, Larkin tends to express his view in a more literal and obvious way, often using people to emphasise this. For example, in *Mr Bleaney* or *The Large Cool Store*, Larkin describes other people's lives – often strangers – from a negative and critical viewpoint, whereas Plath often uses metaphors when expressing her view on life to relate to close family members, particularly her mother which she often refers to as the 'Moon' in her poetry.

[2] In Philip Larkin's *The Large Cool Store* he emphasises the ordinary, mundane lives of the working class through his use of dull adjectives – 'cheap', 'simple', plainly'. He also does this through his use of imagery of the working class being dictated by time ('timed for factory') and all being the same ('low terraced houses'), which emphasises his negative, critical attitude towards living a normal life. This contrasts with Plath's view in *The Munich Mannequins* in which she is very critical of these mannequins – 'terrible' – who promote an ideal image of a woman being perfect due to the fact it is not the way every woman looks. She sees the main duty is a woman's duty to her children – 'blood flood' – which is a stereotypical view and something which women do normally.

Paragraph 1: This is not a bad start at all. There is a clear thesis made about 'place' and a contrast made between literal and metaphorical expression. We have two nominated poems by Larkin for illustrative purposes but no indication yet of which Plath poems will be considered other than those about her mother. This beginning is better than an 'E' grade and comments from the Band Descriptors might appropriately include 'establishes a sense of framework' and 'indicates a comparative approach', both of which indicate a possible D or even C grade essay. However, we need to go further before deciding whether this essay is going to give a 'close focus on the texts' or 'develop a line of argument'. Without clear support for the thesis established, the sound beginning may give way to something much less impressive.

Paragraph 2: Although this second paragraph does give some illustrations for contrast, they are very brief and not clearly contextualised. For instance, what do 'cheap' and' simple' refer to? There is a grammatical point made about word class, although 'plainly' is not an adjective but an adverb. This exposes the candidate's insecure knowledge about grammar, or at the very least it is a careless slip. The contrast between Larkin's and Plath's imagery is, however, not at all clear and the expression of ideas is becoming imprecise and vague. For instance, why does 'low terraced houses' indicate 'a negative, critical attitude towards living a normal life'? Seeing Larkin's choice of language as purely 'negative' is a very lazy and dismissive way to approach his poems and is an error that many candidates make. The idea of what is 'normal' is repeated by the candidate at the end of the paragraph. The point made is that women 'normally' have babies but more comment would be needed to establish how Plath might make a contrast between perfect and normal women. So, there is some implicit awareness that there is a contrast set up between the everyday (normal) and the idealised, but it is not clearly stated. This 'implicit' reference is a common feature of essays in the Lower Band 3 section.

The two poems considered are well chosen, though, and could be very usefully compared since their common theme is the stark contrast between 'perfection' and our everyday experience. The candidate does not take advantage of this, though, and reference to a single word – 'terrible' – in the Plath poem is making very poor use of the metaphorical ideas suggested in the opening paragraph.

[3] This critical persona Plath adopts in *The Munich Mannequins* is similar to Larkin's *Here* in which he is again negative towards people living in the town of Hull: 'plate-glass windows swing doors to their desires', suggesting this is the limit of their ambitions. However, Plath does this in a more obvious way through her use of dramatic words – 'sacrifice' 'terrible' – and far-fetched mocking imagery: 'orange lollies on silver sticks', suggesting that this is something Plath has a very strong disdain for and opinion on. Whereas Larkin uses the negative imagery of the town to reflect his negative imagery of the people who live there which is not as direct as Plath: 'cheap suits, red kitchen-ware', 'raw estates'.

Paragraph 3: The detail in this paragraph is rather better. Both poets are seen as critical, but Larkin is again 'negative' about people while Plath uses 'dramatic words' (again not contextualised) and 'far-fetched mocking imagery'. This argument is consistent with the opening thesis about Plath's use of metaphor, although the reader is beginning to realise that this candidate uses a 'comparative framework which may be partial or simplistic' and is showing strong signs of being in the Lower Band 3 section of marks for AO3 and perhaps, because of the 'broad comments on effects and stylistic points', is in the same area for AO1, too.

Paragraph 4: This paragraph shows a clear example of lazy quotation with a lack of relevant context. Larkin's poem refers to clothes being arranged in 'simple sizes'. The meaning of 'simple' here is 'easy to understand'. The candidate makes the mistake of decontextualising the word and suggesting, wrongly, that this is a criticism of working-class people. This would have been less worrying if the candidate had gone on to explain in what way this was a criticism. Does it suggest they are all stupid and need simple instructions? If so, stating that would at least support an interpretation. It is more likely that 'simple' is intended as a word that shows how easily we are all drawn towards the superficial attractions by our 'young unreal wishes'. The contrast with *Balloons* is a fair one and the comparison of colour imagery is effective. Even here, though, the Larkin quotation isn't quite accurate. It should read 'In browns and greys, maroon and navy'. This error is not an important one in that the sense is not manipulated wrongly, but an examiner looking for 'close reading with a careful illustration of points' would be aware of these little slips as they accumulate and would be very reluctant to think of this essay as a 'thoughtful engagement with the texts' (Band 4) or even that 'points are made but not clearly developed' (Upper Band 3). The comments about *Balloons* are inaccurate, too. The balloons are personified in the poem so that it is they who are 'guileless' rather than the children. Plath's attitude to the balloons bears a similarity to her view of the mannequins in that they are both devices for contrasting human lives with objects invested with human qualities yet which are starkly different. The contrast made by the candidate between the innocence of the child in *Balloons* and Larkin's 'critical view of the world' is underdeveloped and there are much more interesting parallels that could be drawn, especially their shared interest in the ways in which human life somehow falls short of the idealised objects it has created. Larkin's more difficult concept of what it is to be 'natureless in ecstasies' shows the same disappointed falling short as Plath's small son holding what is left of the popped balloon, 'A red/ Shred in his little fist'.

[4] The critical description of the mundane lives of the workers in Larkin's *The Large Cool Store* contrasts with the positive attitude Plath uses in her poem *Balloons*. Larkin associates his views on life through expressing his criticisms of working class people – 'simple' – whereas Plath associates life through her imagery of animals – 'Oval soul-animals'. Larkin's critical attitudes contrast with the innocence of the child – 'guileless' – emphasising the contrast between the child's carefree outlook on life in which she takes a childish delight in the world (what they see is what they get: 'giving a shriek and pop') with Larkin's critical view on the world. This is also emphasised through the use of colours – 'red, green' – when describing the balloons contrasts with Larkin who uses very dull ones – 'brown greys, maroon' – representing how he sees life.

[5] The fact Larkin focuses on working-class people who live normal lives in both his poems could suggest he feels like an outsider. This is particularly evident in *Here* in which Larkin uses positive imagery in the first stanza when describing the landscape of the countryside – 'skies', 'meadows' – and only becomes critical in the second and third stanzas when describing the town: 'stealing flat-faced trolleys', 'fishy-smelling', the repetition of the word 'here' placing the stress on the countryside in which Larkin seems more comfortable. This is also expressed through his use of the words 'loneliness' and 'solitude'. This is similar to *The Munich Mannequins* and Plath's view of seeing the ability to have children as defining a woman – 'blood flood is the flood of love' – where it could be seen that she doesn't want to be alone. She uses imagery such as 'cold', 'snow' and 'darkness', which is often associated with death in Plath's poems. This also creates a sense of isolation and loneliness, 'Nobody's about', suggesting both Plath and Larkin feel isolated.

Paragraph 5: Again, quotations are misappropriated. 'Meadows' offered here as a positive view of the countryside, actually reads 'fields/ Too thin and thistled to be called meadows'. The phrase 'fishy-smelling'/Pastoral' implies a countryside image unexpectedly found in the town (incidentally, this is Hull, a well-known fishing port). The neat distinction the candidate wants to make between Larkin's attitude to countryside and town is partly a bogus one. A little more thought would have provided more apt contrasts, for instance, the 'piled, gold clouds' with the 'grim head-scarfed wives'. Even these contrasts make an unfair distinction in a poem whose main concern is a delight in detailed scenic observation. The sense of isolation that the candidate finds in both Larkin and Plath's work is a fair one although it is the inevitable stance of the writer who must create distance in order to observe. The view of Plath as isolated by her childbearing capabilities and not wanting to be alone is rather difficult to understand.

We are, however, in danger of being over-critical here. On the positive side, the candidate has succeeded in maintaining a comparative framework and made use of examples of imagery and repetition as devices for creating effects. There is no doubt that the candidate knows what is required in a general way. The comparisons are regularly maintained and there has already been reference to imagery, lexical choice, word classes, and repetition, with some attempt to consider the effects they create. It is not, however, a careful reading and the selection of examples too often extracts single words out of context in order to create a simplified set of contrasts that 'lack evidence in places'. Words like 'partial' and 'simplistic' are accurate in the estimation of the essay so far but it does seem to have done enough to be considered a Band 3 essay and therefore with the potential to get at least a grade E.

[6] Both *The Large Cool Store* and *The Munich Mannequins* express views of love and women, Plath's obviously from a female viewpoint and Larkin's a male viewpoint. Larkin doesn't seem to understand love: 'How separate and unearthly love is', whereas Plath only mentions the ability to have children – love doesn't come into it – 'absolute sacrifice'. This also suggested both poets feel isolated – Larkin inexperience in love and Plath hurt by love.

[7] The change in colours used in *The Large Cool Store* to 'lemon, sapphire' presents the idea of trying to be something you're not. This is also expressed through Larkin's use of artificial adjectives: 'natureless', 'synthetic'. This artificiality contrasts with the pureness of the child in *Balloons* who doesn't try to deceive you – 'guileless' – and takes such delight in something as simple as balloons 'giving a shriek and a pop'. This child accepts everything at face value which contrasts with Larkin's criticism where he has to find fault with something – 'unearthly love is'. Both these poems reflect a light-hearted tone both using colloquial language – 'simple' 'out'. However, *Balloons* is optimistic on life and *The Large Cool Store* expresses a pessimistic view on life.

Paragraph 7: The opening evidence of colours and 'artificial adjectives' is convincing enough but beyond that, the rest of the paragraph exposes real weakness. The same quotations are used from *Balloons* with the same simplistic and incorrect reading. The use of the phrase 'unearthly love is' is ungrammatical as it is quoted and a fuller quotation would demonstrate how inaccurate the candidate's description is. Larkin is not finding fault here, he is expressing wonder at a human mystery. The final sentence attempts to remind us that the essay's focus is on the poets' view on life but it is quite wrong to suggest Larkin's poem is pessimistic and Plath's is optimistic. This is a very narrow reading and is dragging the candidate down to Band 2, justifying comments such as 'scattergun approach to analysis', 'superficial ideas' and 'comments on less important links'.

[8] Both *The Large Cool Store* and *The Munich Mannequins* end on a note of uncertainty. Plath ends on a note of false promises: 'The snow has no voice' – suggesting she is always let down by father and husband. Whereas Larkin ends on a note of uncertainty which is typical of Larkin: 'own unreal wishes' – since he often changes his mind throughout his poetry. This is evident in *Here* in which he uses iambic pentameter, changing the rhyme scheme in every stanza: ababcdde. Like Plath in *The Munich Mannequins*, he also refers to death: 'luminously-peopled air ascends'. This metaphor of moving towards heaven suggests this train journey is a metaphor for life.

[9] Both Larkin and Plath seem to be unsatisfied with life, both referring to death. Plath is only positive towards life when seeing it from a child's perspective where they take everything as they see it – 'guileless'. Larkin's over-critical attitude towards leading a normal life ('cheap') suggests he wants to be accepted. Both poets seem to feel isolated and alone whereas Plath inflicts it on herself and Larkin seems so over-critical as he wants to be accepted.

Paragraph 6: This is a very weak paragraph, stating the obvious about the gender of the poets without exploring how this might be expressed. For the first time there is an attempt to contextualise or justify attitudes with brief hints at biographical detail in the final sentence. Since the 'absolute sacrifice' is evidence of love in Plath's poem, the candidate is struggling here to support the theory of isolation set up in the previous paragraph. Candidates are frequently more interested in the biographical details of the lives of Larkin and Plath than in their poems and it is an obvious weakness and lack of focus to pursue this without close support from the poems themselves. In fairness, this is not a trap that this candidate has fallen into in this essay.

Paragraph 8: Again, superficially the comparison seems to be sustained in this discussion of endings but neither quotation used is properly understood or considered in context. Larkin's rhyming pattern in *Here* is not random or 'uncertain' – the pattern matches in stanzas one and three and alternates with stanzas two and four so that no uncertainty exists. The consideration of Larkin's metaphors is valid although there is nothing but 'the snow has no voice' to compare it with in the Plath poem.

Paragraph 9: This final summary attempts to consolidate a thematic link ('death') but then rather clumsily echoes the two misunderstood and decontextualised words from the poems to force the conclusion that has been hinted at earlier.

Examiner's comments on the essay as a whole

It should be clear that, although this essay is disappointing in many ways, it fulfils some of the criteria of the band descriptors for Lower Band 3, which would enable it to achieve Grade E by quite a narrow margin. 'Broad comments', 'simplistic', 'straightforward expression with some errors', 'lacks evidence in places', 'comparative framework used but may be partial/simplistic' all apply to this essay. It goes beyond Band 2 ('limited analysis occurs', 'responds to obvious or broad links or comparison') because it attempts to make comparison of several areas and deals with some literary and linguistic details with some consistency. It is also an essay for which the structure of the paragraphs and the focus on a comparative mode is sufficiently thoughtful that adding more relevant material would be a relatively easy thing to do.

You should be able to recognise how easily the essay could be improved and pushed up into the higher Band 3 areas (which would gain a C or D grade) just by being a little more detailed in support. Often a single word is extracted where quoting the phrase from which it came would immediately have made the argument more convincing.

Practical activity

Look in detail at the comments on each paragraph of the essay. Take each paragraph in turn and identify and highlight the weaknesses. Then decide how you would rewrite this paragraph to make it more effective.

---

16 Other comparative tasks to consider

There are twenty-four texts to choose from in the coursework unit. Clearly, it is not possible to consider every possible permutation of how each of the texts might be combined with another. What follows, however, is a series of pairings of poems/passages from some of the texts on the list. Here is a chance for you to try and write your own comparative essays based on the single extracts from each writer's work. A few suggested points of comparison are made at the end of each pair of extracts to help you to focus in the right way:

Compare the ways in which Jennings and Shakespeare write about parent-child relationships

One Flesh from *Selected Poems* by Elizabeth Jennings

Lying apart now, each in a separate bed,
He with a book, keeping the light on late,
She like a girl dreaming of childhood,
All men elsewhere – it is as if they wait
Some new event: the book he holds unread,
Her eyes fixed on the shadows overhead.

Tossed up like flotsam from a former passion,
How cool they lie. They hardly ever touch,
Or if they do it is like a confession
Of having little feeling – or too much.
Chastity faces them, a destination
For which their whole lives were a preparation.

Strangely apart, yet strangely close together,
Silence between them like a thread to hold
And not wind in. And time itself's a feather
Touching them gently. Do they know they're old,
These two who are my father and my mother
Whose fire from which I came, has now grown cold?

Excerpt from *Hamlet* (Act 3 Scene 4, lines 54–88) by William Shakespeare

Hamlet:
Look here, upon this picture, and on this,
The counterfeit presentment of two brothers.
See, what a grace was seated on this brow;
Hyperion's curls; the front of Jove himself;
An eye like Mars, to threaten and command;
A station like the herald Mercury
New-lighted on a heaven-kissing hill;
A combination and a form indeed,
Where every god did seem to set his seal,
To give the world assurance of a man:
This was your husband. Look you now, what follows:
Here is your husband; like a mildew'd ear,

Blasting his wholesome brother. Have you eyes?
Could you on this fair mountain leave to feed,
And batten on this moor? Ha! have you eyes?
You cannot call it love; for at your age
The hey-day in the blood is tame, it's humble,
And waits upon the judgment: and what judgment
Would step from this to this? Sense, sure, you have,
Else could you not have motion; but sure, that sense
Is apoplex'd; for madness would not err,
Nor sense to ecstasy was ne'er so thrall'd
But it reserved some quantity of choice,
To serve in such a difference. What devil was't
That thus hath cozen'd you at hoodman-blind?
Eyes without feeling, feeling without sight,
Ears without hands or eyes, smelling sans all,
Or but a sickly part of one true sense
Could not so mope.
O shame! where is thy blush? Rebellious hell,
If thou canst mutine in a matron's bones,
To flaming youth let virtue be as wax,
And melt in her own fire: proclaim no shame
When the compulsive ardour gives the charge,
Since frost itself as actively doth burn
And reason panders will.

Some points of comparison:

■ the use of iambic pentameter

■ the fading of passion in human life

■ children's idea of their parents as young people

■ the lexical choices

■ the use of metaphor.

Which other poems/passages might be suitable for further comparison on this theme?

■ Compare the ways in which Duffy and Irving write about religion

Prayer from *Mean Time* by Carol Ann Duffy

Some days, although we cannot pray, a prayer
utters itself. So, a woman will lift
her head from the sieve of her hands and stare
at the minims sung by a tree, a sudden gift.

Some nights, although we are faithless, the truth
enters our hearts, that small familiar pain;
then a man will stand stock-still, hearing his youth
in the distant Latin chanting of a train.

Pray for us now. Grade I piano scales
console the lodger looking out across
a Midlands town. Then dusk, and someone calls
a child's name as though they named their loss.

Darkness outside. Inside, the radio's prayer –
Rockall. Malin. Dogger. Finisterre.

An excerpt from *A Prayer for Owen Meany* by John Irving

> I am doomed to remember a boy with a wrecked voice—not because
> of his voice, or because he was the smallest person I ever knew,
> or even because he was the instrument of my mother's death, but
> because he is the reason I believe in God; I am a Christian because
> of Owen Meany. I make no claims to have a life in Christ, or with
> Christ—and certainly not for Christ, which I've heard some zealots
> claim. I'm not very sophisticated in my knowledge of the Old
> Testament, and I've not read the New Testament since my Sunday
> school days, except for those passages that I hear read aloud to me
> when I go to church. I'm somewhat more familiar with the passages
> from the Bible that appear in The Book of Common Prayer; I read
> my prayer book often, and my Bible only on holy days—the prayer
> book is so much more orderly.
>
> I've always been a pretty regular churchgoer. I used to be a
> Congregationalist—I was baptized in the Congregational Church,
> and after some years of fraternity with Episcopalians (I was
> confirmed in the Episcopal Church, too), I became rather vague in
> my religion: in my teens I attended a "nondenominational" church.
> Then I became an Anglican; the Anglican Church of Canada has
> been my church—ever since I left the United States, about twenty
> years ago. Being an Anglican is a lot like being an Episcopalian—so
> much so that being an Anglican occasionally impresses upon me the
> suspicion that I have simply become an Episcopalian again. Anyway,
> I left the Congregationalists and the Episcopalians—and my country
> once and for all

Some points of comparison:

- certainty/uncertainty in considering religion
- patterns of security which are like religion
- the inspirations of prayer
- the use of metaphor
- the sentence structures.

Which other poems/passages might be suitable for further comparison on this theme?

Compare the ways in which Collins and Swift write about history

Fishing on the Susquehanna in July from *Taking Off Emily Dickinson's Clothes* by Billy Collins

I have never been fishing on the Susquehanna
or on any river for that matter
to be perfectly honest.

Not in July or any month
have I had the pleasure–if it is a pleasure–
of fishing on the Susquehanna.

I am more likely to be found
in a quiet room like this one–
a painting of a woman on the wall,

a bowl of tangerines on the table–
trying to manufacture the sensation
of fishing on the Susquehanna.

There is little doubt
that others have been fishing
on the Susquehanna,

rowing upstream in a wooden boat,
sliding the oars under the water
then raising them to drip in the light.

But the nearest I have ever come to
fishing on the Susquehanna
was one afternoon in a museum in Philadelphia

when I balanced a little egg of time
in front of a painting
in which that river curled around a bend

under a blue cloud-ruffled sky,
dense trees along the banks,
and a fellow with a red bandanna

sitting in a small, green
flat-bottom boat
holding the thin whip of a pole.

That is something I am unlikely
ever to do, I remember
saying to myself and the person next to me.

Then I blinked and moved on
to other American scenes
of haystacks, water whitening over rocks,

even one of a brown hare
who seemed so wired with alertness
I imagined him springing right out of the frame.

An excerpt from *Waterland* by Graham Swift

Children, there is a theory of history which may be called – to borrow a word from the ancient Greeks – the theory of hubris. This doctrine provides that there can be no success with impunity, no great achievement without accompanying loss; that no Napoleon can go carving up the map of Europe without getting his comeuppance.

You sneer. Who administers this grand and rough justice? The gods? Some supernatural power? This is getting all too much like fairy-tales again. Very well. But even nature teaches us that nothing is given without something else being taken away. Consider water, which, however much you coax it, this way and that, will return, at the slightest opportunity, to its former equilibrium. Or consider the handsome wife of Thomas Atkinson, formerly Sarah Turnbull, of Gildsey. Between the years 1800 and 1815 she bears Thomas three sons, two of whom live and one of whom dies; and a daughter, who lives, but only till her sixth year, for the techniques of land-drainage may have improved considerably but medical science is still in its infancy.

Some points of comparison:

- the sense of private history as linked to a wider world
- the contrast of private musing (Collins) with public address (Swift)
- the use of multiple modifying clauses
- the contrast of tone
- the use of factual detail.

Which other poems/passages might be suitable for further comparison on this theme?

Compare the ways in which Levy and Heaney write about British traditions

An excerpt from *Small Island* by Andrea Levy

My mirror spoke to me. It said: "Man, women gonna fall at your feet." In my uniform of blue – from the left, from the right, from behind – I looked like a god. And this uniform did not even fit me so well. But what is a little bagging on the waist and tightness under the arm when you are a gallant member of the British Royal Airforce? Put several thousand Jamaican men in uniform, coop them up while, Grand Old Duke of York style, you march them up to the top of the hill and then back down again and they will think of nothing but women. When they are up they will imagine them and when they are down they will dream of them. But not this group I travelled with to America. Not Hubert, not Fulton, not Lenval, not James, not even me. Because every last one of us was too preoccupied with food. The only flesh we conjured was the sort you chewed and swallowed.

This was war. There was hardship I was prepared for – bullet, bomb and casual death – but not for the torture of missing cow-foot stew, not for the persecution of living without curried shrimp or pepper-pot soup. I was not ready, I was not trained to eat food that was prepared in a pan of boiling water, the sole purpose of which was to rid it of taste and texture. How the English built empires when their armies marched on nothing but mush should be one of the wonders of the world. I thought it would be combat that would make me regret having volunteered, not boiled-up potatoes, boiled-up vegetables – grey and limp on the plate like it had been eaten once before. Why the English come to cook everything by this method? Lucky they kept that boiling business as their national secret and did not insist that people of their colonies stop frying and spicing-up their food.

Blackberry-Picking from *Selected Poems 1965–87* by Seamus Heaney

Late August, given heavy rain and sun
For a full week, the blackberries would ripen.
At first, just one, a glossy purple clot
Among others, red, green, hard as a knot.
You ate that first one and its flesh was sweet
Like thickened wine: summer's blood was in it
Leaving stains upon the tongue and lust for
Picking. Then red ones inked up and that hunger
Sent us out with milk cans, pea tins, jam-pots
Where briars scratched and wet grass bleached our boots.
Round hayfields, cornfields and potato-drills
We trekked and picked until the cans were full,
Until the tinkling bottom had been covered
With green ones, and on top big dark blobs burned
Like a plate of eyes. Our hands were peppered
With thorn pricks, our palms sticky as Bluebeard's.

We hoarded the fresh berries in the byre.
But when the bath was filled we found a fur,
A rat-grey fungus, glutting on our cache.
The juice was stinking too. Once off the bush
The fruit fermented, the sweet flesh would turn sour.
I always felt like crying. It wasn't fair
That all the lovely canfuls smelt of rot.
Each year I hoped they'd keep, knew they would not.

Some points of comparison:

- the sensations of food
- the contrasting confidence of the speakers
- the close detail
- the sense of being outside the common experience
- the choice of verbs.

Which other poems/passages might be suitable for further comparison on this theme?

Compare the ways in which Chaucer and Atwood portray women's roles in society

An excerpt from *The Wife of Bath's Prologue and Tale* by Geoffrey Chaucer

And in his wey it happed hym to ryde,	995
In al this care under a forest syde,	
Wher as he <u>saugh</u> upon a daunce go	
Of ladyes foure and twenty, and yet mo;	
Toward the whiche daunce he <u>drow ful yerne</u>,	
In hope that som wysdom sholde he lerne.	1000
But certeinly, <u>er</u> he came fully there,	
Vanysshed was this daunce, he <u>nyste</u> where.	
No creature <u>saugh</u> he that bar <u>lyf</u>,	
Save on the grene he <u>saugh</u> sittynge a wyf –	
A fouler <u>wight</u> ther may no man <u>devyse</u>.	1005
Agayn the knyght this olde wyf <u>gan</u> ryse,	
And seyde, "Sire knyght, <u>heer forth ne lith no wey</u>.	
Tel me what that ye seken, <u>by your fey</u>!	
<u>Paraventure</u> it may the bettre be,	
Thise olde folk kan <u>muchel</u> thyng," <u>quod</u> she.	1010
"My <u>leeve mooder</u>," <u>quod</u> this knyght, "certeyn	
<u>I nam but deed</u>, but if that I kan <u>seyn</u>	
What thyng it is. that wommen moost desire.	
<u>Koude ye me wisse</u>, I wolde <u>wel quite youre hire</u>."	
"<u>Plight</u> me thy <u>trouthe</u>, heere in myn hand," <u>quod</u> she,	1015
"The nexte thyng that I <u>requere</u> thee,	
Thou shalt it do, if it lye in thy myght,	
And I wol telle it yow, <u>er</u> it be nyght."	
"Have heer my <u>trouthe</u>," <u>quod</u> the knyght, "I grante."	
"Thanne," <u>quod</u> she, "<u>I dar me wel avante</u>	1020
Thy <u>lyf</u> is <u>sauf</u>; for I wol stonde therby,	
Upon my <u>lyf</u>, the queene wol seye as I.	
Lat se which is the proudeste of <u>hem</u> alle,	
That wereth on a <u>coverchief or a calle</u>,	
That dar seye nay of that I shal thee teche.	1025
Lat us go forth withouten lenger speche."	
Tho <u>rowned she a pistel</u> in his ere,	
And bad hym to be glad and have no fere.	

An excerpt from *The Handmaid's Tale* by Margaret Atwood

Today, despite Rita's closed face and pressed lips, I would like to stay here, in the kitchen. Cora might come in, from somewhere else in the house, carrying her bottle of lemon oil and her duster, and Rita would make coffee–in the houses of the Commanders there is still real coffee–and we would sit at Rita's kitchen table, which is not Rita's any more than my table is mine, and we would talk, about aches and pains, illnesses, our feet, our backs, all the different kinds of mischief that our bodies, like unruly children, can get into. We would nod our heads as punctuation to each other's voices, signaling that yes, we know all about it. We would exchange remedies and try to outdo each other in the recital of our physical miseries; gently we would complain, our voices soft and minor key and mournful as pigeons in the eaves troughs. I know what you

Modern language

saugh: saw
drow ful yerne: drew eagerly
er: before
nyste: did not know
lyf: life
wight: person/creature
devyse: 1. look upon, 2. tell
gan: began to
heer forth ne lith no wey: there's no way on from here
fey: on your honour
paraventure: perhaps
muchel: many
quod: said
leeve mooder: dear mother
I nam but deed, but: I am dead unless
seyn: say
koude ye me wisse: if you could tell me
wel quite youre hire: pay you well for your time
plight: pledge
trouthe: promise
requere: ask
I dar me wel avante: I am sure
sauf: safe
lat se: let them say
hem: them
coverchief or a calle: types of hats
rowned she a pistel: she whispered a message

mean, we'd say. Or, a quaint expression you sometimes hear, still, from older people: I hear where you're coming from, as if the voice itself were a traveler, arriving from a distant place. Which it would be, which it is.

How I used to despise such talk. Now I long for it. At least it was talk. An exchange, of sorts.

Or we would gossip. The Marthas know things, they talk among themselves, passing the unofficial news from house to house. Like me, they listen at doors, no doubt, and see things even with their eyes averted. I've heard them at it sometimes, caught whiffs of their private conversations. Stillborn, it was. Or, Stabbed her with a knitting needle, right in the belly. Jealousy, it must have been, eating her up. Or, tantalizingly, It was toilet cleaner she used. Worked like a charm, though you'd think he'd of tasted it. Must've been that drunk; but they found her out all right.

Or I would help Rita make the bread, sinking my hands into that soft resistant warmth which is so much like flesh. I hunger to touch something, other than cloth or wood. I hunger to commit the act of touch.

But even if I were to ask, even if I were to violate decorum to that extent, Rita would not allow it. She would be too afraid. The Marthas are not supposed to fraternize with us.

Fraternize means to behave like a brother. Luke told me that. He said there was no corresponding word that meant to behave like a sister. Sororize, it would have to be, he said. From the Latin. He liked knowing about such details. The derivations of words, curious usages. I used to tease him about being pedantic.

Some points of comparison:

- women's behaviour towards each other
- the roles dictated to women by men
- the specialised wisdom of women
- the lexical choice
- the narrative style/point of view.

Which other passages in each text might be suitable for further comparison on this theme?

17 Some frequently asked questions (with answers)

What happens if I write less than 2,000 words?

There are no marks deducted for writing below the word limit but you will be self-penalising by not having developed your argument as fully as you might have.

What happens if I write more that 2,500 words?

The task is to write an essay that is between 2,000 and 2,500 so writing more than this is an indication that you have not shown the discipline required of the coursework task. Again, points are not deducted for going over the limit but the structural tightness and focus of your essay may suffer as a result. The teacher or examiner reading your essay has every right to stop reading before the end if you have clearly ignored the word limit. In many walks of life – university, journalism, office reporting – you will not make a good impression if you pay no attention to the length of the piece of writing requested. Get into good habits now.

How much can my teacher help me with the coursework essay?

Obviously you will have had plenty of discussion with your teacher about possible themes and the choosing of appropriate passages and poems in class. You will also submit your own choice of theme and chosen poems or passages for your teacher's approval before you begin writing. When you have written a first draft of your complete essay, your teacher will write some comments and annotations on your essay, which will help you to improve it. It may be that one or two paragraphs can be improved or that you haven't sustained a comparison throughout or that you have paid too much attention to one of the texts to the neglect of the other. Once this first draft has been annotated, you are on your own. It is not helpful to do many drafts in which you tinker with a few minor points each time and your teacher should not be involved in that final process.

What evidence of drafting must I submit?

The first draft which has been annotated by your teacher will be submitted alongside the finished product of your essay. It should be possible to see how you have responded to your teacher's advice between the first draft and the final essay. There are no points awarded, however, for the drafting procedure; your final essay should be evidence enough. A draft must, nevertheless, be included.

Can I use the internet for information?

You may find plenty of material on the internet that gives you some contextual background for your writing. Remember, however, that your task is to write a comparative essay with the emphasis on close detailed literary and linguistic analysis. You will not find such an essay on the internet but you will find other material. Beware of websites that appear to offer you ready-made essays at a price; the quality is often very poor and they are extremely likely to be irrelevant to the coursework task. By all means include critical opinion about the passages and poems about which you are writing but be sure to acknowledge it in the bibliography at the end of your essay.

Are a bibliography and critical writing essential to a good essay?

Absolutely not. Some candidates will be able to weave wider reading effortlessly into their analyses but most candidates will be distracted by such an approach. Wider reading should give you pleasure in the A2 year and should inform your close comparative analysis without dominating or replacing it. Remember, be very sparing in your use of biographical details; they are largely distracting to the success of this kind of essay.

Context is mentioned under AO3 which makes up 50 per cent of the marks. Why is it being played down?

As explained earlier in this guide, context refers to a number of areas. Especially when writing about other genres (prose, drama), you will have to explain the context of the passage you have chosen to analyse so that its wider relationship to the text can be understood. The central feature of AO3 is the comparison, establishing the relationships between texts. When aspects of lexis or sentence structure are discussed in your essay, you may need to refer briefly to the period in which the texts were written in order to explain archaic constructions or a shift in meaning. That is, of course, valid contextualisation.

Should I give page references for the poems/passages I write about?

No. There are a number of different publications of the set texts so page numbers may be meaningless. Instead, you are required to photocopy the poems and passages about which you write and attach them to your final submitted essay. In this way, you will be reminded to focus on a few specific areas rather than the whole text AND, if you have an unusual selected poems text, for instance, teachers and moderators will know exactly what you are referring to in your essay.

How many poems or passages should I write about?

The directive 'Write a lot about a little not a little about a lot' applies to all four of the units in A level English Language and Literature. You need a lot of discipline in order to do the job properly and that means limiting your essay to about three poems and three passages at the most. If you choose more than this, your argument will be diluted and you will be in danger of lacking sufficient close detailed reading to be awarded a good mark.

Are you saying I could get away with just reading a couple of poems or a page or two of a novel in order to do the job properly?

Of course not! Your selection of poems and passages will only come after you have made a thorough study of both your chosen texts. Only in this way will you have any kind of feel for the stylistic and thematic qualities of the two authors. Wide reading will inform a close critical analysis of a very small section of the texts. Be careful though; the temptation may be to try to show off the broad knowledge you have of the texts but this will dilute your essay which is quite a short one. It is possible that an outstanding candidate could, theoretically, 'get away with' reading very little but an outstanding candidate will have developed some affection for literature by the second year of study and will never want to settle for such a strategy.

Any final tips?

You have developed many analytical skills during the AS year. Don't forget what you have learned and use it to select and write about your texts. By the A2 year, most candidates have really begun to understand the analytical techniques they only partly 'got' at AS. You should have plenty of time to work on your coursework in the A2 year. Enjoy it. Read more than you have to. Apply critical judgements and analysis to everything you read. Make yourself a better person. Good luck.

Useful framework tools

When you are exploring and analysing a text, or when you are writing your own commentary, you need to use relevant framework terms to enable you to demonstrate your understanding effectively. The following glossary is organised into five sections which cover the five important elements in any analysis.

1 Overview

The following terms are useful in presenting an overview of a text, and ought to be explored before you move to a closer and more detailed examination:

Aim/purpose	The reason why the text has been written. This can often only be deduced from a close examination of the language and form. The writer could, for example, be trying to argue a case, persuade us of a point of view or emotionally move us in some way.
Attitudes	The writer's point of view in relation to the subject matter. Does the way that the author feels about the subject or topic come across?
Audience	The people the writer had in mind when writing the text. Is it, for example, clearly aimed at either men or women? Is it for children or for older people, or for the general reader?
Context	The circumstances in which or for which the text was written. The recasting exercise, for example, requires you to rewrite a text that was written in, and for, a specific context and create a new text for a different context.
Domain	The type of writing to which a text belongs, for example, journalism, literature, advertising, law, conversation.
Mode	The medium chosen for the text. It could be spoken, written or a mixture of the two.
Tenor	The relationship between the writer/speaker and the addressee. Tenor is characterised by its degree of formality. For example, a legal document will carry a formal tenor, while the tenor of a conversation between a husband and wife is likely to be informal.
Theme	The key idea or ideas that form the core 'message' of the text.
Tone	The attitude the writer or speaker reveals towards the reader or listener. For example a tone which is humorous, witty, ironic, cynical, superior, patronising or flattering could be adopted.
Topic	The part of the sentence or utterance which deals with what it is about.

2 Discourse

Discourse is a term that refers to any piece of language, written or spoken, and there are some important elements to think about before you look closely at specific features:

Structure

Juxtapositioning	Placing a word, phrase or sentence next to another to achieve a specific stylistic effect.
Layout	The way the text has been ordered or structured on the page.
Form	This can refer to both external and internal features: **External**: What genre has been chosen? ■ **Prose**: the genre could be novel, essay, letter, article, document, drama. ■ **Verse**: lyric, sonnet, dramatic monologue, occasional verse. **Internal**: What is the inner design? ■ **Prose**: consider organisation, balance, climax, sentence structure, use of rhythm, etc. ■ **Verse**: think about the rhythm, for example: *iambic rhythm*: a weak beat followed by a strong beat; *trochaic rhythm*: a strong beat followed by a weak beat; *anapaestic rhythm*: two weak beats followed by a strong beat. ■ **Stanza form and rhyme scheme**: some of the more straightforward could include *blank verse* (unrhymed lines of 10 syllables with iambic rhythm), *couplets* (rhyming pairs of lines), *free verse* (different metres and variable rhythm substituted for a definite metre), *sonnet* (a fourteen line poem with a specific rhyme scheme and structure).

Narrative stance

First person address	The writer may choose to write from the point of view of the central character (as in *Great Expectations*) and present events through his or her eyes. This will involve extensive use of the first person pronoun (I/we) and is often a more personal approach.
Third person address	The writer may take the view of the omniscient narrator (as in *Things Fall Apart*). This will involve the use of the third person pronoun (he/she/they).
Narrative voice	The way the writer/speaker chooses to address the audience.
Point of view	The attitude the writer/speaker takes towards the subject, for example, enthusiastic, serious, cool, interested/uninterested, biased/unbiased.

Features of speech

Adjacency pairs	Linked utterances produced by different speakers, such as questions and answers, commands and responses, etc.
Chaining	The linking together of adjacency pairs to form a longer unit of Discourse.
Deixis	Linguistic pointing. Deixis allows a speaker to point at places, times and individuals in a conversation. Typically that would include words like 'this', 'here', 'there' (place), 'now', 'yesterday' (time) and 'he', 'you' (individuals).
Feedback	The responses to an utterance from someone else. Feedback could include monitoring or interaction features as well as longer utterances.
Fillers	Non-fluency features such as '*um*' and '*er*', which speakers employ to avoid long pauses or silences.
Hedges	Any device used by a speaker to reduce the impact of an utterance, for example '*I am not sure* but …' or 'That is *rather poor*'.
Initiation	The way in which someone begins a conversation or talk.
Non-fluency features	Features that result from the unprepared nature of speech, such as hesitations, unintended repetitions, false starts and fillers.
Paralinguistic features	Non-linguistic variables in speech, such as tone of voice, emphasis and intonation.
Phatic speech	Language we use to enable social contact rather than convey a literal meaning, such as 'It's a nice day today' or 'How are you keeping?'
Tag questions	A short question attached to the end of an utterance, seeking some sort of agreement or confirmation, for example, 'It's a lovely day, isn't it?'
Turn taking	The way in which speakers regulate their contributions to a conversation, some people giving precedence to others, some taking precedence over others.

Rhetoric

Originally a taught subject, rhetoric is the art of speaking, and uses many devices which are found elsewhere in this glossary. All of the following could be used rhetorically to enhance speech: alliteration, anaphora, antithesis, apostrophe, assonance, cataphora, hyperbole, irony, metaphor, metonymy, onomatopoeia, oxymoron, paradox, personification and simile.

Rhetoric	Language used in a structured way with the aim of convincing or persuading someone to agree with a certain point of view or take a certain action.
Anaphora	Anaphoric references point backwards in a text. In rhetoric it refers specifically to the repetition of a word or phrase at the beginning of successive sentences.
Apostrophe	An address directed at one person or a group of people.

Bathos	A descent from the elevated to the trivial for humorous effect.
Cataphora	Cataphoric references point forward in a text.
Metonymy	The substitution of the name of an attribute for the thing itself, for example, the crown = the monarch, as in James Shirley's *Death the Leveller*, 'Sceptre and crown must tumble down …'.
Rhetorical questions	Questions which do not require a response from the listener and are so framed as to suggest the answer the speaker wants, for example, 'And just what is this government doing to stamp out crime?' (This invites the response 'nothing'.)

Pragmatics

Pragmatics	The study of meaning in context. For example, a question such as 'Are you ready yet?' could take on different meanings depending on the context and who was being addressed. It could be a straightforward enquiry, or could mean, 'Hurry up I've been waiting ages'.

3 Lexis

It is essential you refer in detail to the language of the text, using some of the following terms:

Word classes

Open classes	These include nouns, full verbs, adjectives and adverbs, and are referred to as open classes because we often coin new words to add to them.
Closed classes	These include determiners, pronouns, prepositions, conjunctions, auxiliary verbs, interjections and enumerators. The closed classes have a fairly fixed membership and new words are rarely invented to add to the list.
Adjective/modifier	Adjectives modify or limit meaning of a noun, for example, 'a small, black chair'.
Adverb	Adverbs qualify verbs, adjectives or other adverbs, and generally deal with place (here/there) time (today/now) manner (carefully/slowly) and degree (rather/quite).
Determiner	Determiners identify or determine what we are referring to, and are used with a noun (e.g. *this* hat, *those* shoes, *many* people, *that* man, *my* book).
Noun	Nouns refer to: ■ people, objects, places, substances (concrete nouns) ■ concepts, events, states, activities (abstract nouns).

Pronoun	Pronouns are words used to replace nouns. There are a number of sub-sections: personal (*I/me*), possessive (*mine*), demonstrative (*this*), reflexive (*myself*), emphatic (*myself*), relative (*who/which/that*), interrogative (*who?*). Pronouns differ from determiners in that they replace nouns (for example, I like <u>that</u>), not identify nouns (I like <u>that</u> car).
Verb (auxiliary/ modal)	Auxiliary verbs help the main verb to communicate person, number and tense. The primary auxiliaries are 'be', 'have' and 'do', and can also function as main verbs. For example, 'have' can be used as an auxiliary verb ('I <u>have</u> bought you an ice-cream') or as a main verb ('I <u>have</u> a bike'). The modal auxiliaries (such as 'can', 'may' and 'will') do not function as main verbs.
Verb (finite)	This generally refers to the main part of the verb, which varies with tense, mood, number, person for example, 'he sings', 'they sang').
Verb (non-finite)	This refers generally to the parts of the verb that do not vary, such as the infinitive (to sing) and the participle (singing).

Diction

Anglo-Saxon	Words which derive from Anglo-Saxon roots generally have a vigorous, earthy, strong and concrete feel (for example, '*a hearty welcome*')
Latinate	Words which derive from Latin roots may have an elevated, majestic, literary or sometimes ponderous feel (for example, '*a cordial reception*').
Colloquial	Colloquial diction refers to relaxed, ordinary language and can often add a fresh, racy feel to a text, or if badly used could be stale or clichéd.

Semantic variation

Allusion	A reference to a person, place, event, work of literature, etc.
Ambiguity	Language which has more than one possible meaning or interpretation. Poets often use ambiguity to add depth of meaning to their poems
Antithesis	Contrasting ideas or words which are balanced against each other (for example, 'Not that I loved Caesar less, but that I loved Rome more', *Julius Caesar* by Shakespeare).
Antonym	Words which are opposite in meaning (for example, big/ little).
Cliché	A stale over-used expression that lacks originality and freshness (for example, 'He has eyes like a hawk').
Collocation	Two or more words that have been placed together or which appear together as part of a set phrase, for example, 'pitch black', 'sweet dreams'.
Connotation	The meanings that have become attached to words through frequent association.
Denotation	The dictionary definition of a word.

Emotive language	Language which is specifically chosen to appeal to the reader's or listener's feelings or emotions.
Hyperbole	Exaggeration for effect, often extravagant.
Imagery	The use of language to create an image or sense impression in the mind of the reader or listener. A discussion of imagery will require a consideration of connotation, simile and metaphor.
Irony	Language used to mean the opposite of what it appears to mean. It is often used to indicate the difference between a true and supposed condition, and must not be confused with sarcasm which shares some of its features but is spoken and intended to hurt or wound the listener. Irony usually implies two audiences, only one of which understands the true meaning of what is being said or written.
Metaphor	Implied comparison, in which one thing is said to be another, for example, 'Life's but a walking shadow' (*Macbeth*).
Oxymoron	A clash of opposites, for example, 'bitter sweet' or 'I must be cruel to be kind'.
Paradox	An apparent contradiction.
Pathetic fallacy	The tendency in literature to credit nature with human feelings or emotions or to reflect human feelings or emotions.
Personification	Attaching human characteristics to an inanimate object. This is often indicated by the use of a capital letter. Examples include 'Grim visag'd War' or 'England expects every man to do his duty'.
Repetition	The repeating of words, phrases or clauses for specific effects.
Sarcasm	The essence of sarcasm is that it is intended to hurt the listener by using words which are often ironic and bitter.
Semantic field	Words which are closely connected through their meaning share the same semantic field. A thesaurus groups words together in their semantic fields.
Simile	Stated comparison using the words 'like' or 'as'.
Symbolism	Using one thing to represent something else. For example, the rose is used to represent England, the thistle Scotland, the daffodil Wales and the shamrock Ireland.
Synonym	Words which share the same or almost the same meaning.

Register

Register	A variety of language distinguished according to use in different contexts and for different purposes or audiences.
Colloquial language	The language of everyday speech which is often lively, energetic and racy. At its worst it can be careless and slovenly.
Emotive language	Language which aims to involve and engage the emotions or feelings of the reader or listener.

Slang	Original or invented language or new expressions, which at its best adds life and vigour to language. Slang terms for the verb 'to die' would include 'kick the bucket', 'pop your clogs', 'push up the daisies'. It develops many forms including varieties such as Cockney rhyming slang (*Apples and pears*'/'*stairs*'). It should not be confused with careless, colloquial or regional language.
Tenor	The relationship between the speaker and the addressee, which is characterised by the degree of formality.

4 Grammar

An accurate understanding of the way in which grammatical features are used to express meaning is a key discriminator between the average and the good answer.

Syntax

Syntax	Sentence structure and organization.
Simple sentence	A sentence which contains a single clause which includes a finite verb.
Compound sentence	A sentence which contains two or more clauses linked by the coordinating conjunctions, and, but, (n)either, (n)or.
Complex sentence	A sentence which contains two or more clauses linked by subordinating conjunctions, such as 'although', 'as', 'because', 'that', 'which' or 'who', but does **not** contain any coordinating conjunctions.
Compound-complex sentence	A sentence which contains three or more clauses, which contain at least one coordinating and at least one subordinating conjunction.
Minor sentence	A group of words which begins with a capital letter and ends with a full stop but which does not contain a finite verb.

Tense

The significance of the use of the tense in a piece of discourse is worth commenting on.

Tense	The part of the verb that indicates the present, the future or the past.

Standard/non-standard features

The use of non-standard language features in a piece of discourse is worth commenting on.

5 Phonology

Awareness of the sounds of language is important for both written and spoken texts:

Prosodic features

Prosodic features	Variations in stress, emphasis, rhythm and intonation.
Rhythm	Rhythm can be used to refer to the natural flow of the spoken language with its variety of stress and emphasis, or, more specifically and technically, to the rhythmic patterns employed by poets to achieve specific effects (see **Form**).
Caesura	A break or pause within a line of poetry. This is often used to add a dramatic effect to the verse.
End Stop	A line of poetry with a clear pause at the end of the line. This separates the lines and enables poets to make links between connected lines.
Enjambement	A line of poetry that runs on. This often gives poetry the sound of natural speech, and is often used in connection with caesura.
Intonation	Variation of the pitch and rhythmic patterns of the voice in speech.
Stress	The emphasis given to words and phrases during speech.

Pronunciation

Accent	An identifiable way in which utterances are pronounced, which may relate to language and social class.
Dialect	A variety of language distinguished according to the user. It may be regional or social but generally involves variations in vocabulary and grammar, as well as in pronunciation.
Idiolect	A person's individual speech characteristics.
Received pronunciation (RP)	Originally the spoken language which was 'received' at court, it has come to refer to the pronunciation used by educated speakers whose speech gives no clue to their region of origin.
Standard English	Refers to vocabulary and grammar used by educated speakers of English which gives no indication of specific class or regional variations.

Tone

Writers or speakers will reveal their attitude to the reader or listener through the tone which may be, for example, witty, ironic, sarcastic, cynical, patronising, self-effacing, etc.

Sound

Writers or speakers use the sounds of language to help them convey their feelings, ideas, attitudes, etc. The following are worth noting:

Alliteration	The repetition of consonant sounds (for example, 'The bare black cliff clang'd round him', *Morte d'Arthur*, Tennyson).
Assonance	The repetition of vowel sounds (for example, 'The lone and level sands stretch far away', *Ozymandias*, Shelley).
Onomatopoeia	The use of language in which the meaning of the word is reflected in the sound (for example, 'clang', 'hiss').

Glossary

Adverbial phrase: a phrase containing information about how, where or when an action takes place, for example, 'I read books *nearly every day*'.

Aim or purpose: the reason why the text has been written. The writer could, for example, be trying to argue a case or persuade the audience to have a certain point of view.

Alliteration: the repetition of a consonant sound, for example, 'the lovely ladies'.

Allusion: a reference to another work of literature or other source by a writer. The writer may well assume that the reader has some knowledge of the work referred to and will understand the allusion.

Ambiguity: when language has more than one possible meaning or interpretation. Poets often use ambiguity to add depth of meaning to their poems.

Analyse: to make distinctions between and comment on the different elements of a work.

Antithesis: when phrases or sentences are contrasted, for example, '*We will win* the game. *We will not lose.*'

Antithetical: opposite and contrasting.

Apostrophe (rhetorical): a figure of speech in which concrete or abstract things or ideas are addressed as if present, for example, 'O Love! How can you treat me so!'

Argument: a connected series of ideas, backed up by relevant facts, which tries to make a case, and convince us of its truth and validity.

Assonance: repeated vowel sounds.

Asyndetic list: a form of list, in which there is no conjunction (such as 'and' or 'but') separating the final two items. This can give an open-ended feel to the list, perhaps suggesting there is more that could be added. The opposite of this is a syndetic list, such as 'At the market I bought apples, oranges, pears *and* bananas'.

Audience: the readers the writer had in mind when writing the text.

Caesura: a pause in any part of a line of verse, usually, but not always, indicated by a punctuation mark. Its function is far more complex than merely 'a pause for thought'; among many functions, it can draw attention to particular lexis or create emotional emphasis.

Coda: a musical term which describes a completion or rounding off.

Collocation: two or more words that have been placed together or which appear together as part of a set phrase; examples include 'crystal clear', 'cosmetic surgery' and 'red wine'.

Colloquialism: language that may be used in ordinary conversation but is not appropriate in formal or literary contexts.

Complex sentence: a sentence with two or more clauses linked by subordinating conjunctions.

Compound sentence: a sentence with two or more clauses linked by co-ordinating conjunctions.

Connotation: the associations and feelings we attach to words in addition to their core meanings;

for example, although 'smile' and 'grin' refer to similar facial expressions, the word 'smile' has connotations of warmth and friendship, whereas the word 'grin' may have connotations of falseness, malice or stupidity.

Context: the social situation, including audience and purpose, in which language is used; this situation is an important influence of the language choices made by speakers and writers.

Declarative sentence: a sentence that makes a statement.

Denotation: the primary, literal meaning of a word or phrase.

Domain: the type of writing to which a text belongs, for example, journalism, literature, advertising, law, conversation.

Dialect: a variety of a particular language, characterised by distinctive features of accent, grammar and vocabulary, used by people from a particular geographical area or social group.

Discourse markers: words or phrases which give structure to speech or writing, enabling a writer or speaker to develop ideas, relate points to each other or move from one idea to the next, for example, 'however', 'likewise', 'in addition', 'in contrast', 'nevertheless', 'furthermore', 'therefore'.

Dynamic verbs: verbs which describe physical actions, such as 'jump'.

Emotive language: language which is specifically chosen to appeal to the reader's or listener's feelings or emotions.

Emphasis: stress laid on a word or phrase by a speaker to indicate its special meaning or importance.

Enjambement: continuity of the sense and rhythm from one line of verse to the next without end-stopping. It does not just 'help the poem to flow' but can create a variety of effects such as the creation of a conversational style or the suspending of meaning to a later point in the poem.

Exclamation: an expression of emotion.

External referencing: will point to another text or texts which can be connected to the discourse through content, theme or idea, and which help to illuminate the writer's or speaker's meaning in some way.

False start: an aspect of normal non-fluency in language. A speaker may begin an utterance unit in one way and then immediately change the focus, for example, 'we put on our coats (.) it we were cold'.

Feedback: the responses to an utterance from someone else. Feedback could include monitoring or interaction features as well as longer utterances.

Figurative language: language which draws an imaginative comparison between what is described and something else, resulting in an image which cannot literally be true, but which may enable us to perceive something more vividly or allow us greater insight into the story or character. See simile, metaphor and personification.

Filler: a sound such as 'erm', 'um' and 'er', that speakers use to fill pauses in speech. Many speakers also use expressions such as 'y'know' and 'like' as verbal fillers.

Formal: a formal text is one that rigidly follows certain rules or traditions of form. An informal text is usually more relaxed.

Framework: In the study of language and literature, this refers to structures around which you build your analysis. Individual frameworks may be: metaphor, lexis, grammar, etc.

Genre: a class or category of text, with its particular conventions or language, form and structure; for example, short story, science fiction novel, Shakespearean comedy.

Graphology: the layout of a text, with use of such features as typeface.

Half-rhyme: a rhyme in which end consonants match but the preceding syllable does not, for example, 'blind/bland', 'foot/fate'.

Hedge: a word or phrase such as 'maybe', 'perhaps' or 'sort of', used to soften the impact of what is said, or to make speech sound more polite.

Hesitation: apparent indecision in an utterance, often characterised by a pause or an unintended repetition, for example, 'I I I'm not sure'.

Hyperbole: deliberate exaggeration.

Iamb: a metrical foot (or unit) with the rhythm: unstressed/stressed (x /).

Iambic pentameter: a line of verse with five iambic feet.

Imagery: in literary terms, imagery refers to the pictures created by a writer's choice of language, for example, their use of metaphor or personification.

Imperative sentence: a sentence that gives a command.

Internal referencing: often uses pronouns to point to something within the discourse. There are three types: *Anaphoric references* point backwards in a text. The reader or listener needs to think back to make sense of an utterance (e.g. *'The blow* was hard and *it* caused a black eye'); *Cataphoric references*: point forward in a text, and the reader or listener needs to be on the alert for a future reference (e.g. *'Those* were *major problems* for the economy') [Remember that cats jump forward]; *Exophoric references*: direct the reader or listener outside the text and often need some form of physical gesture to make the meaning clear (e.g. 'The mouse was *this* tiny').

Intonation: variation of the pitch and rhythmic patterns of the voice in speech.

Irony: a mismatch or discrepancy between what is written or said and what is actually meant.

Juxtaposition: to place side by side; in texts, writers may juxtapose ideas to create interesting or surprising effects.

Layout: the way the text has been ordered or structured on the page.

Lexical choices: the vocabulary selected by a writer to create a specific tone or effect.

Lexis: the choice of vocabulary in a text or the total stock of words in a language.

Listing: deliberately placing a number of items next to each other to ensure they are memorable for either listeners or readers.

Long vowel/short vowel: the vowels have long and short versions which can combine to create phonological effects. Long vowels can be heard in lexis like pl<u>a</u>te, s<u>ee</u>m, s<u>igh</u>, l<u>oa</u>d, tr<u>u</u>e and short vowels in c<u>a</u>t, b<u>e</u>t, s<u>i</u>t, d<u>o</u>t, b<u>u</u>t.

M

Main clause: a part of a sentence that is grammatically independent and may exist alone or alongside a subordinate clause.

Metaphor: a direct comparison drawn between two different things as if the subject really is the thing it is being compared to; for example, 'her hands were ice-blocks' or 'he was a bear of a man'.

Meter: a pattern of stressed and unstressed syllables, for example, iamb (x /) and trochee (/ x). The number of stresses in a line are described as mono- (1),di- (2), tri- (3), tetra- (4), penta- (5) meters.

Minor sentence: groups of words that begin with a capital letter and end with a full stop but do not contain a verb.

Modal verb: an auxiliary verb expressing necessity or possibility, for example 'could', 'will', 'should', 'must'.

Mode: the medium of communication used, usually speech or writing.

Modifier: a word or phrase which, when use in conjunction with another word, provides readers or listeners with additional detail or greater precision about the sense of that word.

Monitoring: monitoring features appear in speech as part of the interaction with a physically present addressee, and indicate the speaker's awareness of the addressee's presence, for example, 'you know' and 'I mean'.

Monosyllabic words: words with only one syllable.

Mood: the atmosphere resulting from the tone set by the writer.

N

Narrative: an account of connected events.

Narrative voice: the tone or style a narrator chooses to use to address the audience, which gives us an impression of the narrator's character.

Neologism: an invented word.

O

Object: in grammar, the person or thing being directly affected by the action.

Onomatopoeia: the use of words that sound like what they mean, for example, 'quack', 'hiss'.

Oral poetry: the tradition of reading poetry aloud that dates back to illiterate societies in which it was the only form of transmission.

P

Pantheism: the belief that God is everything and everything is God. Descriptions of nature by some poets will reflect this philosophy.

Paradox: an idea that seems to contradict itself, such as 'ignorance is bliss'.

Paralinguistic features: non-verbal variables in speech such as tone of voice, emphasis, intonation.

Past tense: tense related to time gone by.

Patterns/patterning: a regular order or arrangement of elements in the text to try to ensure they are memorable for either listeners or readers.

Pause: a short break in a spoken text, the duration of which is recorded in seconds, for example (2.0).

Personification: a form of metaphor where something which is not human is endowed with human characteristics; for example, 'the windows stared blankly'.

Phrase: in the hierarchy of grammatical units, the phrase comes between the word and the clause; there are five types of phrase:
Noun phrase (e.g. the red dress)
Verb phrase (e.g. will be running)
Adjective phrase (e.g. nice hot sweet)
Adverb phrase (e.g. quite inexcusably)
Prepositional phrase (e.g. wherever and whenever).

Polysyllabic words: words with more than one syllable.

Present tense: tense referring to time now existing.

Prosodic features: variations in speech such as stress, emphasis, rhythm and intonation.

R

References/referencing: a reference points to something which is either within or outside the specific piece of discourse.

Register: a type of language defined in terms of its appropriateness for the type of activity or context in which the language is used, including the purpose, audience and situation of a piece of speech or writing.

Repair: a self-correction in spontaneous speech.

Repetition: repeating words or phrases for emphasis or to create a rhetorical effect.

Rhetoric: the technique of using language persuasively in order to influence the opinions and behaviour of an audience.

Rhetorical parallelism: phrases or sentences of similar construction and ideas, for example, 'We will win the game. We will become champions'.

Rhythm: the natural flow of the spoken language with its variety of stress and emphasis, or more specifically and technically the rhythmic patterns employed by poets to achieve certain effects.

S

Semantic field: a group of words within a text relating to the same topic; for example, tyre, brake pedal, starter motor and exhaust are all from the semantic field of cars.

Sibilance: repeated use of the consonant 's', for example, 'the silvery snake slithered sinuously'.

Simile: an imaginative comparison drawn between two different things, linked with the words 'like' or 'as'; for example, 'her hands were as cold as ice' or 'the man was like a bear'.

Simple sentence: a sentence with only one clause.

Slang: original or invented language or new expressions. Slang terms for the verb 'to die' would include 'kick the bucket', 'pop your clogs', 'push up the daisies', etc. It should not be confused with careless, colloquial or regional language.

Stanza: a group of lines together in a poem, sometimes called a 'verse'.

Stative verbs: verbs which describe states of being and thought processes, such as 'to be', 'to think' or 'to seem'.

Stress: the emphasis given to words and phrases during speech.

Structure: the total contribution of all the parts to the whole. This may be seen in terms of chapters, scenes or verses. It can also refer to other structures, for example, the lexical patterning, the rhyme scheme, the phonological patterns.

Subject: in grammar, the person or thing acting on the verb.

Subordinate clause: this depends on the main clause; for example, in the sentence 'I went to a salesroom where I saw a great sports car.' The clause 'where I saw a great sports car' cannot stand alone.

Subjunctive: a verbal form or mood expressing hypothesis, for example, 'if I were rich I would buy a house'.

Syndetic list: a form of list in which a conjunction (such as 'and' or 'but') separates the final two items. For example, 'At the market I bought apples, oranges, pears *and* bananas'.

Synaesthesia: the mixing of sensations, for example, 'bitten by blue light', 'the blinding echo of the sky'.

Synecdoche: a part standing for the whole, for example, 'I see a sail on the horizon' ('sail' instead of 'ship'), 'fingers gripped the wall' ('fingers' instead of 'a person').

Syntactic(al): related to the ordering of the parts of a sentence, clause or phrase.

Syntax: the way words are combined to form sentences.

T

Tenor: the relationship between the writer/speaker and the addressee. The tenor is characterised by its degree of formality. For example, a legal document will carry a formal tenor, while a conversation between a husband and wife is likely to be informal.

Theme: the ideas suggested by a piece of writing, often recurring during the narrative.

Thesis: a proposition to be proved. The initial argument of an essay that will be developed and justified in later paragraphs.

Tone: the mood or feeling of a text conveyed by the writer.

Triplet: a pattern of three repeated words or phrases.

U

Utterance: a unit of spoken language, the end of which is indicated by a pause or a change of speaker. This term is often used to describe a 'spoken sentence', as an utterance may not follow the expectations and grammatical conventions of a written sentence.

Index

Key terms and their page numbers are in **bold**

Acknowledgements

The authors and publishers wish to thank the following for permission to use copyright materials:

Extract from *Advanced Conversational English* by Crystal and Davy, published by Pearson Education Limited (1975). Copyright © Pearson Education Limited; Bloomsbury and John Irving for an extract from *A Prayer for Owen Meany* by John Irving, Bloomsbury (1989); Carcanet and Elizabeth Jennings for poem *One Flesh* from *Selected Poems* by Elizabeth Jennings, Carcanet (1979); Faber and Faber Ltd. for poem *Mr Bleaney* from *The Witsun Weddings* by Philip Larkin (1964); Faber and Faber Ltd for poems *The Hanging Man* and *Wintering* from *Ariel* by Sylvia Plath (1965); Faber and Faber Ltd for *Blackberry-Picking* from *Death of a Naturalist* by Seamus Heaney (1980); Extract from *For Whom the Bell Tolls* by Ernest Hemingway, published by Jonathon Cape. Reprinted by permission of the Random House Group Ltd; Extract from *Hotel World* by Ali Smith, Hamish Hamilton 2001, pages 3–4. Copyright © Ali Smith, 2001. Reproduced by permission of Penguin Books Ltd; *I felt a Funeral* from *The Poems of Emily Dickinson*, by Emily Dickinson, edited by Thomas H. Johnson. Reprinted by permission of Harvard University Press; *Inventory* from *Dreaming Frankenstein and Collected Poems* by Liz Lochhead (1984). Reprinted by permission of Birlinn Limited; *Mending Wall* and *The Death of the Hired Man* from *The Poetry of Robert Frost* edited by Edward Connery Lathem, published by Jonathon Cape. Reprinted by permission of The Random House Group Ltd; *Nineteen Eighty Four* by George Orwell (Copyright © George Orwell, 1949). Reprinted by permission of Bill Hamilton as the Literary Executor of the Estate of the Late Sonia Brownell Orwell and Secker & Warburg Ltd; Pan Macmillan for an extract *Fishing on the Susquehanna in July* from *Taking Off Emily Dickenson's Clothes* by Billy Collins. Copyright © Billy Collins (2000); Penguin and Graham Greene for an extract from *The Invisible Japanese Gentlemen* by Graham Greene (1965); *Prayer* is taken from *Mean Time* by Carol Ann Duffy, published by Anvil Press Poetry (1993); Sinclair-Stevenson and Jane Gardam for an extract from *The Iron Coast* by Jane Gardam (1994); Extract from *Small Island* by Andrea Levy. Reproduced by permission of Headline Publishing Group Limited; Extract from *The Accidental Tourist* by Anne Tyler, published by Chatto and Windus. Reprinted by permission of The Random House Group Ltd; Extract from *The Handmaid's Tale* by Margaret Atwood, published by Jonathan Cape. Reprinted by permission of The Random House Group Ltd; *The Naming of Parts* by Henry Reed from *Collected Poems* by H. Gardner by permission of Oxford University Press; Extract from *Waterland* by Graham Swift, reproduced by permission of A. P. Watt Ltd on behalf of Graham Swift; *Death of a Salesman*, © 1949 Arthur Miller. Reproduced by permission. All rights reserved.

Every effort has been made to contact the copyright holders and we apologise if any have been overlooked. Should copyright have been unwittingly infringed in this book, the owners should contact the publishers, who will make corrections at reprint.